The Campus History Series

UNIVERSITY OF NEW MEXICO

On the Cover: The University of New Mexico (UNM) women's basketball team's history began on December 22, 1898, with an intramural game between the Gladiators and the Olympians, both composed of UNM students. Shortly after, they secured a 4-2 victory against Las Cruces College at the First Street Armory, marking the start of the women's basketball Rio Grande Rivalry. By 1901, the team had grown in prominence, posing for a team photograph on a dirt lot, while eating lunch, captained by Kate Cunningham. Florence Chapin, an elocutionist and physical director, provided physical training with her innovative system, helping the team dominate New Mexico basketball, becoming champions in 1902. Despite early success, UNM faculty restricted women's teams from traveling outside Albuquerque by 1912, limiting broader competition opportunities. (Courtesy of the Center for Southwest Research, University Libraries, University of New Mexico.)

Cover Background: The Albuquerque International Balloon Fiesta, taking place every October, brings a unique tradition to the University of New Mexico campus, where the sky above becomes a canvas of color. This event not only celebrates Albuquerque's deep-rooted connection to hot air ballooning but also cements its reputation as a leading center for ballooning worldwide. (Courtesy of the Center for Southwest Research, University Libraries, University of New Mexico.)

The Campus History Series

University of New Mexico

Amber Lane and Portia Vescio

ARCADIA
PUBLISHING

ISBN 978-1-4671-6260-9
Hardback ISBN 978-1-5402-9977-2

Published by Arcadia Publishing
Charleston, South Carolina

Printed in the United States of America

Library of Congress Control Number: 2025931958

For all general information, please contact Arcadia Publishing:
Telephone 843-853-2070
Fax 843-853-0044
E-mail sales@arcadiapublishing.com

Visit us on the Internet at www.arcadiapublishing.com

To all past, present, and future alumni

CONTENTS

ACKNOWLEDGMENTS

Founded in 1889, the University of New Mexico sits on the traditional homelands of the Pueblo of Sandia. The original peoples of New Mexico—Pueblo, Navajo, and Apache—since time immemorial have deep connections to the land and have made significant contributions to the broader community statewide. We honor the land itself and those who remain stewards of this land throughout the generations and also acknowledge our committed relationship to Indigenous peoples. We gratefully recognize our history (UNM Indigenous Peoples' Land and Territory Acknowledgment).

All images are from the Center for Southwest Research, University Libraries, University of New Mexico, unless stated otherwise.

Introduction

The University of New Mexico has evolved into a leading institution that serves as both an educational and a cultural cornerstone of the Southwest. Established on February 28, 1889, UNM's history is deeply intertwined with the development of the New Mexico Territory, which has been defined by its diverse cultural, economic, and geographical landscape. The university's establishment addressed the pressing educational needs of the region's residents. Elias S. Stover, UNM's first president, oversaw the construction of Hodgin Hall in 1892, marking the university's physical and symbolic beginnings. From its humble beginnings, the university's trajectory has been marked by a growing influence on regional and national scholarship, particularly in fields relating to the Southwest such as anthropology, archaeology, history, and the arts. While the architectural landscape of the campus has undeniably shaped its physical identity, the academic programs, faculty, students, community, and evolving campus have played just as significant a role in shaping UNM's legacy. In its early years, UNM faced significant challenges, including the lack of formal secondary education among its prospective students. This necessitated the creation of a preparatory curriculum, which remained in place until 1896, when Clarence Herrick, UNM's second president, began transitioning the institution toward true university-level education. Under William G. Tight, UNM's third president, the university established a unique identity by emphasizing Southwestern studies and adopting the Pueblo Revival architectural style. Tight's decision, though initially controversial, to align the campus's architecture with New Mexico's Indigenous and Hispanic heritage solidified the university's physical and cultural connection to the region. University architect Van Dorn Hooker once remarked that the campus architecture is "a conscious reflection of this land, its history, and its culture," a statement that resonates with anyone who steps onto the campus for the first time. It's immediately apparent that UNM is unlike any other university. The Pueblo style has also developed throughout the decades, with five distinct styles on campus that play off the vernacular architecture of Spanish missions and New Mexican pueblos, creating its own vocabulary of carefully studied features and design compositions that are meant to evoke a sense of place and regional feeling. The university's growth mirrored New Mexico's journey toward statehood on January 6, 1912, a milestone that brought increased resources and recognition. By 1922, UNM had earned college accreditation, transitioning from a small territorial school to a respected institution of higher learning. During the 1920s, enrollment grew steadily, bolstered by an influx of students after World War I. By 1928, UNM had firmly established itself as a significant educational and cultural force, laying the groundwork for future expansion.

One pivotal figure in UNM's early development was Anita Osuna Carr, the first Hispanic woman on the university faculty. From 1924 to 1933, Carr taught Spanish and French, advocated for bilingual education, and worked to preserve New Mexico's Hispanic and Latin American heritage. She founded the New Mexico Folklore Society and helped establish the New Mexico Art League, further cementing UNM's commitment to fostering cultural connections. Under Pres. James F. Zimmerman (1927–1945), UNM expanded its focus on fields relevant to the unique region, such as Southwestern history, including anthropology and archaeology, and Latin American studies. Zimmerman emphasized the importance of studying New Mexico's heritage and its broader regional context. This shift was reflected in both the curriculum and the university's archaeological fieldwork, particularly through the efforts of Edgar Lee Hewett, a prominent archeologist. Hewett's work on the Antiquities Act of 1906 laid the foundation for the preservation of Chaco Culture and the establishment of Chaco Culture National Historical Park. Other early faculty members, such as Florence Hawley Ellis, who helped lay the groundwork for New Mexico's archaeology programs, and scholars from other disciplines, contributed to the establishment of UNM as a hub for research in these fields. UNM's commitment to diversity and inclusion gained momentum during the mid-20th century. By the 1960s and 1970s, the institutional focus on regional and minority studies led to the creation of specialized programs such as Chicano Studies, Africana Studies, and Native American Studies to address the educational needs and interests of students. By the 1990s, UNM boasted one of the largest populations of Hispanic and Native American students and faculty in the United States. A 1995 study highlighted that the number of full-time Hispanic faculty at UNM was four times the national average, and the number of Native American faculty was five times greater. UNM's expansion has not been just academic. In the 1960s, the university underwent significant physical development as part of a strategic plan to support its growing academic offerings. A new campus layout, which included the creation of a north campus for medical facilities and a south campus for athletic and research units, aimed to facilitate the increased demand for both academic and extracurricular spaces. This reorganization was accompanied by further construction of new buildings, such as the Student Union Building, the Law School, and the Medical Center. The central campus was to be situated so that all classes were within a 10-minute walking distance, emphasizing accessibility and convenience. Amidst this expansion, the addition of the Duck Pond has become a beloved feature of the campus, enhancing its natural beauty and providing a space for students, faculty, and visitors to gather, study, reflect, and connect with nature.

The university also extended its reach beyond Albuquerque with satellite campuses in Los Alamos, Gallup, Zuni, and Valencia County, each serving as a localized center for academic programs. The arts also flourished during this time. UNM's photography program, established in the early 1960s, gained national recognition under the leadership of Van Deren Coke and then Beaumont Newhall. The program attracted renowned faculty and developed a world-class photography collection, now housed in the UNM Art Museum. The Jonson Gallery and the Tamarind Institute further elevated UNM's reputation in the arts. In music, figures such as Marilyn Tyler, Jane Snow, Kurt Frederick, and Grace Thompson Edmister contributed to the department's growth. Edmister, who chaired the music department from 1925 to 1942, became the first woman to conduct a city symphony and a predecessor to the New Mexico Symphony Orchestra. UNM has also been home to numerous influential alumni, including Leslie Marmon Silko, Rudolfo Anaya, Denise Chávez, Tony Hillerman, Lois Duncan, and Deb Haaland, the first Native American US cabinet secretary. These individuals have significantly contributed to literature, politics, and cultural preservation. UNM has also played a critical role in preserving New Mexico's linguistic heritage. Sabine Ulibarrí, Spanish as a Heritage Language (SUSHL), led by Damian Vergara Wilson, focuses on the unique dialect of Traditional New Mexican Spanish. Developed in isolation, this dialect blends elements of medieval Spanish, Mexican Spanish, indigenous languages, and English. The program emphasizes learning from familial and local traditions, fostering pride in New Mexico's unique linguistic legacy and cultural connection to the language. Today, UNM stands as a nationally recognized institution that blends cultural, historical, and academic perspectives with innovation and rigor. Programs in the humanities, sciences, and professional fields, such as law, engineering, and medicine, also continue to excel. The university's campus has expanded to accommodate modern needs while maintaining a deep respect for its cultural roots. Through its commitment to diversity, academic excellence, and community engagement, UNM not only honors its heritage but also ensures a vibrant and dynamic future in the Southwest.

One

The Early Years, 1889–1928

The University of New Mexico was founded on February 28, 1889, during a transformative period in the New Mexico Territory. Established in Albuquerque to address the region's educational needs, UNM began under the leadership of its first president, Elias S. Stover, with the construction of Hodgin Hall in 1892. Stover's tenure also saw the establishment of a gymnasium in 1895, which supported the growth of athletics, including basketball, baseball, football, and track and field, fostering early school spirit. Early challenges, such as the lack of formal secondary education, led to the creation of a preparatory curriculum, which remained in place until 1896. In 1897, under Clarence Herrick, UNM's second president, the university began offering college-level courses and constructed Hadley Hall, providing additional classrooms for UNM's first science building. William G. Tight, who became president in 1901, ushered in a transformative era. Tight shifted the campus's architectural style from Victorian to Pueblo Revival, aligning UNM with the region's Indigenous and Hispanic heritage. This bold decision, though controversial, became a defining feature of the university's identity. He also expanded the campus with new dormitories and a heating plant, all in the Pueblo Revival style, and introduced Arbor Day. UNM's growth mirrored New Mexico's journey to statehood in 1912, which brought increased resources and recognition. Under David Spence Hill (1919–1927), the university implemented rigorous academic standards and expanded its infrastructure. The library, originally housed in Hodgin Hall, was moved to a dedicated Library Annex, reflecting UNM's commitment to academic growth. Pioneering faculty like Helen E. Murphy, the first female department chair in biology, broke barriers in academia, while student soldiers training on campus during World War I highlighted the university's growing importance. By 1922, UNM earned accreditation from the North Central Association of Colleges and Schools, marking its transformation into a respected university. By the late 1920s, UNM had established itself as a prominent educational and cultural force in the Southwest, with a growing, diverse student body and an expanding curriculum. These early achievements laid the foundation for UNM's continued growth and influence in the decades to come.

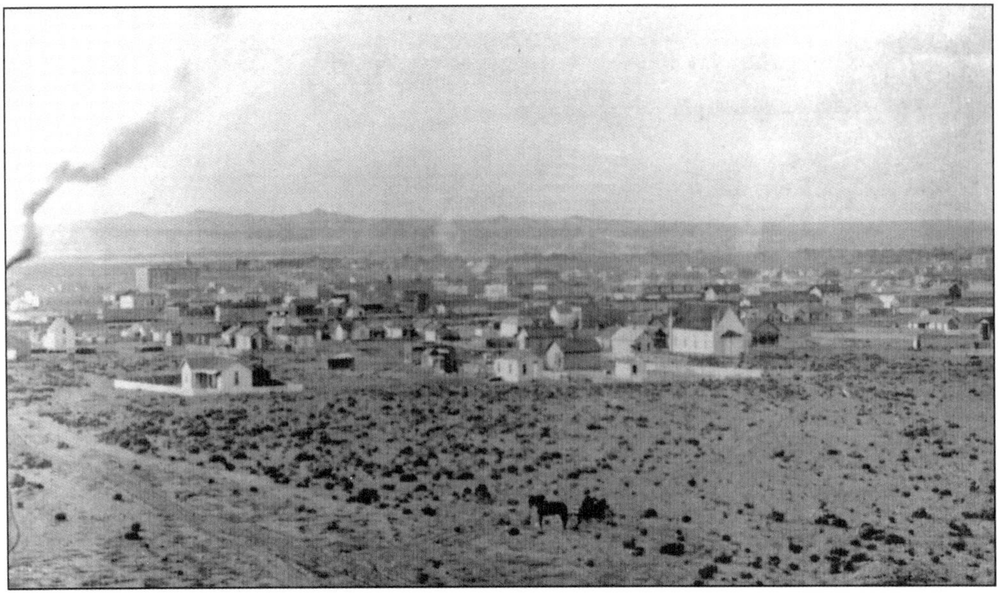

This early photograph is of Albuquerque looking west in 1889. UNM was established by an act of Territorial Legislature on February 28, 1889. The Enabling Act specified that the institution should be located east of Albuquerque on not less than 20 acres of land and that the institution should become the state university at the time statehood was obtained.

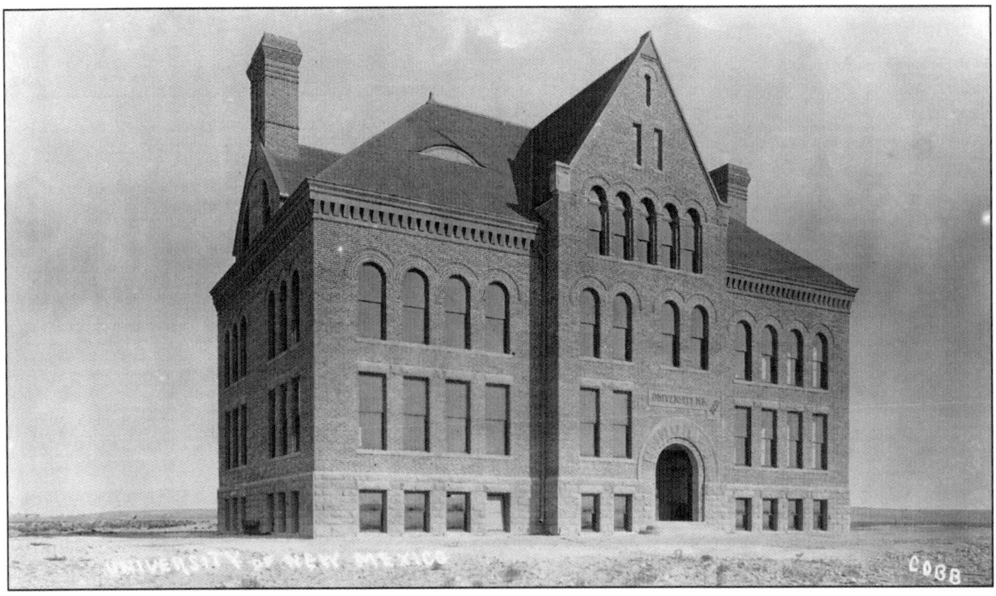

Opened as a summer school on June 15, 1892, the university's Main Building symbolized New Mexico's educational aspirations in 1892. Fall classes began on September 21, and the 75 students enrolled that fall embodied hopes to enrich the region still regarded as the "Wild West" and advance statehood. Renamed in 1936 to honor Charles Hodgin, a long-serving faculty member, the building marked a transformative era for higher education in the territory.

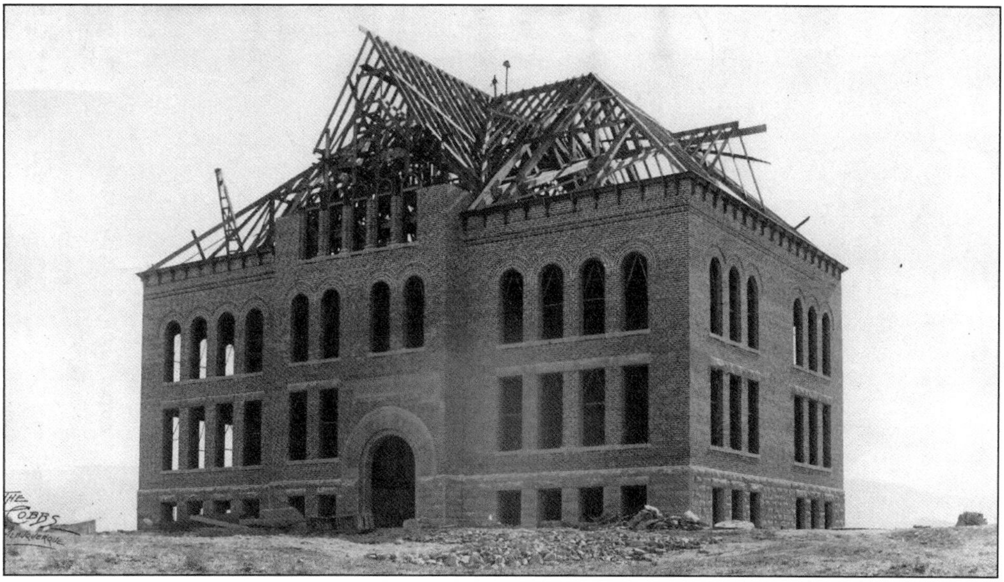

Despite ongoing construction, UNM opened to students on June 15, 1892, with lectures held off-campus. Most of the 75 students enrolled took preparatory classes to address the poor state of secondary education in the territory. This preparatory curriculum remained in place until 1896. By the fall, the building was ready, and enrollment had reached 108. Many of the students aimed to teach in the territory's schools.

William G. Tight, a scholar of Pueblo culture, remodeled the Main Building in 1908 to reflect a vernacular, regionally distinctive architectural style. Tight replaced the popular Romanesque red brick with features inspired by Indigenous architecture, aligning the campus more closely with its Southwest environment. Rodey Hall, a 500-seat auditorium, was added nearby. Hodgin Hall was added to the National Register of Historic Places in 1973, solidifying its historical significance.

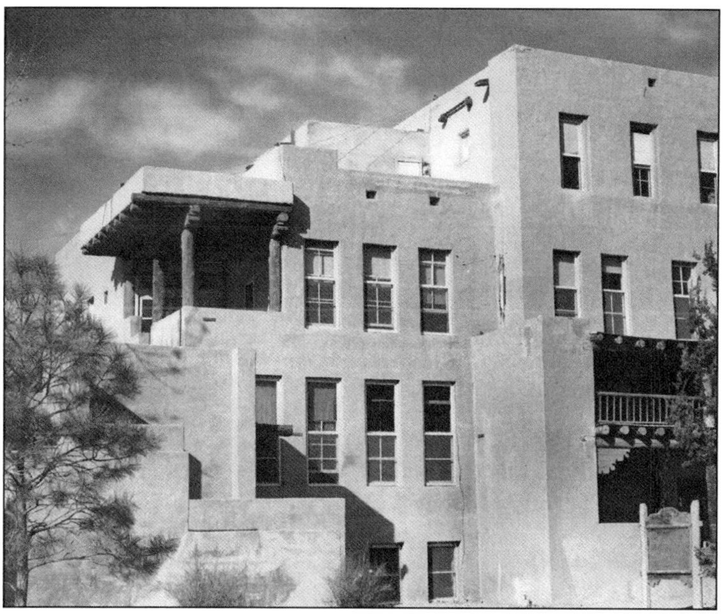

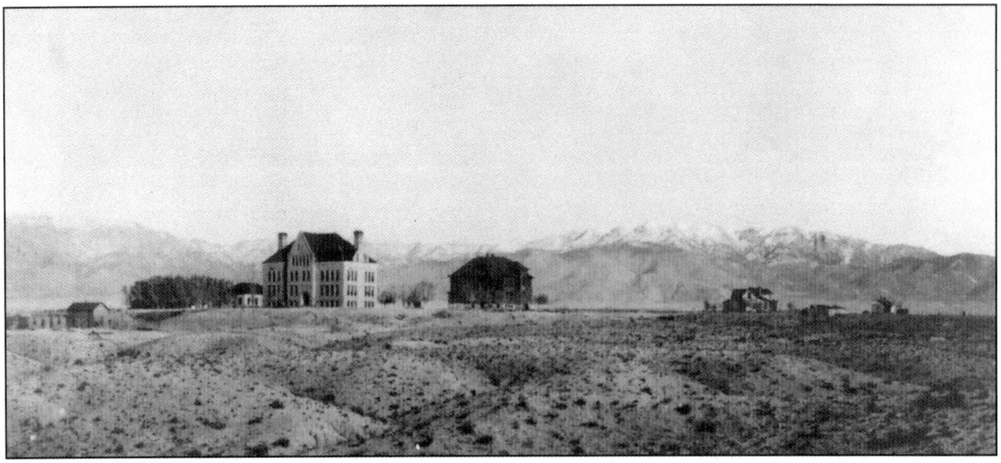

Hodgin Hall held all of the functions of a university inside it. This versatile structure housed classrooms, offices, a library on the first floor, four recitation rooms on the second floor, a large room used for assemblies, and later a girls' gymnasium on the third floor. The basement housed bathrooms, a lunchroom, living quarters for the university custodian, and in later years, physics and chemistry labs and a home economics department.

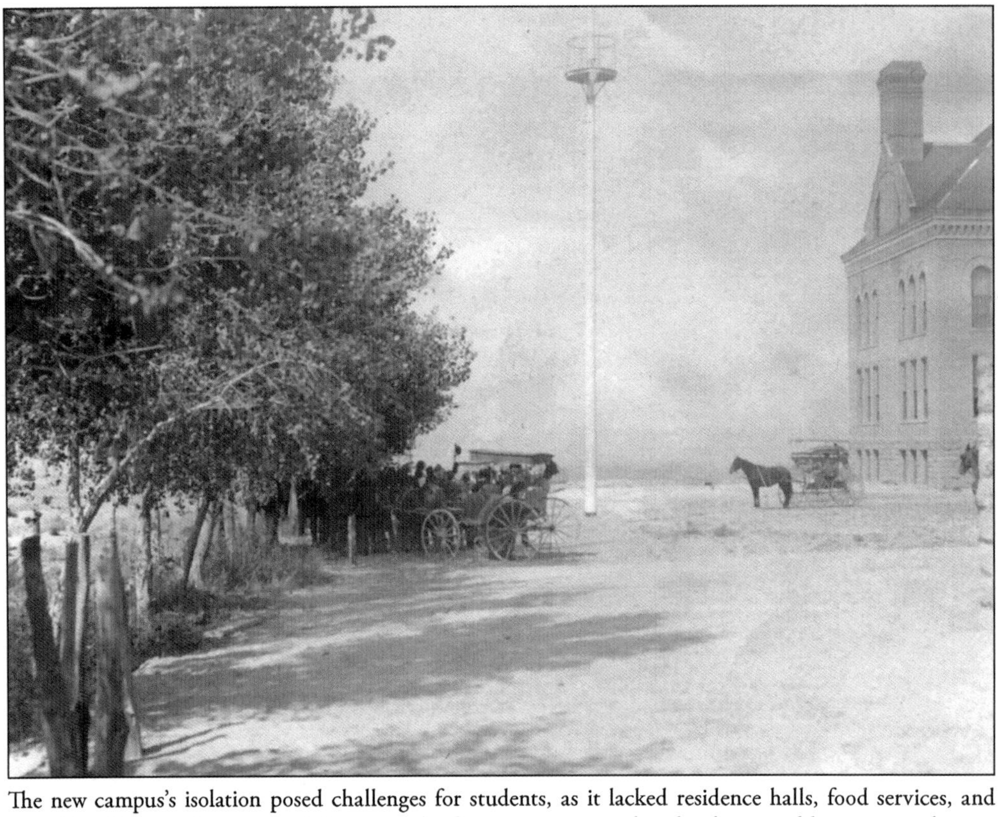

The new campus's isolation posed challenges for students, as it lacked residence halls, food services, and amenities. Most students walked the two miles from town, as travel with a horse and buggy was a luxury. UNM did provide some transportation; students could pay a five-cent fare to ride a buggy drawn by four horses up to the university, which was overseen by Josephine Parsons.

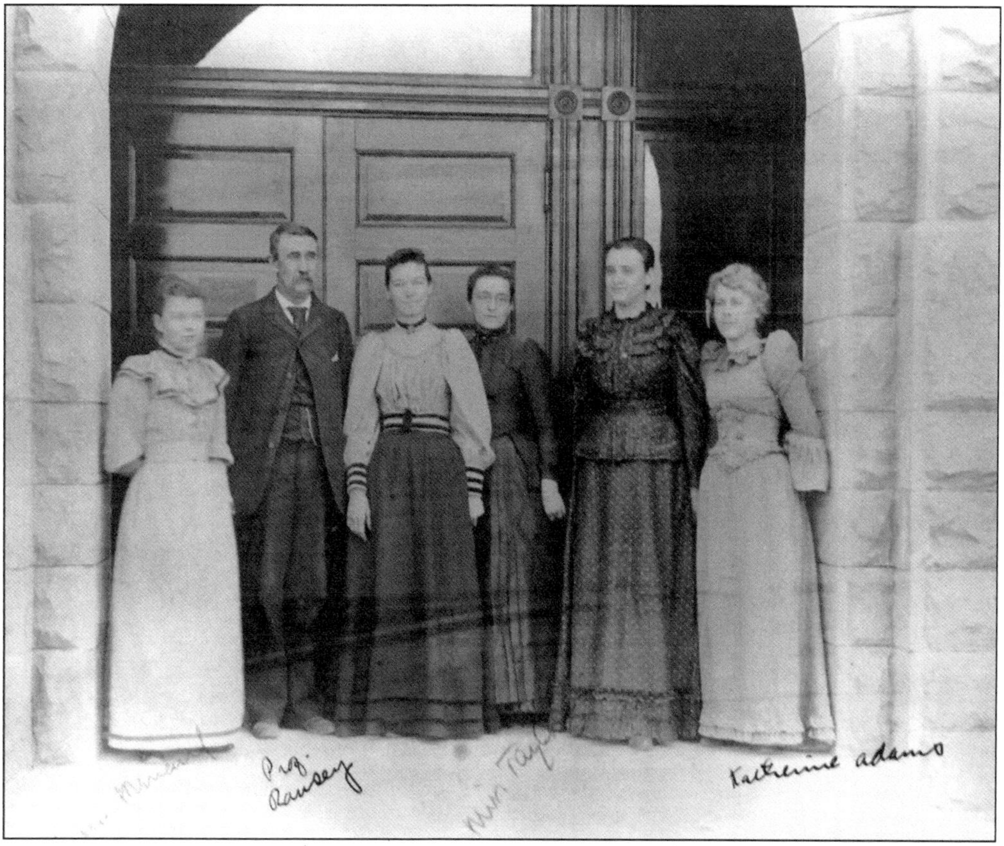

In the fall semester of 1892, George Ramsey, principal of the preparatory and normal departments, led UNM's academic affairs while teaching mathematics and physics. The first six faculty members included five master's degree holders: Ramsey, Alcinda Morrow (English and Spanish), Marshall R. Gaines (Latin and natural sciences), Albert Christy (elocution), G.R. Stouffer (accounting), and student Andrew Groh (German and French). This photograph features two of UNM's first graduates, Katherine Adams and Bessie Menaul. In the second year, the university hired new faculty, bringing the total to eight, with four being women.

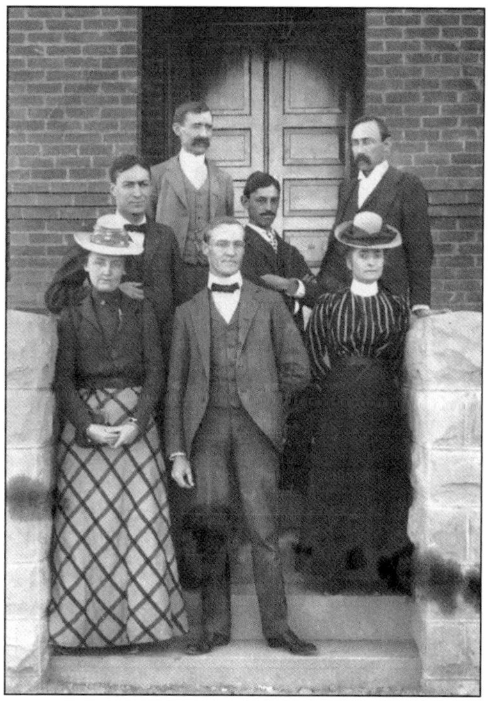

Dean Charles E. Hodgin served 28 years as principal of the Normal School as well as dean and vice president of the School of Education. A member of UNM's first graduating class of 1894, he was also one of the organizers of the Educational Association of New Mexico Territory. This 1893 photograph, showing him on the left on the steps of the administration building, honors his lasting legacy, with Hodgin Hall later named in his honor.

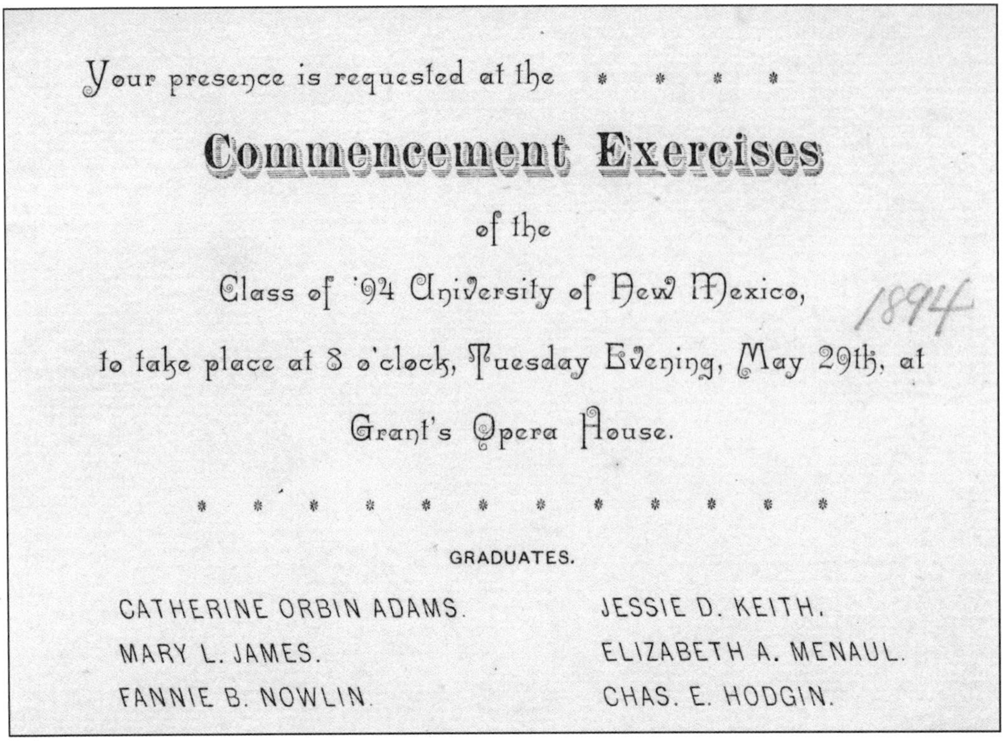

Your presence is requested at the * * * *

Commencement Exercises

of the

Class of '94 University of New Mexico, 1894

to take place at 8 o'clock, Tuesday Evening, May 29th, at

Grant's Opera House.

* * * * * * * * * * * *

GRADUATES.

CATHERINE ORBIN ADAMS. JESSIE D. KEITH.

MARY L. JAMES. ELIZABETH A. MENAUL.

FANNIE B. NOWLIN. CHAS. E. HODGIN.

At the spring 1894 commencement, the first graduates of the University of New Mexico were six recipients from the normal department. Among them were five women and one man, each receiving a bachelor of arts in pedagogy. Since the university was not yet prepared to offer full college courses, these graduates had completed some coursework elsewhere at other universities to meet the requirements. Most of the 140 students enrolled at UNM at the time were barely ready for the preparatory program. This cohort marked UNM's initial commitment to teacher training and education, also reflecting the growing role of women in academia during the late 19th century. Their achievement laid the foundation for the expansion of academic programs and the advancement of higher education in the territory.

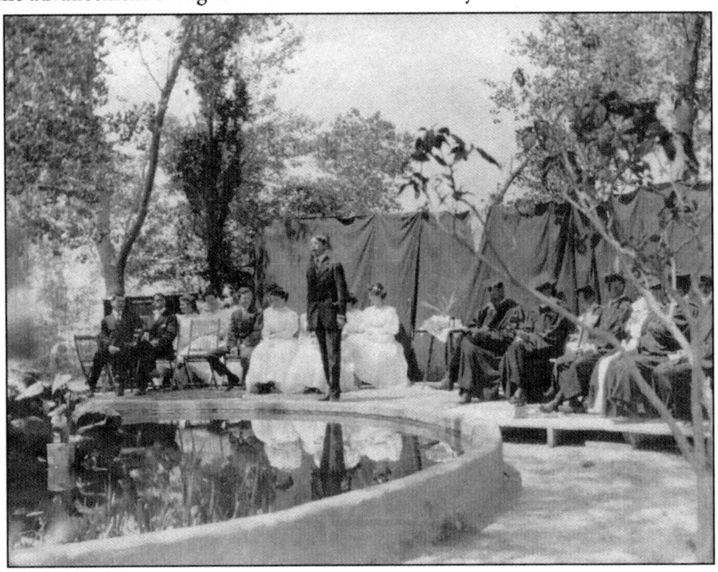

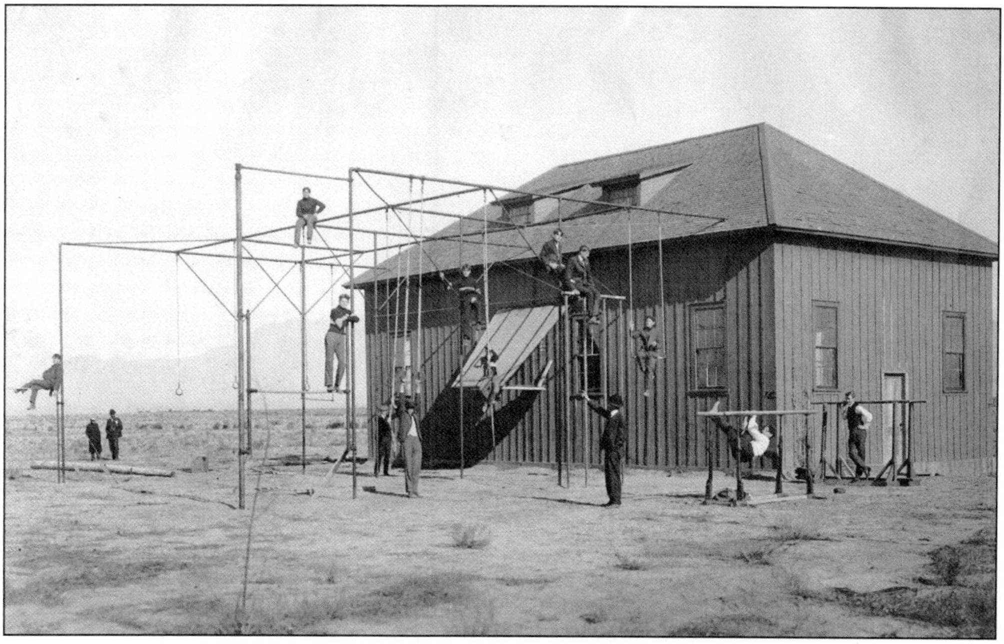

The gymnasium, from 1895, was a substantial frame building with an outdoor gymnasium constructed of iron pipes affording a framework to which trapezes, running rings, horizontal bars, chest bars, and parallel bars were attached. In this 1895 photograph, students engage in physical activity at the first gymnasium on the University of New Mexico campus. The simple wooden structure was one of the earliest spaces dedicated to student recreation and fitness.

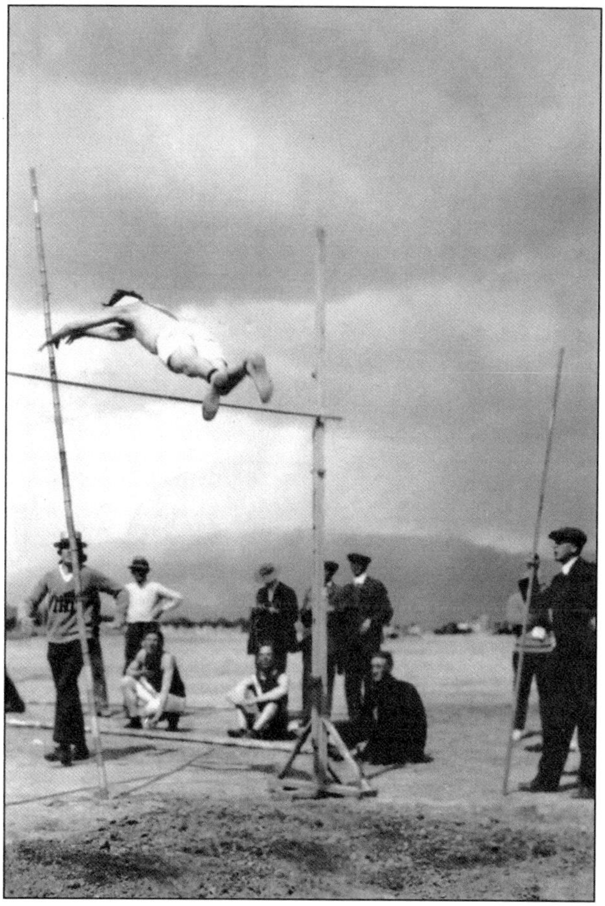

An early glimpse into UNM's athletic history, this c. 1900 photograph captures a student pole vaulter in action. As one of the few organized sports at the time, track and field events like pole vaulting offered students a chance to engage in competitive athletics. The makeshift equipment and outdoor setting reflect the humble beginnings of sports at UNM before the establishment of formal athletic programs and facilities.

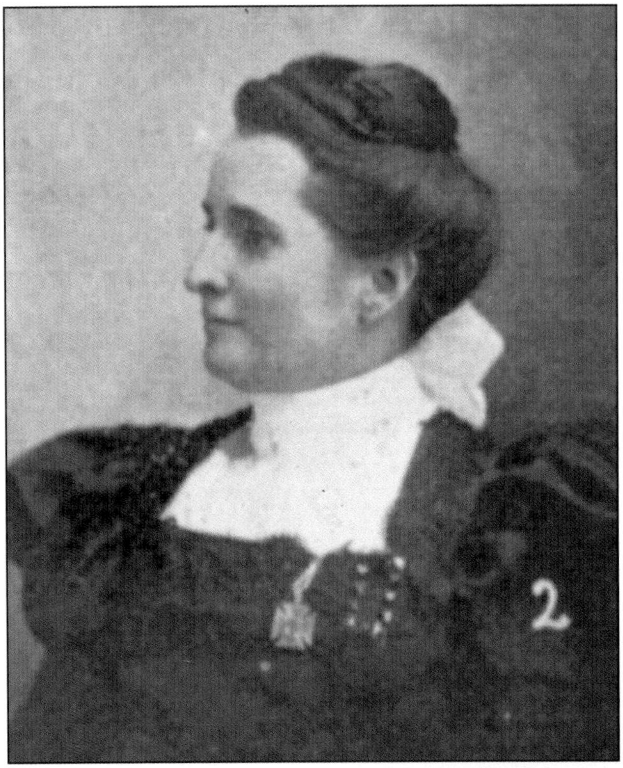

Josephine S. Parsons served the University of New Mexico from 1894 to 1927, holding various roles, including instructor of mathematics and principal of the commercial department as early as 1893. She earned her bachelor of arts in 1904. In recognition of her significant contributions, Parsons Hall and Parsons Grove were later named in her honor.

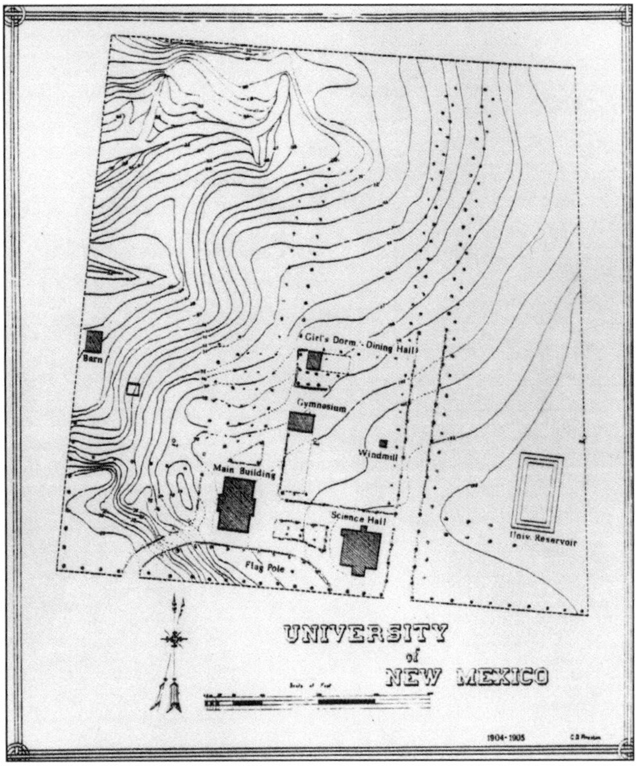

This 1904–1905 map highlights the original 20-acre site chosen by the Territorial Legislature for the University of New Mexico. Located on the east mesa, this modest parcel laid the foundation for what would become a sprawling and architecturally unique campus. In these early days, the university's vision and layout were just beginning to emerge, setting the stage for its future growth and development.

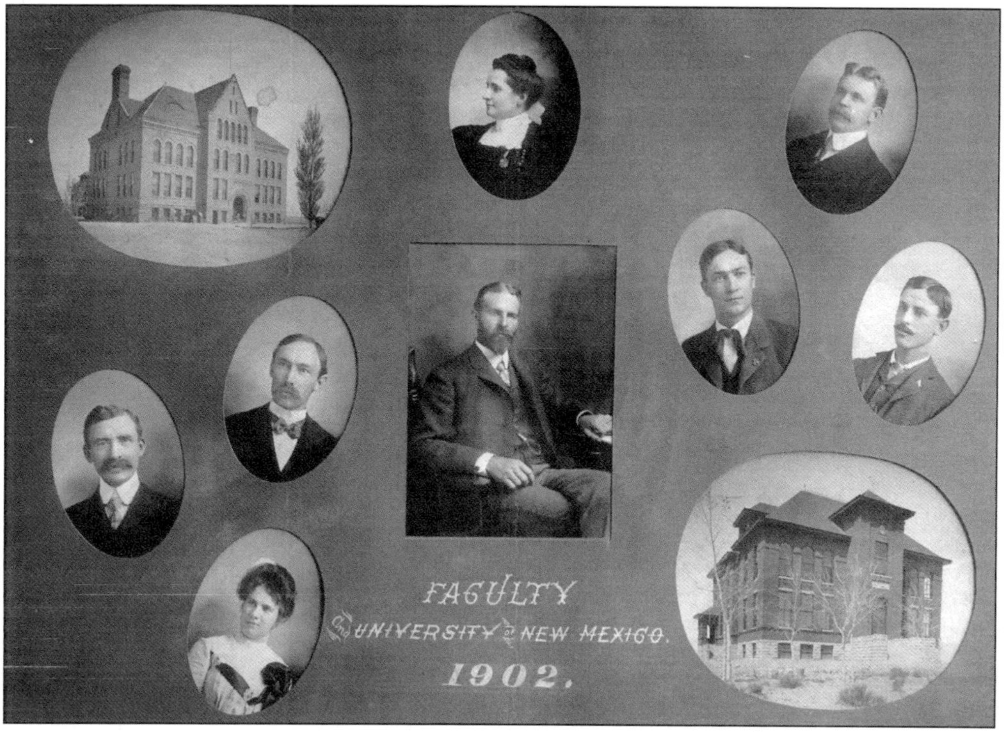

This 1902 photograph captures the early faculty of the University of New Mexico, with Pres. William G. Tight seated at the center. Tight, who served as president from 1901 to 1909, was instrumental in shaping UNM's early identity. He advocated for a campus architecture inspired by the Pueblo Revival style, leaving a lasting influence on the university's aesthetic.

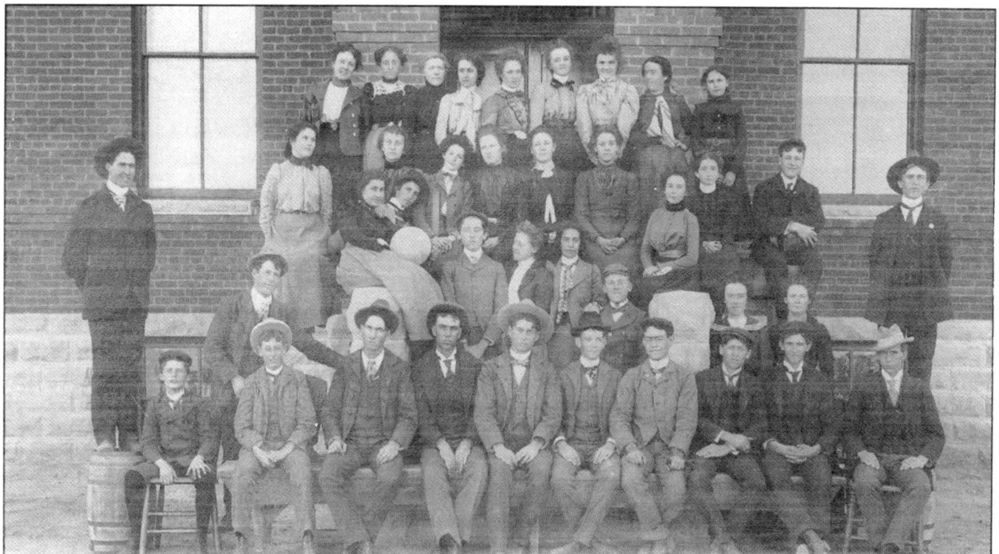

The University of New Mexico's 1901 graduating class featured a small but pioneering group of students. Pictured here are the graduates who helped shape the institution's early academic tradition. Their accomplishments reflected the university's early emphasis on teacher education and regional service, with a focus on preparing educators to serve the growing public school system in New Mexico.

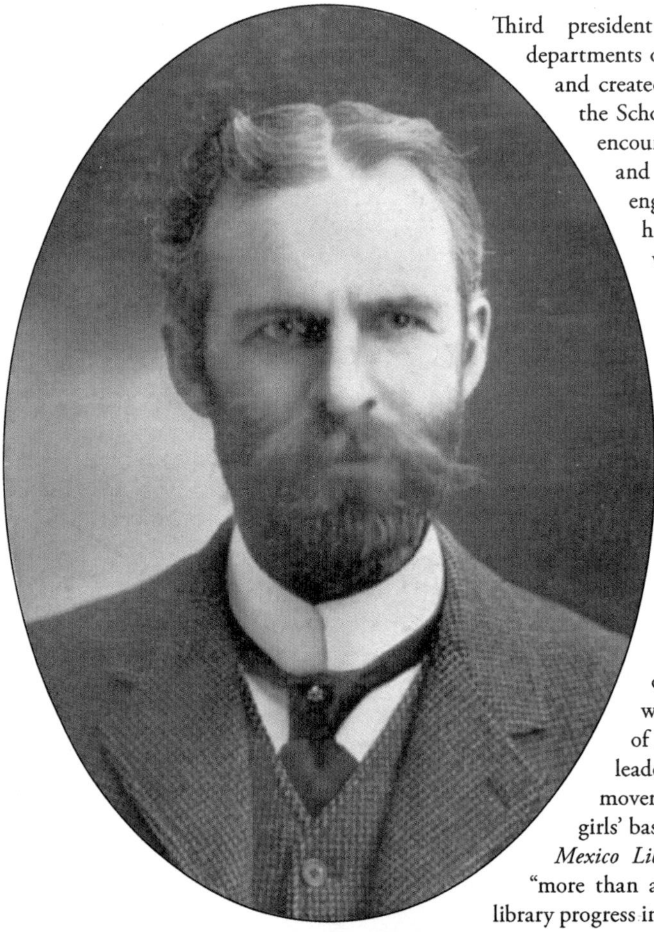

Third president William Tight expanded the departments of philosophy, language, and science and created the School of Music in 1902 and the School of Engineering in 1906. He also encouraged the formation of sororities and other academic and social clubs for engineering and drama students, while his campus beautification projects were also significant.

This photograph shows Julia Asplund with President Tight. Beginning in 1903, she was UNM's official first librarian and the first woman to serve on the UNM Board of Regents. She was one of the foremost leaders of the New Mexico suffrage movement as well as a history teacher and girls' basketball coach. According to the *New Mexico Library Bulletin* from 1958, Asplund "more than any one person, was responsible for library progress in New Mexico."

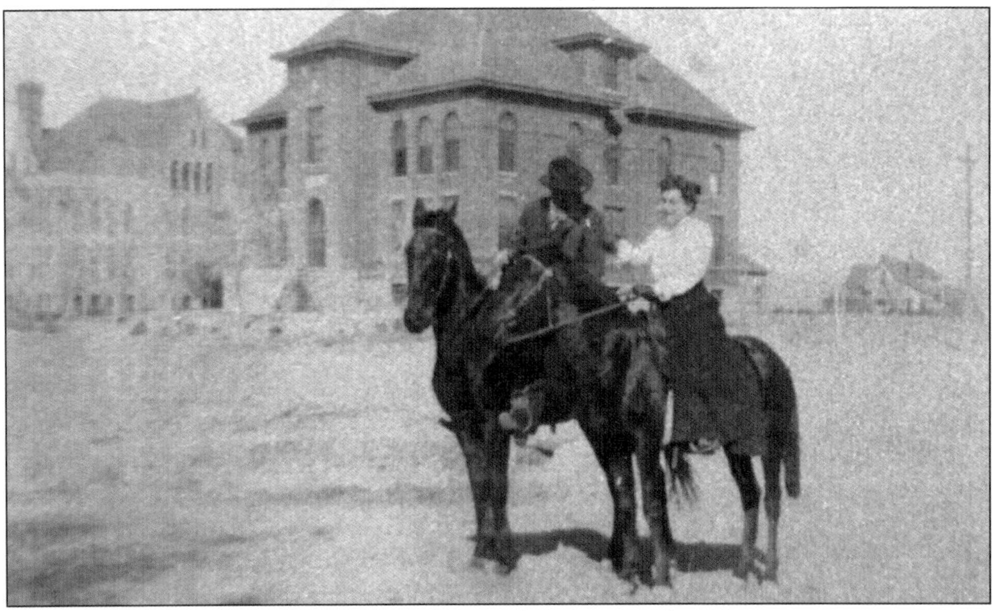

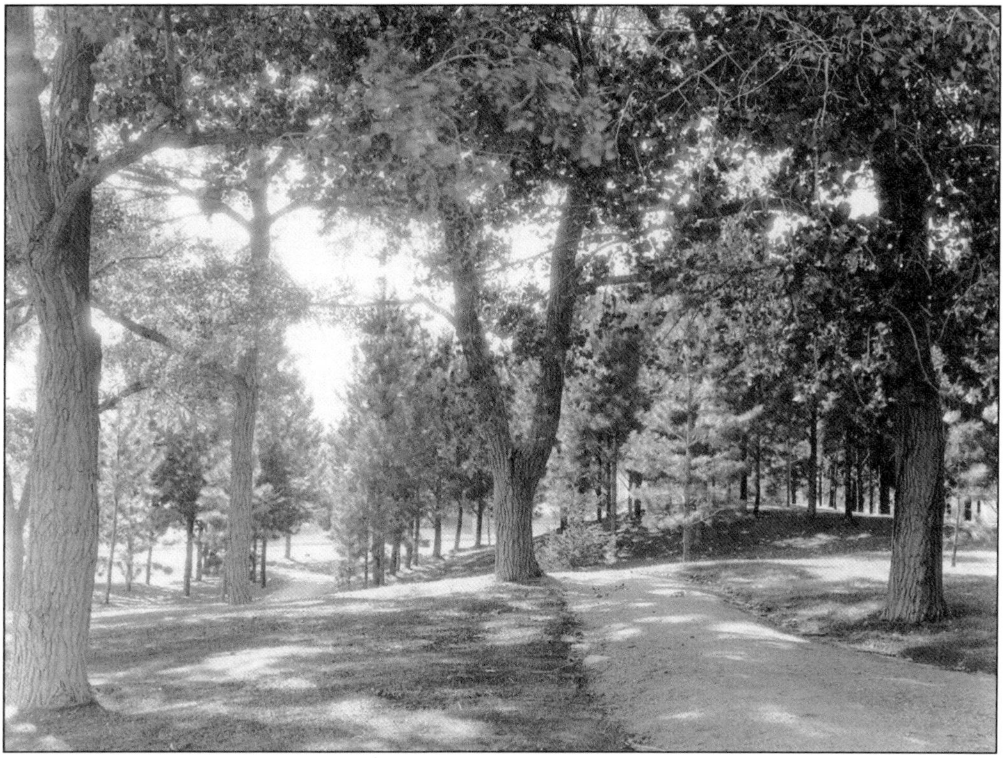

The University of New Mexico owes much of its charm and beauty to the more than 5,000 defining trees that grace its campus, a legacy that began under third president Tight. In 1904, Tight launched an annual Arbor Day event where faculty, students, societies like the Estella Society, and community members transplanted ponderosa pines from the Sandia Mountains behind Hodgin Hall, forming what would come to be known as Tight's Grove. Tight believed that the beautification of the campus would foster a more conducive academic environment, and these are now the oldest trees on campus. He also oversaw the planting of other plants like rose bushes, honey locusts, and yuccas, further enriching the landscape. The installation of a reservoir in 1905 secured irrigation. His commitment to integrating New Mexico's cultural heritage extended to his promotion of Pueblo-style architecture. In 1994, the State of New Mexico designated the UNM campus an arboretum and provided protections for its over 200 species of trees, preserving Tight's vision. The largest tree on campus is a Siberian elm that is over 80 feet tall.

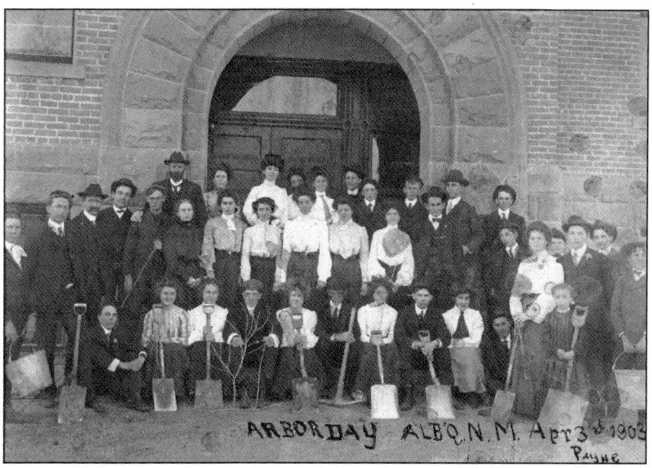

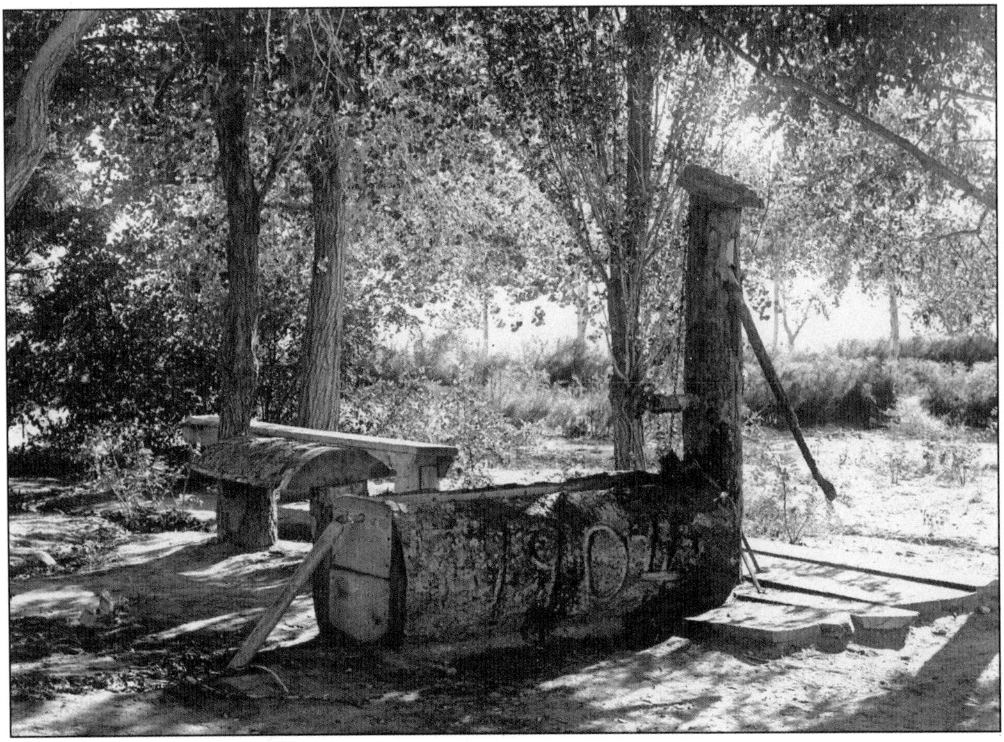

It was a custom of the graduating classes to leave something in the way of a class memorial. The custom was started by the class of 1904, which left a rustic pump that was situated near the avenue leading from the Main Building to Hadley Hall.

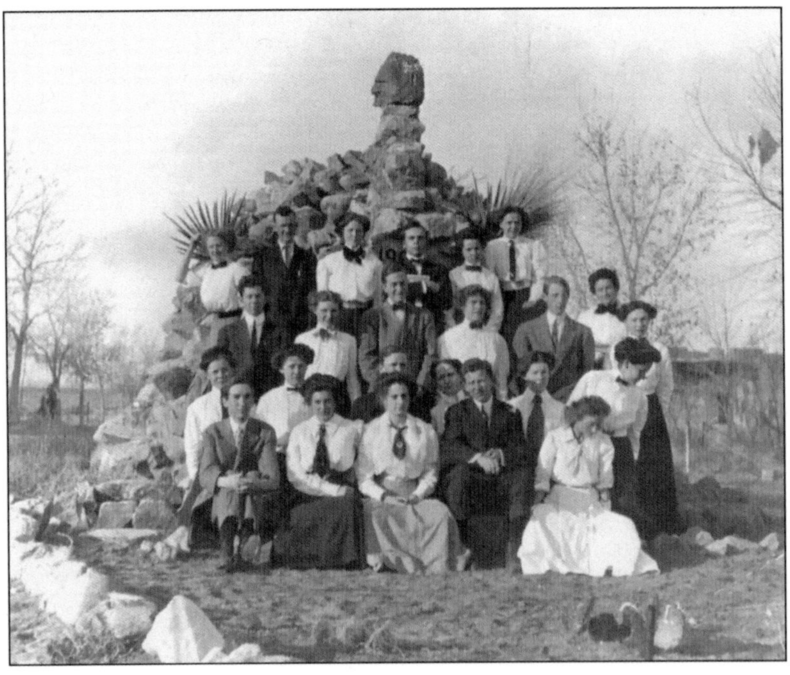

The class of 1907 left a sundial that bore a Native inscription: "Short the day and great the work. I tarry not for the slow." Many graduating classes took the opportunity to pose and take class pictures on the sundial.

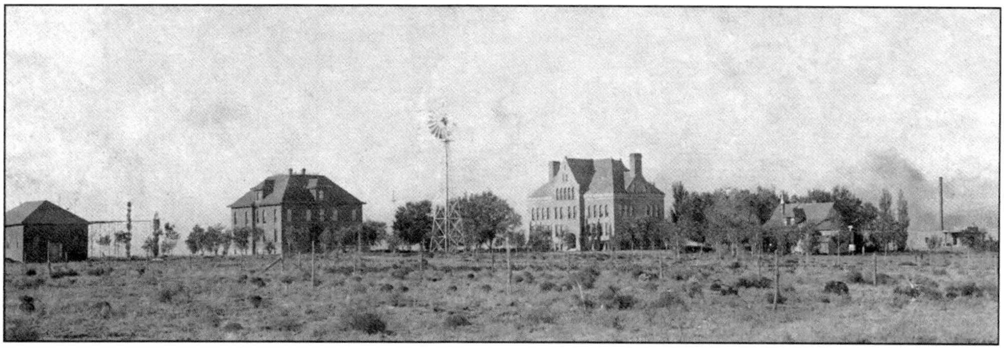

This photograph shows the entire campus as it was in 1906 before the remodeling of Hodgin Hall and before the fire in Hadley Hall. The first building erected on campus in the Pueblo Revival style was the boiler plant seen at the far right.

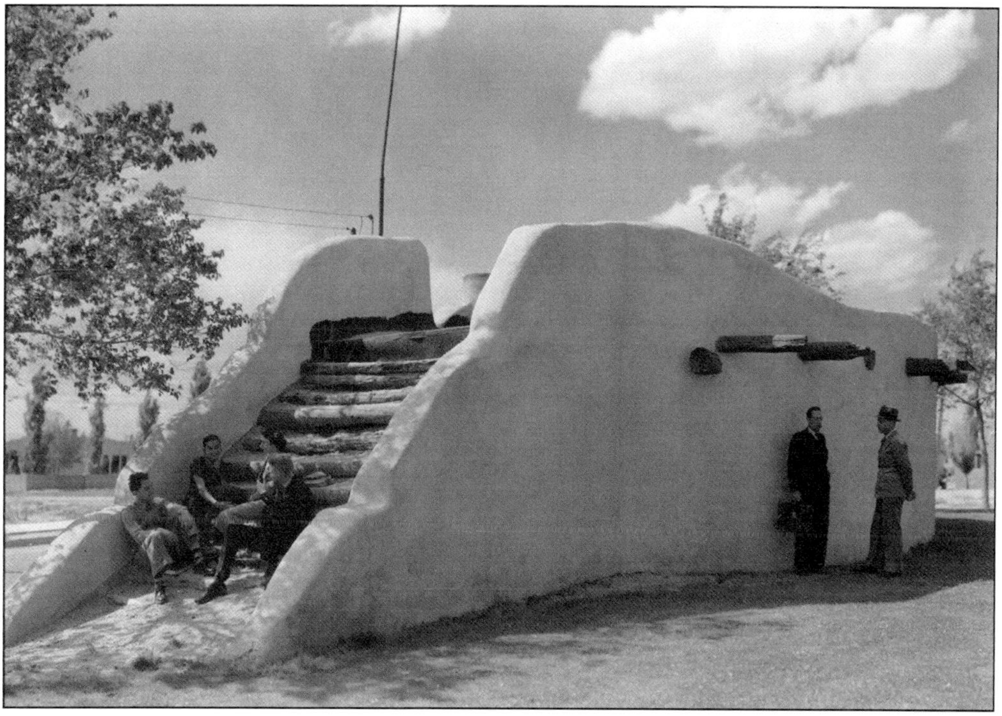

The Estufa, built in 1907–1908 by a local fraternity, stands as a key feature of the University of New Mexico's Albuquerque campus. Serving as the Pi Kappa Alpha chapter house since 1915, the structure draws on Pueblo kiva design, marking the start of Pueblo Revival architecture on campus. With adobe walls, vigas, and a unique roof entrance, it was listed in the National Register of Historic Places in 1988.

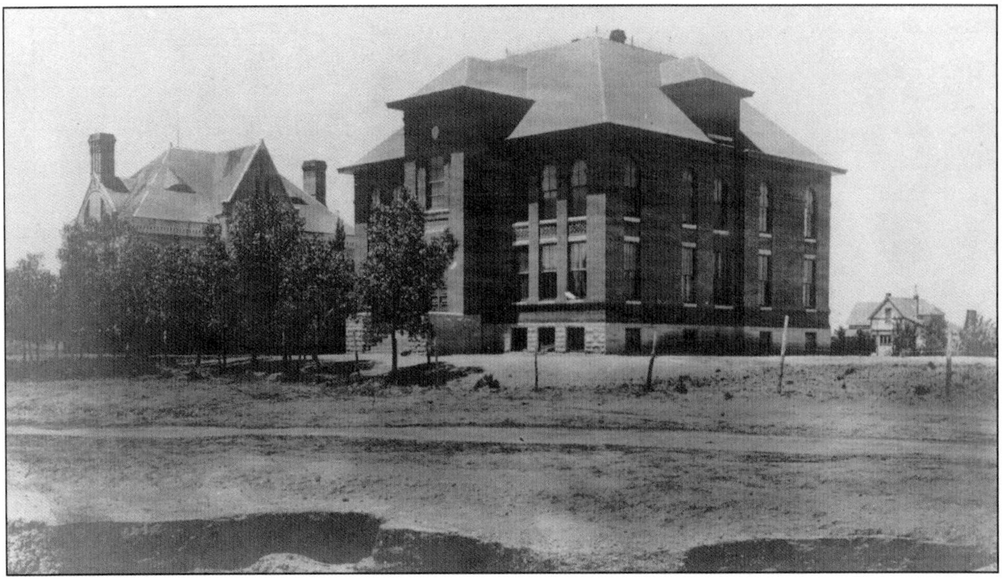

Second president Herrick made significant contributions to the University of New Mexico by establishing the College of Literature and Arts in 1899 (later Arts and Sciences). He introduced a Spanish language program for rural schools, created a bacteriology lab to combat tuberculosis, and implemented a teacher training program for Albuquerque's public schools. Herrick also oversaw the construction of Hadley Hall, UNM's first science building, which included laboratories, an herbarium, lecture rooms, and offices.

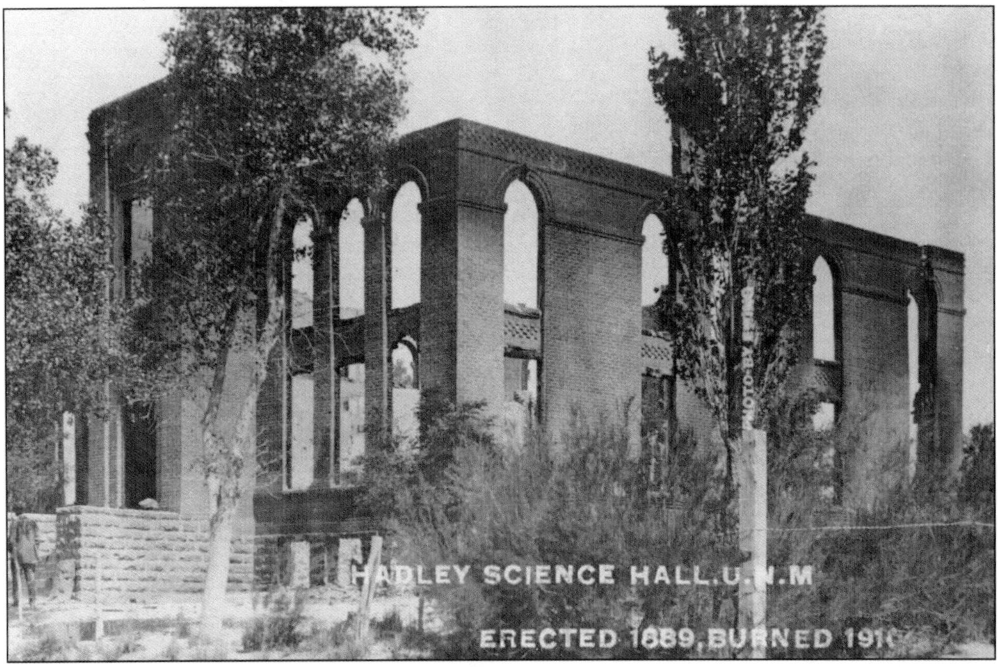

On May 23, 1910, a devastating fire at Hadley Hall destroyed valuable collections, including President Herrick's geological collection, the botanical collection, and the Ethnological Museum's ancient specimens. Gold and silver ores were melted down, and the mineralogy collection, which had been part of the St. Louis World's Fair exhibit, was also lost. Additionally, engineering and science equipment, as well as William Tight's personal papers and library, were destroyed. Access to the building was hindered by difficult road conditions.

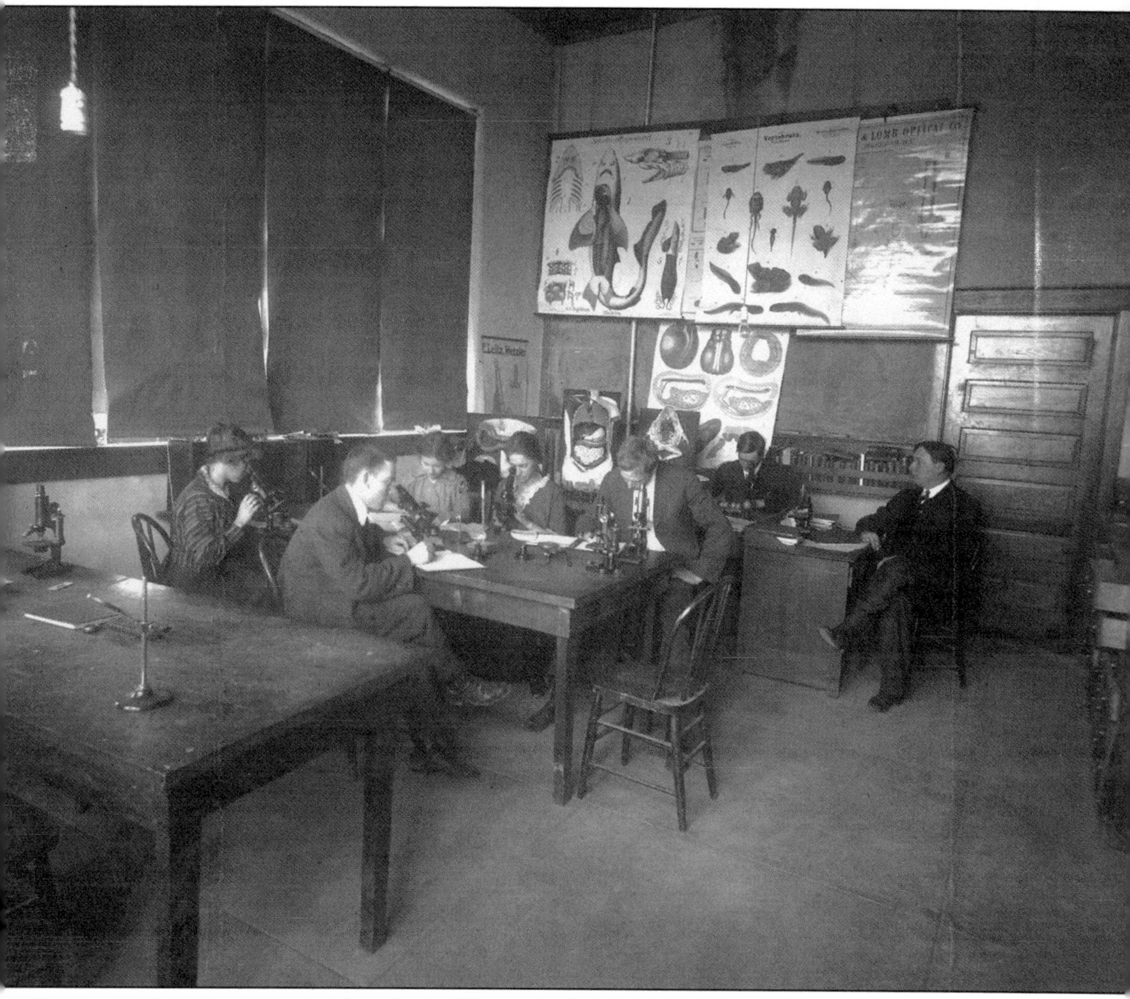

Biology has been a cornerstone of academic offerings at the University of New Mexico since 1892, shortly after its founding. Early courses emphasized physiology, botany, and zoology, reflecting a strong commitment to scientific education. The biology department achieved significant milestones, including having an all-female faculty of Dr. Edna Mosher and Dr. Elsie Foster and the appointment of Helen Elizabeth Murphy as the first female department chair in 1923. A trailblazer, Murphy graduated from Cornell University with a bachelor of science in 1917 and earned her doctorate in 1920 while serving as a graduate instructor in biology. The department awarded its first master of science degree in 1928 and its first doctorate in 1952, the same year Dr. Edward Castetter—namesake of the current biology building—joined as professor and chair. Under Murphy's leadership and through the contributions of early faculty, the department grew, ultimately expanding its curriculum and research scope. Today, it remains integral to UNM's mission, advancing biological sciences through education and innovation.

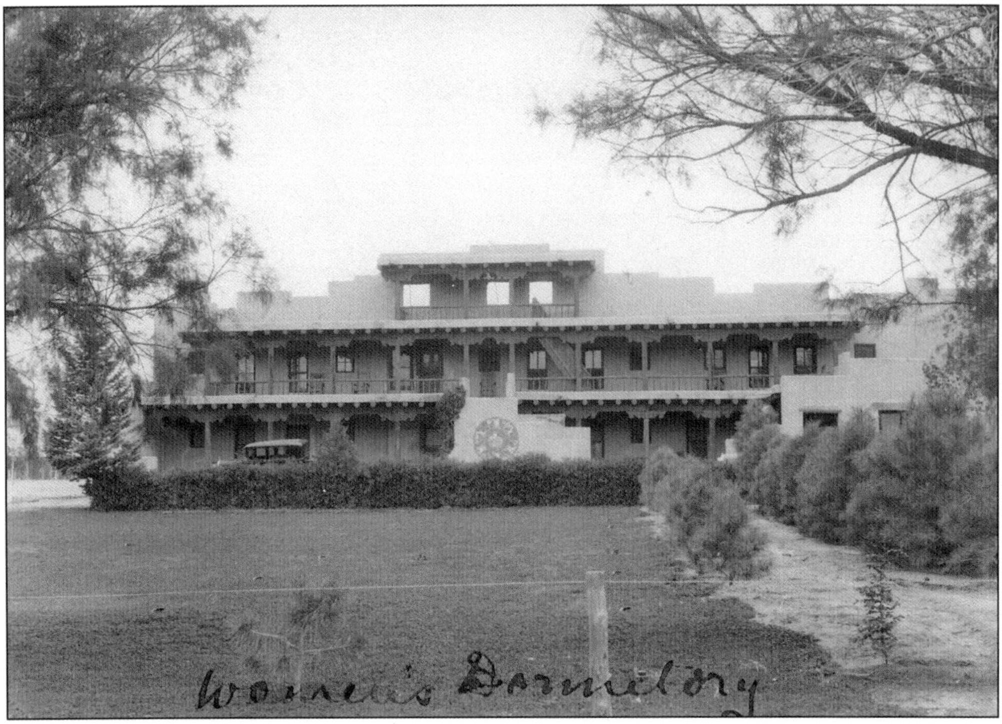

The University of New Mexico's first dorms, Hokona Hall (maiden butterfly), seen here, and Kwataka Hall, were built in 1906 in the Pueblo Revival style. These buildings featured distinctive elements like buttressed walls, projecting vigas, and stepped parapets. Inside, they were furnished with Navajo rugs and rustic furniture and included electric lighting and a solar-heated water system. The roofs were concealed with Spanish-style beehive ovens, or *hornos*. Hokona Hall, which housed 30 women, featured large symbols inspired by Hopi pottery designs by President Tight and English teacher Ethel Hickey.

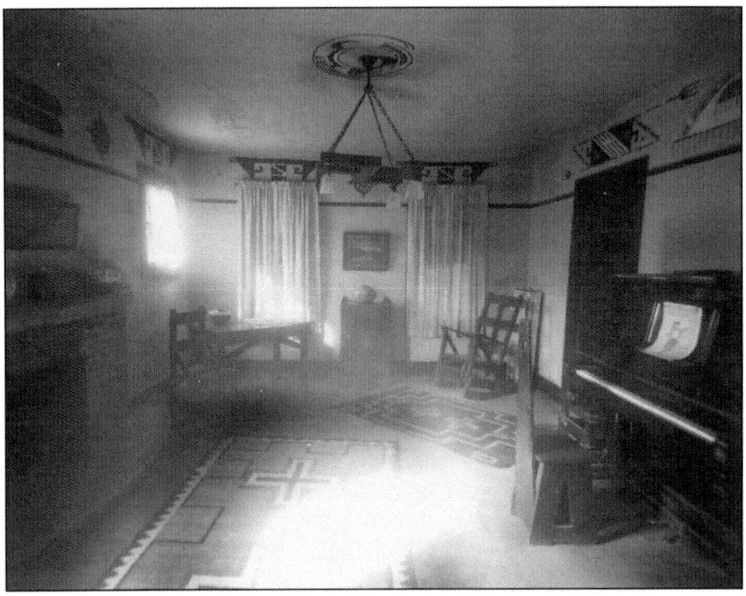

The interior of Hokona Hall showcases the Pueblo Revival style that defines much of UNM's architectural identity. Originally serving as a women's dormitory, Hokona Hall's design incorporated traditional Southwestern elements such as adobe-style walls and carved wooden beams. Rooms were arranged in suites with two bedrooms and a study room.

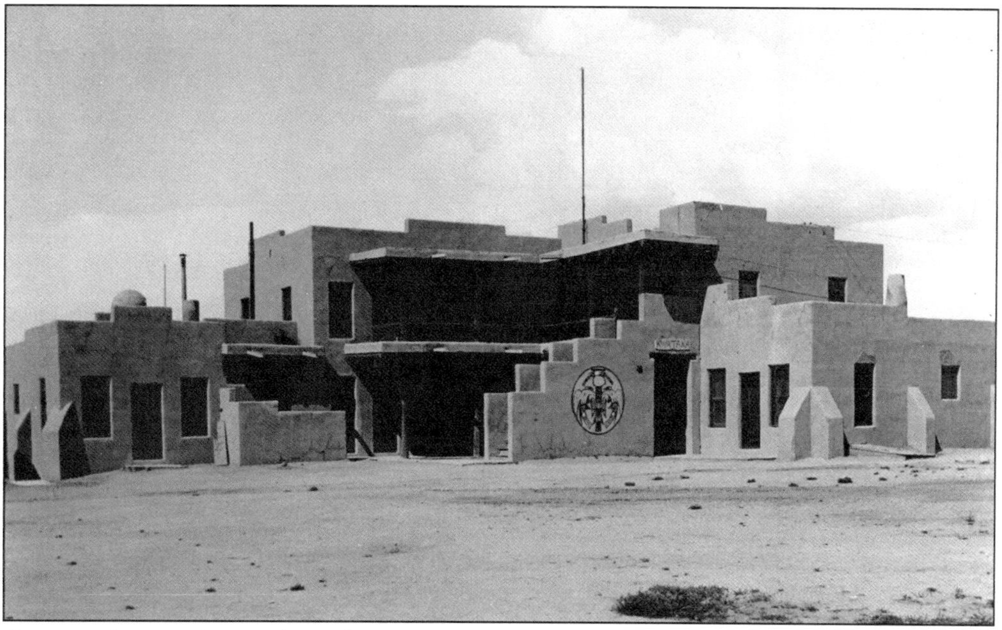

Constructed in 1906, Kwataka Hall (man eagle) was one of the University of New Mexico's earliest dormitories. Reflecting the Pueblo Revival style, the building symbolized the university's effort to incorporate regional Indigenous architectural traditions into its campus. The hall housed 24 male students and became an important part of the early campus community. Its design marked the beginning of a cohesive architectural vision at UNM.

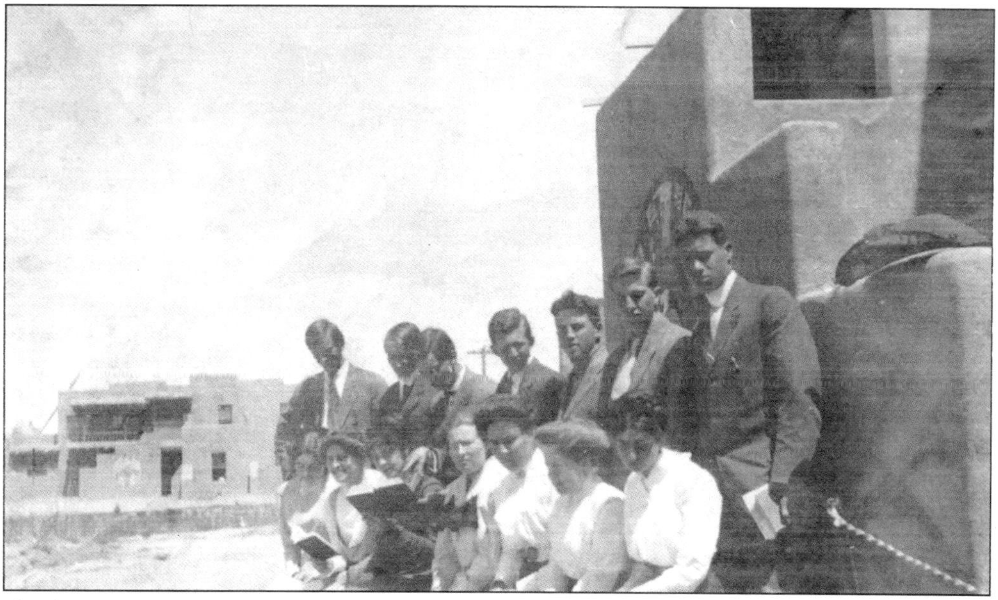

The dormitories not only provided essential housing but also served as spaces for social interaction and personal development among the early generations of UNM students. The girls would often invite the boys to their dormitories, and vice versa, for parties.

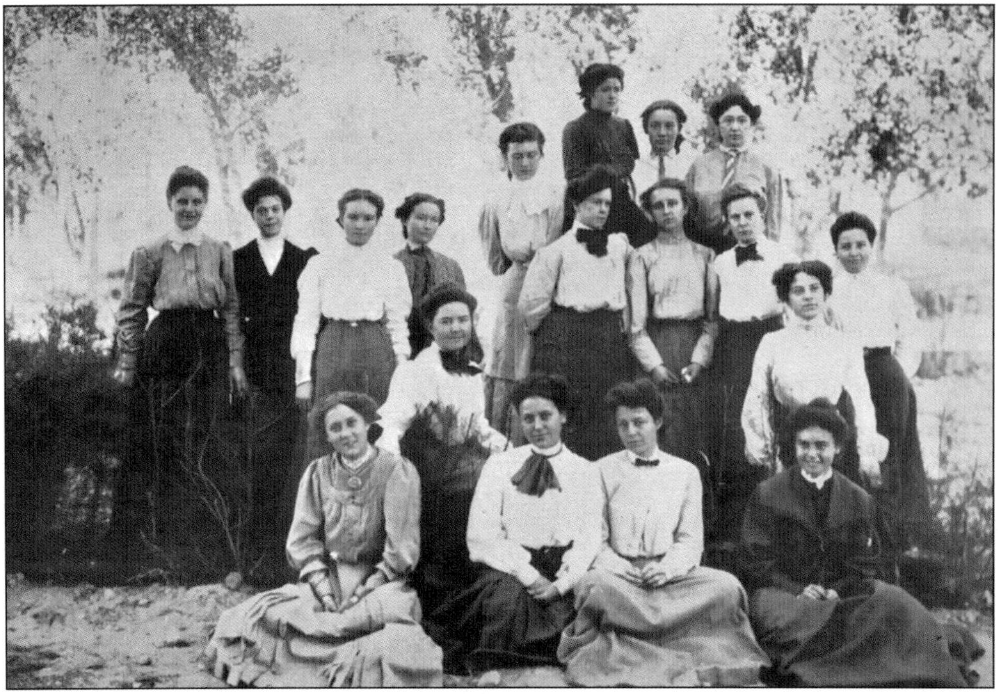

Founded in 1898, the Estrella Society was one of the University of New Mexico's oldest organizations for women, lasting until 1924. It served as a platform for young women dedicated to literary pursuits, fostering intellectual growth and women's rights advocacy during a time of limited educational opportunities. The society supported female students and contributed to expanding their presence in higher education.

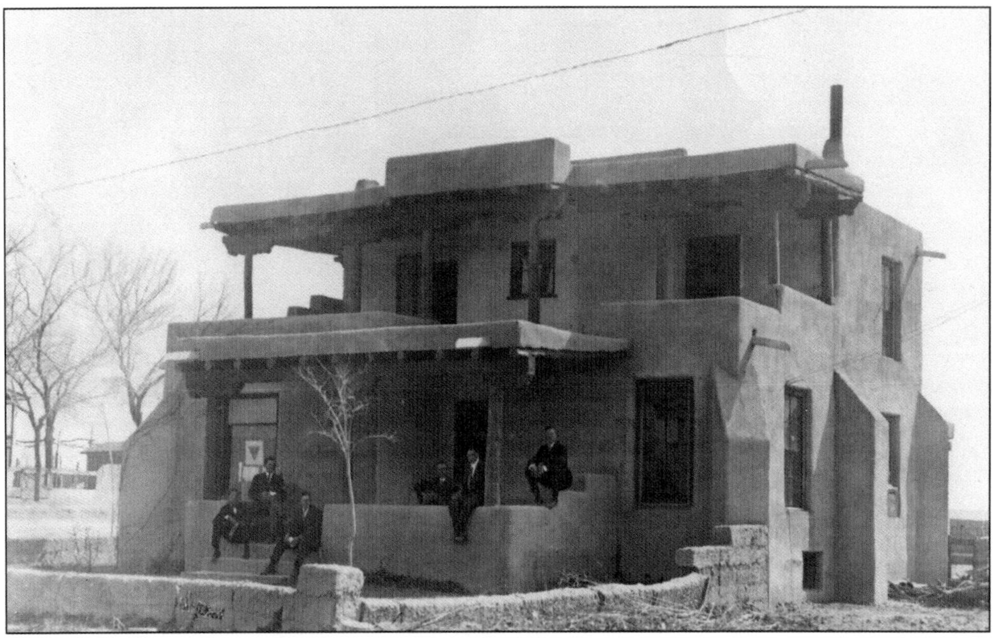

This photograph shows the Sigma Tau Fraternity in front of former president Tight's house. The house at 1916 Central Avenue was used by fraternities and sororities until it was razed in August 1964.

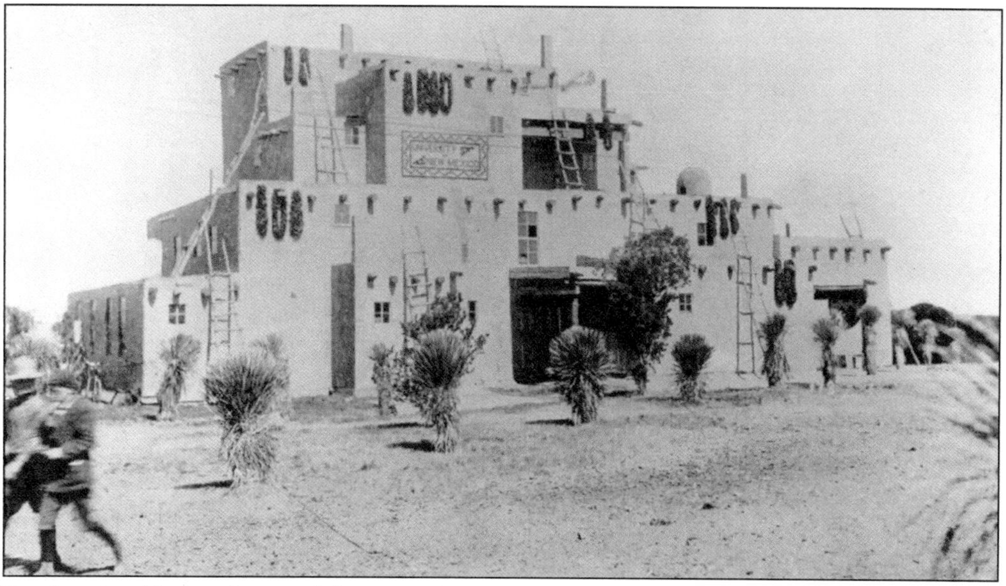

For the 1908 Territorial Fair exhibition, Tight wanted to advertise to the citizens of the territory the adaptability of the Pueblo style of architecture. He, the faculty, and students erected a wood-frame movie set building for the fair. It was an attempt to show New Mexicans their architectural heritage.

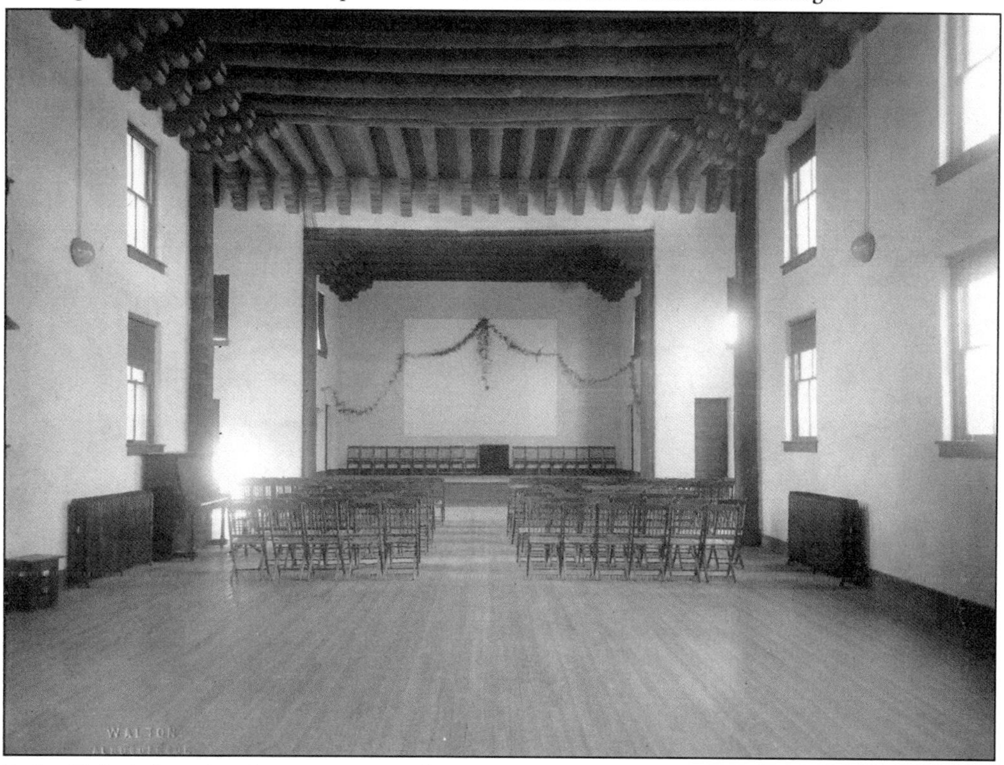

Rodey Hall, dedicated on January 23, 1909, honored Judge Bernard S. Rodey, a key figure in the creation of the University of New Mexico. Designed to resemble the Taos Church, it served multiple purposes over the years, including a chapel, auditorium, and archaeology museum. In 1933, it became home to the drama department. Unfortunately, by 1971, the building was deemed unsafe and demolished.

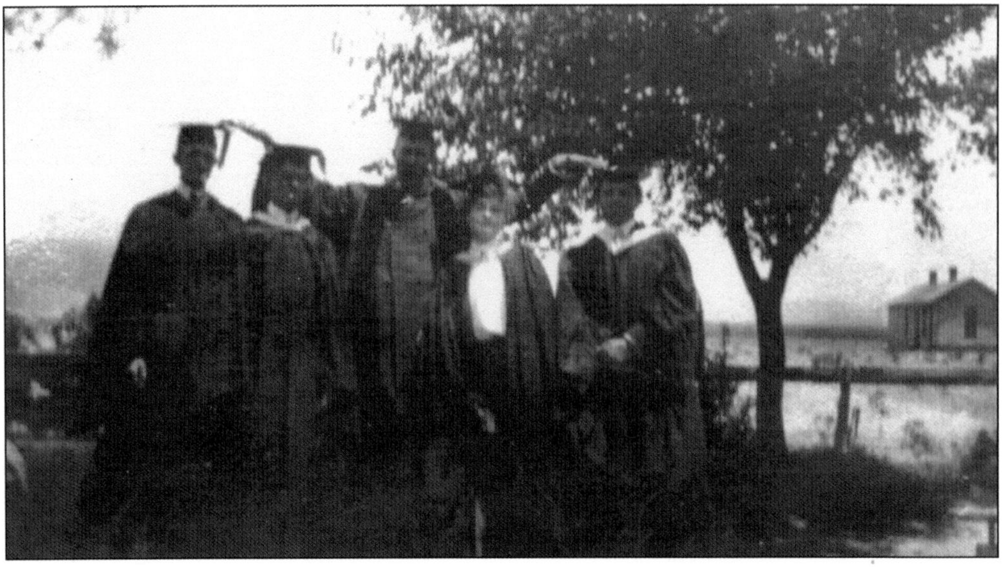

In this photograph, President Tight is standing with some 1908 graduates. This class was the largest graduating class since the university's foundation. Graduation was held in the opera house, where Tight passed out diplomas.

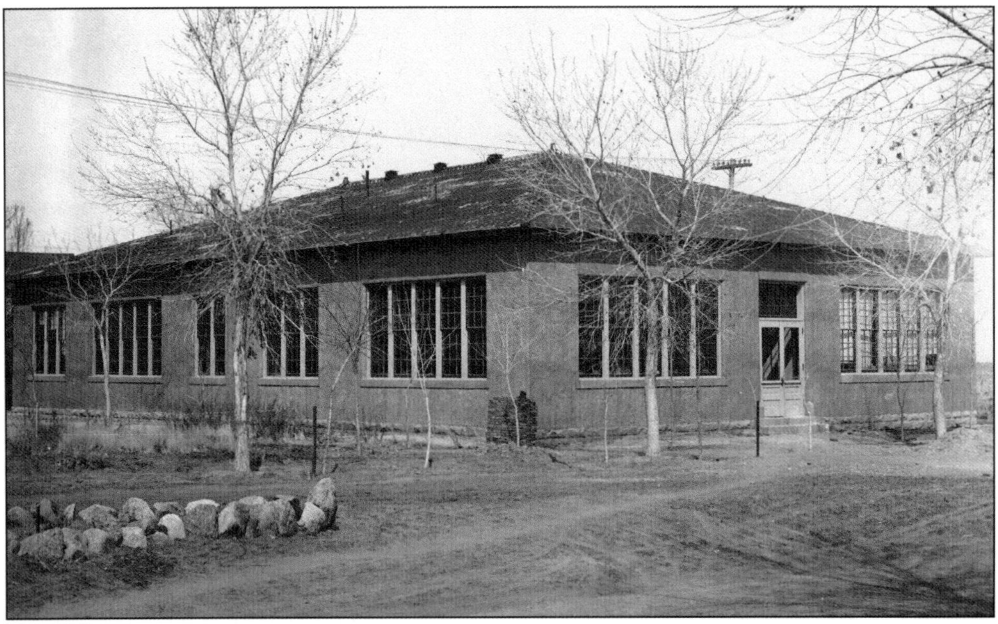

Tight's successor, Edward D.M. Grey, president from 1909 to 1912, was not at all interested in continuing the Spanish-Pueblo Revival architecture and rejected it as the campus style. The only building project completed under his presidency was the construction of the new College Engineering building in 1911 to replace the fire-ravaged Hadley Hall.

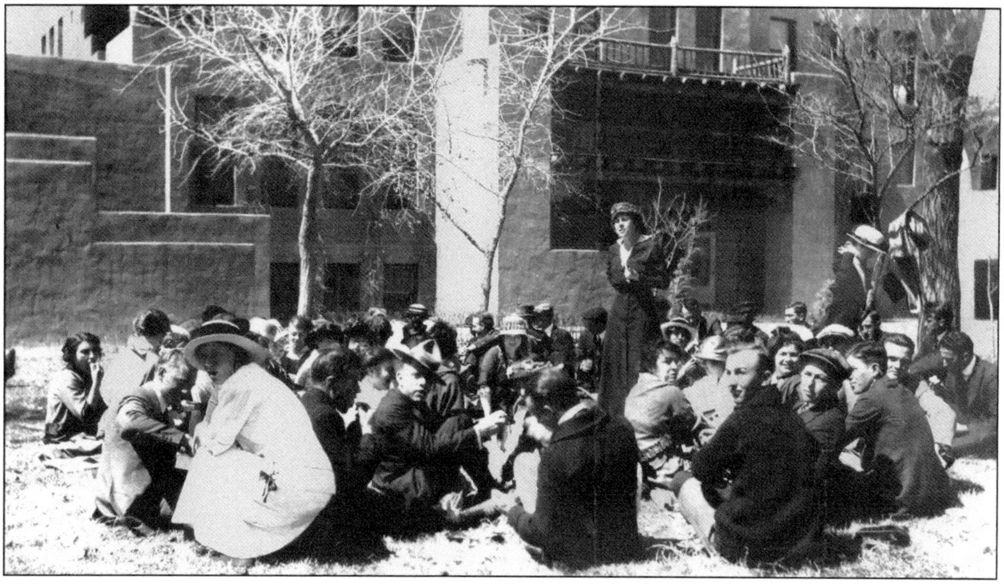

An early graduating class from the University of New Mexico, around 1915, poses in front of Hodgin Hall. The modest size of the class reflects the university's early years, when it served primarily local students in a small but growing Albuquerque community. Hodgin Hall, the university's first building, symbolizes the humble beginnings of what would become a major research institution.

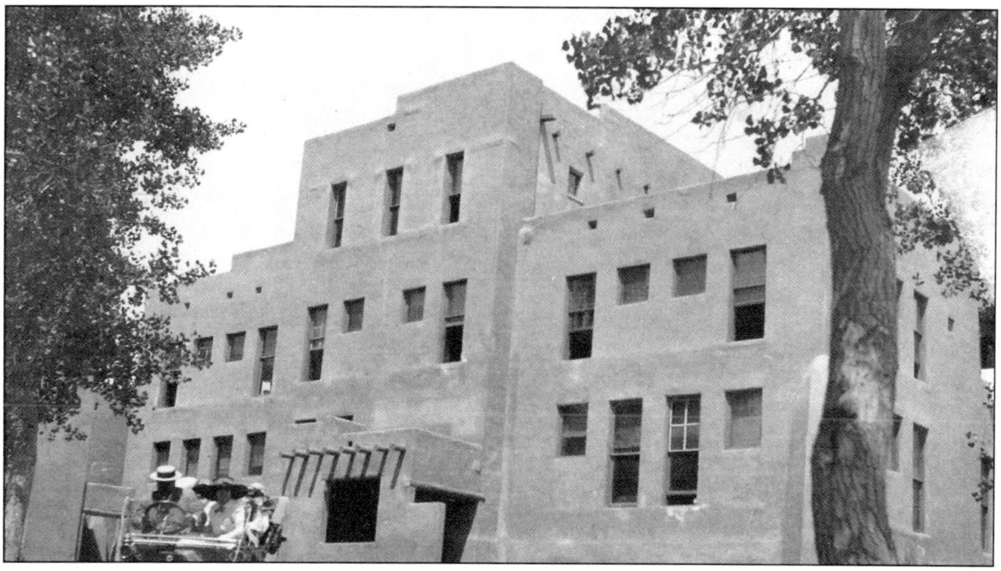

During the tenure of David R. Boyd, the fifth president of the University of New Mexico, the institution underwent substantial changes. When Boyd assumed his role, Albuquerque had evolved significantly from its earlier days as a frontier railroad town. The city's population was increasing, and modern conveniences like streetcars, cars, and paved roads were becoming commonplace. Under Boyd's leadership, the university's campus expanded from 25 to 300 acres, mirroring Albuquerque's progression into a more modern urban center.

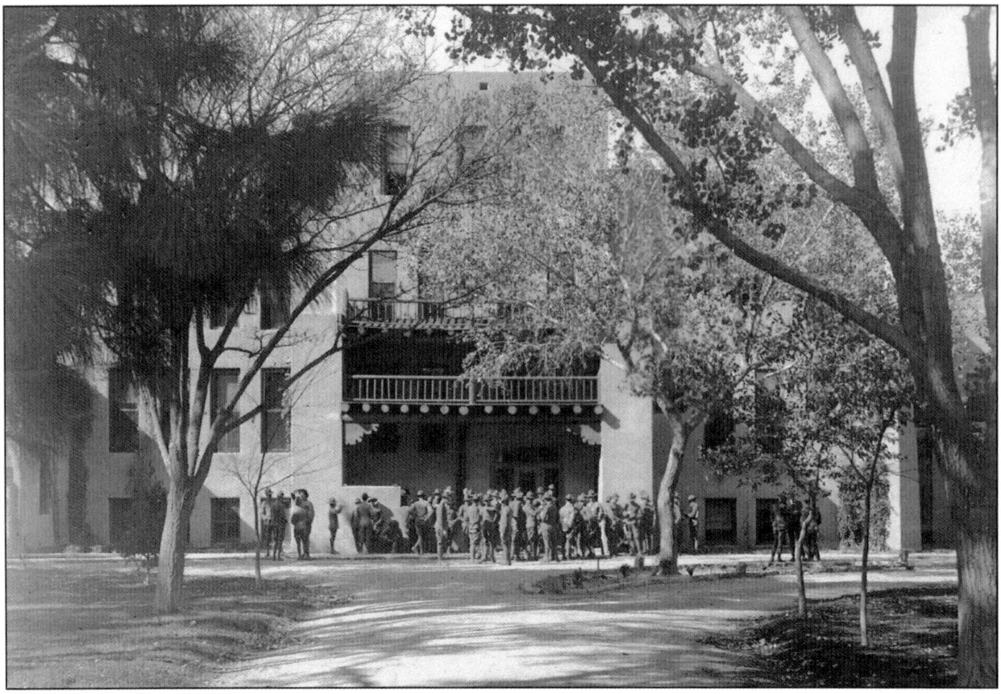

World War I caused significant disruptions to the growth of the University of New Mexico, with many construction projects delayed. As the United States approached war, universities like UNM adapted to wartime needs. In 1917, the university introduced the Student Army Training Corps (SATC), providing military training to male students in fields like engineering and medicine. At the same time, Battery A of the New Mexico National Guard established Camp Funston on the eastern edge of the campus, setting up temporary barracks and stables and using Kwataka Hall for officer housing. About 160 young men ages 18 to 21 were stationed at the camp. By the mid-1920s, overcrowding in university facilities prompted the construction of several new buildings, including the Library Annex in 1925, Parsons Hall for biology in 1928, and Yatoka Hall, a men's dormitory, also completed in 1928. In 1929, a lecture hall and dining hall were added, along with the Carlisle Gymnasium, named in honor of a student who died during World War I.

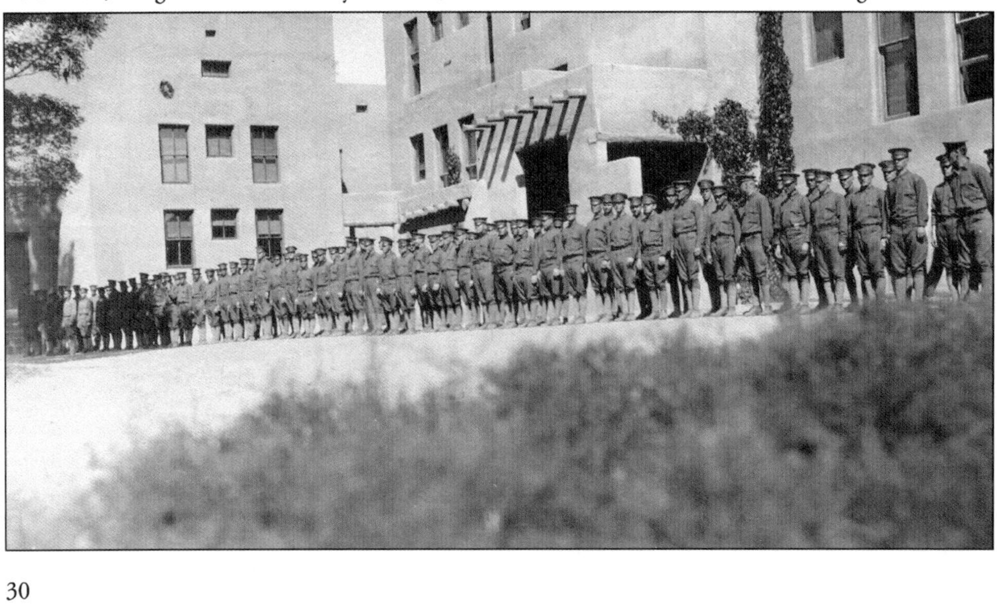

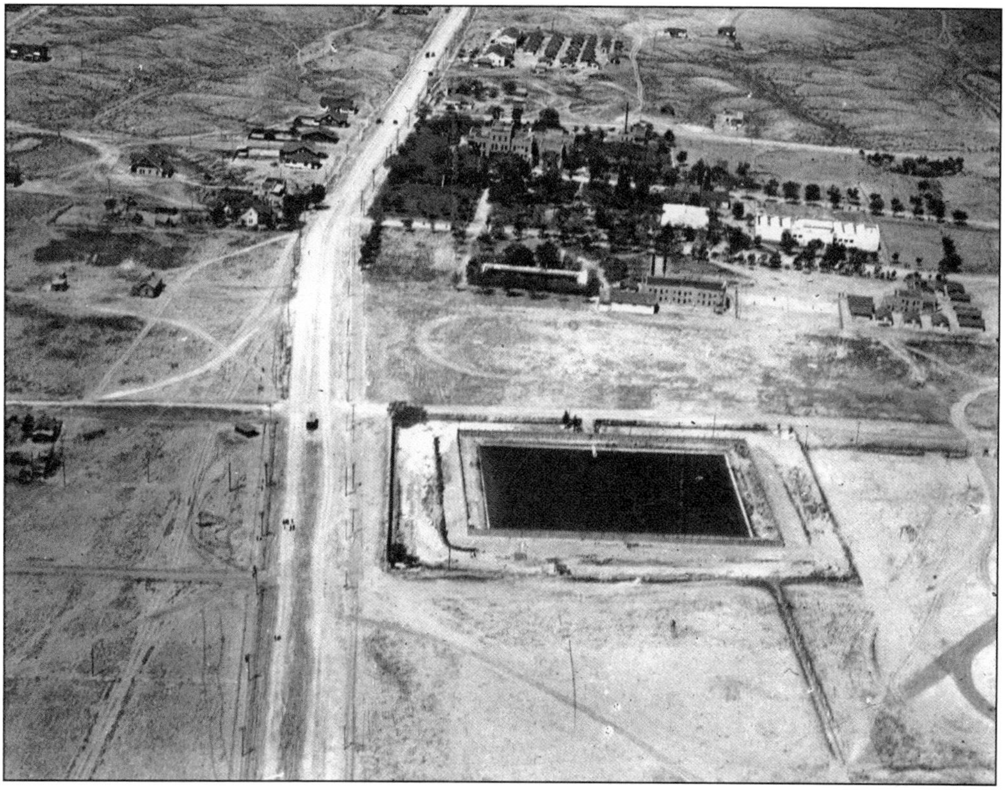

This is likely the first aerial photograph capturing the campus as it was in the 1920s. The few visible residences are situated on the south side of Central Avenue. The first university reservoir was built in 1905, primarily for irrigation purposes, and was lined with brick five feet below the water line. Its installation meant more plants, flowers and trees and better working conditions. Students also enjoyed the reservoir for recreational use, swimming in the summer and ice skating or playing hockey in the winter. A new city reservoir, seen in both photographs, was built on the old site in 1924. It fulfilled the needs of Albuquerque and its vicinity, and its opening was celebrated with a band.

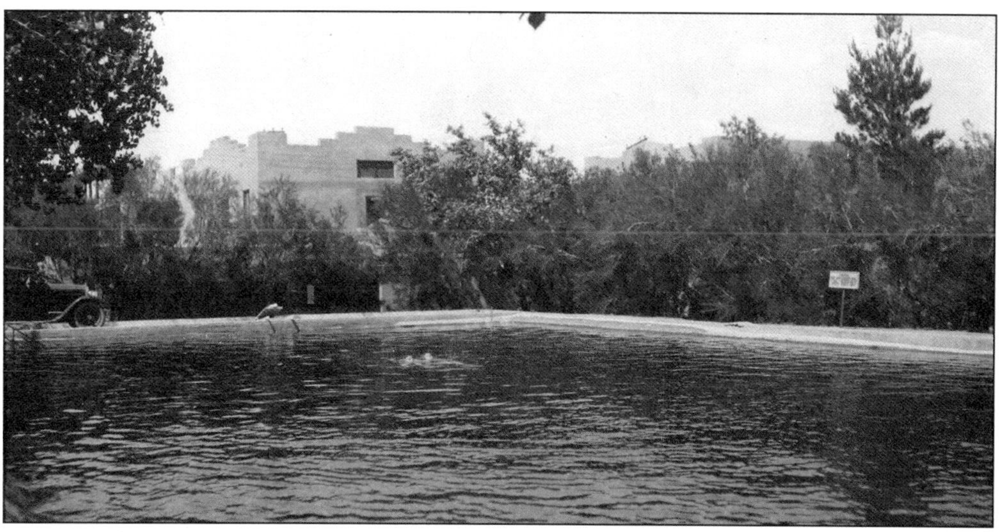

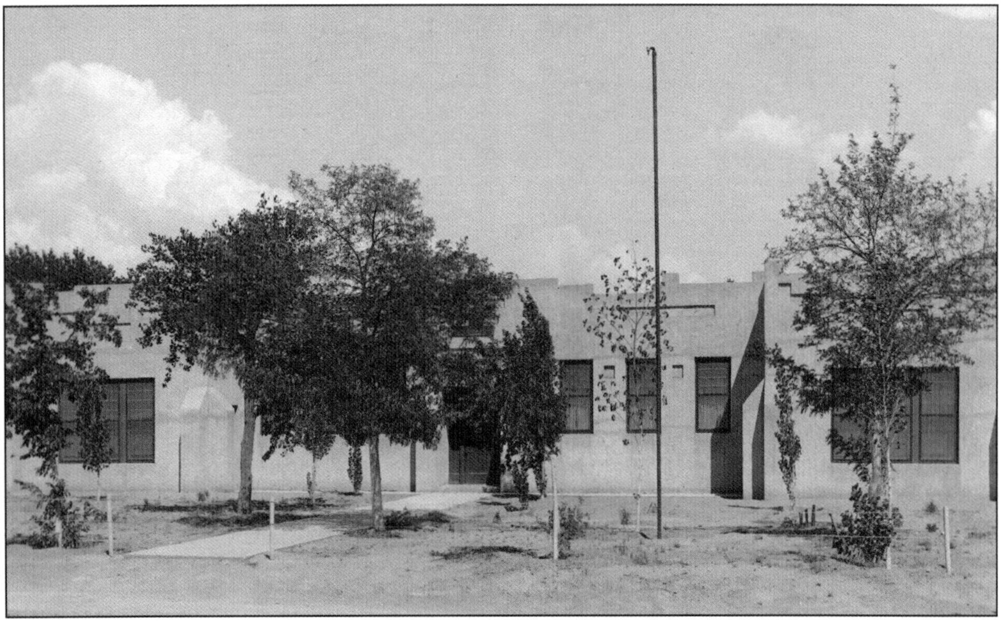

Sara Raynolds Hall, built in the Mayan Pueblo Revival style, was originally home to the Home Economics Department, which historically promoted literacy and employability for women and was linked to the suffrage movement. Listed in the National Register of Historic Places and the New Mexico Register of Cultural Properties, it was dedicated on Mother's Day in 1920. The building combines Mayan details with Art Deco influences and is the only building on campus in this distinctive style.

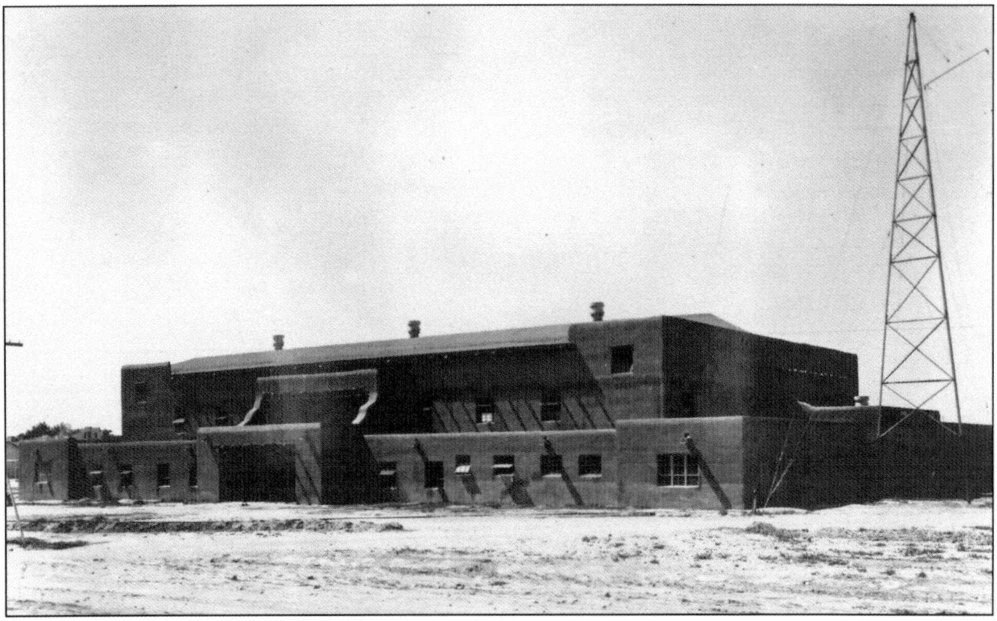

Radio broadcasting began on campus shortly after World War I. In 1921, UNM acquired surplus wireless telegraph and telephone equipment, and students built two steel towers. On December 16, 1921, the first broadcast aired, featuring weather reports. Carlisle Gym was constructed around the radio station facilities. The equipment was capable of sending messages up to 1,000 miles and receiving from as far as Washington, DC. Concerts were held weekly in Rodey Hall, attracting listeners from across Albuquerque.

At the request of sixth president David Spence Hill, a large illuminated "U" was originally installed atop the administration building, later relocated to the front of Hodgin Hall. Constructed from tin, with 25 lights on each side, it cost approximately $200.

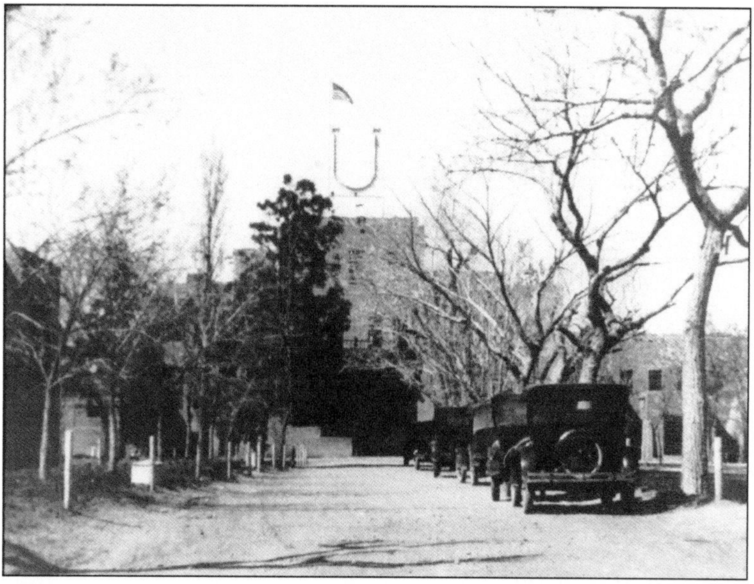

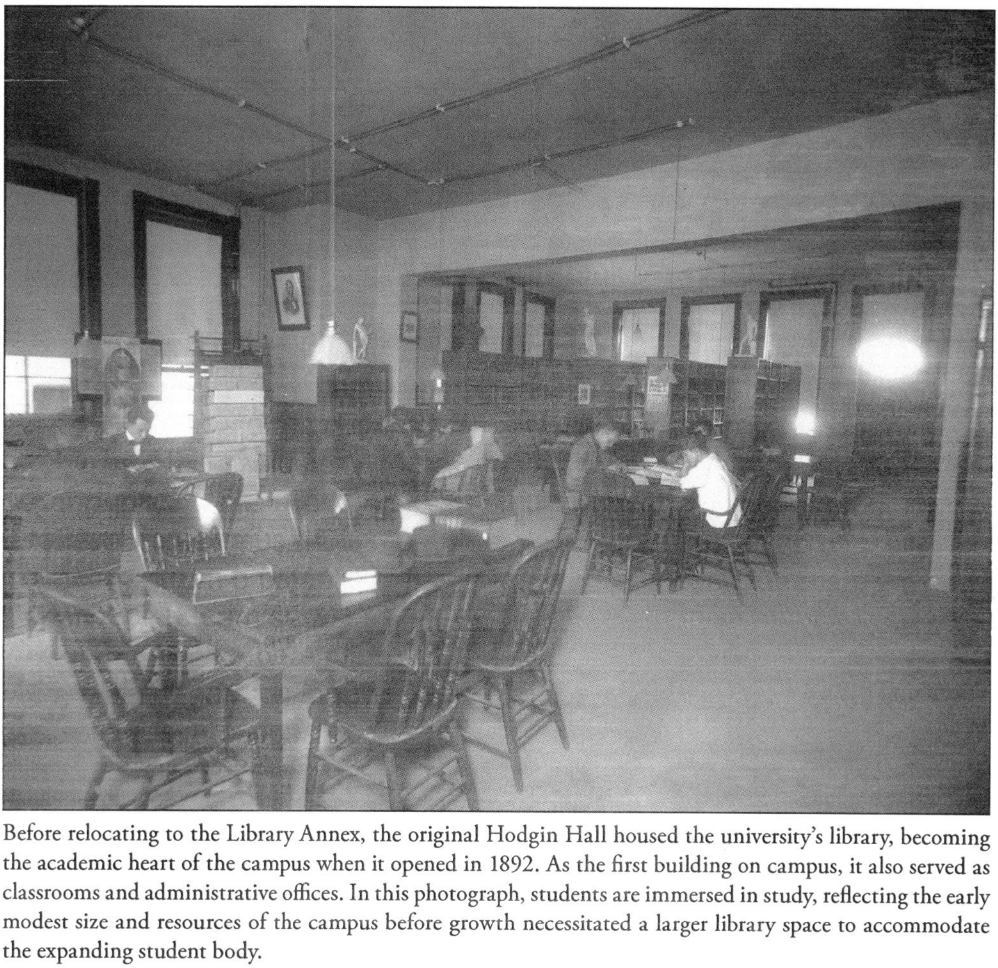

Before relocating to the Library Annex, the original Hodgin Hall housed the university's library, becoming the academic heart of the campus when it opened in 1892. As the first building on campus, it also served as classrooms and administrative offices. In this photograph, students are immersed in study, reflecting the early modest size and resources of the campus before growth necessitated a larger library space to accommodate the expanding student body.

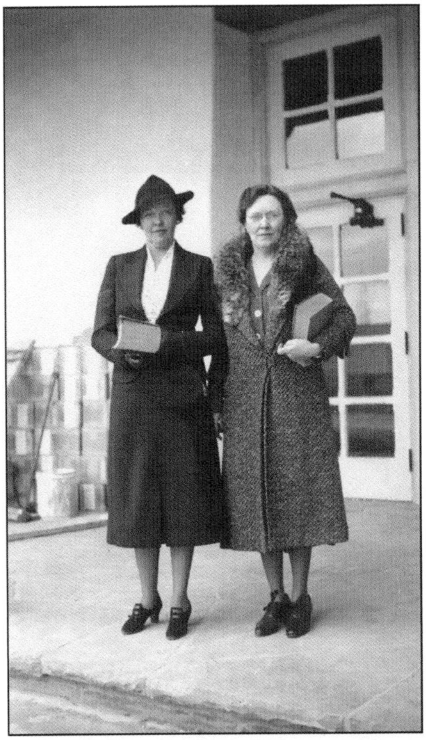

Construction of the new library began in 1924 on the site of the former Hadley Hall. Wilma Loy Shelton (right), seen here with Willa Zimmerman, was instrumental in its development. In addition to managing dormitories and supervising social functions, she enforced university rules and oversaw the overcrowded library, making her essential to the university's operations. Inaugurated in 1926, the library quickly outgrew its original purpose, and it was repurposed as an art annex in 1938.

The Library Annex, opened in 1926, was one of the most modern libraries in the Southwest. With a staff of four, it featured rooms for cataloging, newspapers, and unpacking, plus a reading room for over 100 readers. Designed to accommodate the growing student body and book collection, the building also marked the shift toward Pueblo Revival architecture on campus. Its construction was approved by the board of regents in 1924, thanks to librarian Wilma Loy Shelton's efforts.

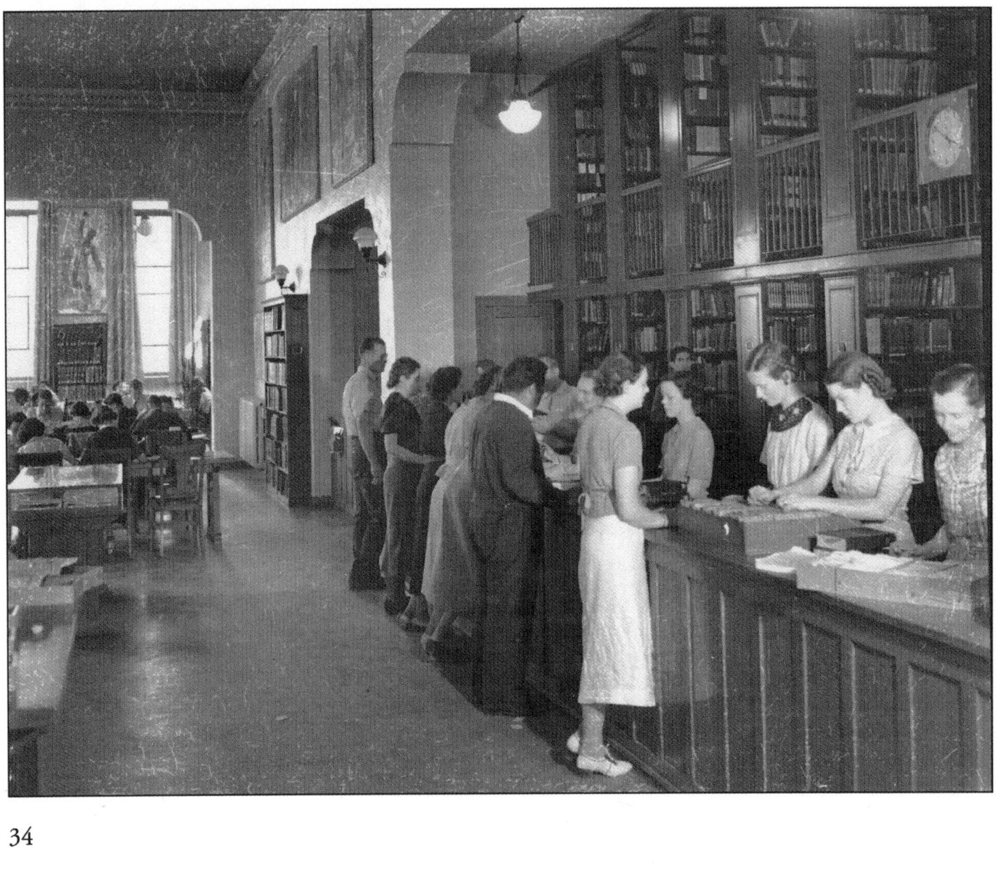

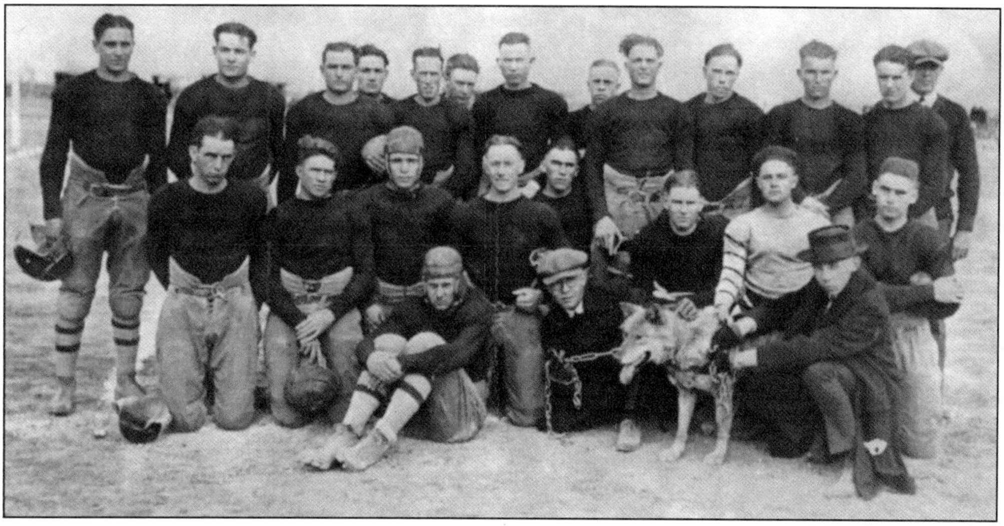

This 1921 group portrait of the UNM Lobo football team captures a significant moment in university history, featuring a live wolf, the team's namesake. Among the players is future UNM president Tom L. Popejoy, second row far left, who would go on to lead the university during a period of tremendous growth and development.

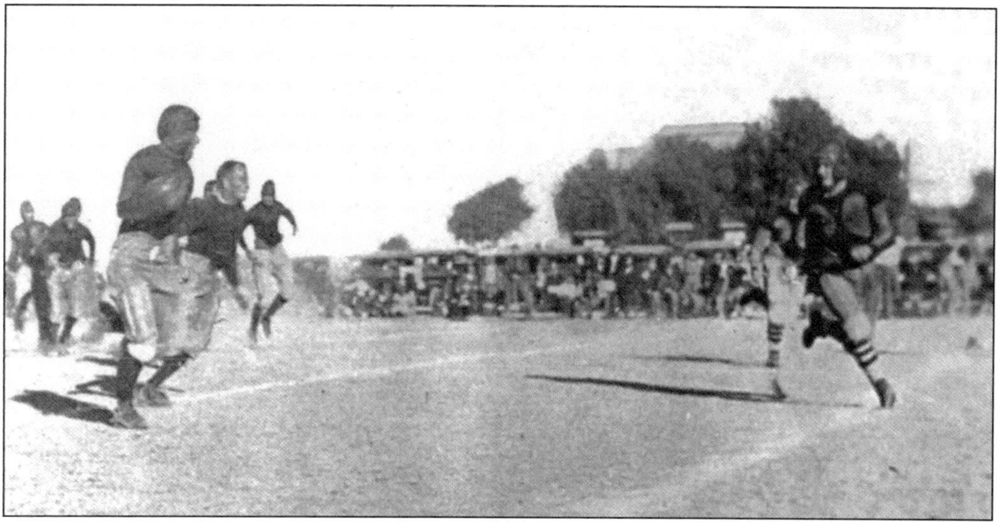

During his time at UNM, Popejoy, here in for the tackle, excelled in football, never missing a practice and notably scoring the game-winning field goal in 1924 that defeated Arizona 3-0. A 1925 graduate in economics, he was active on campus as president of Sigma Chi, was a member of the debate team, and served as graduate manager of athletics. In 1968, he received an honorary doctor of law degree from the University of Arizona.

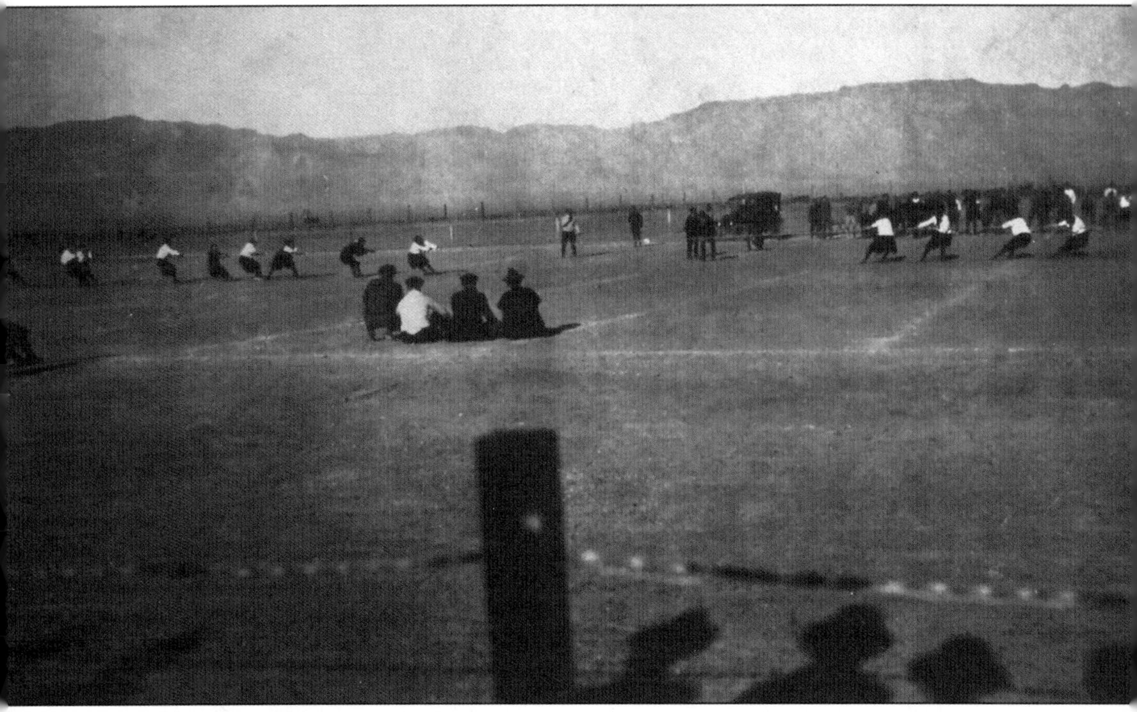

Tug-of-war was part of Arbor Day celebrations and later became a popular feature at track meets, played on University Field. Competitions included not only track teams but also rivalries between departments. For instance, the engineering department often faced off against the combined arts, philosophy, and sciences (APS) department, adding a fun and spirited element to campus events. These matches were a highlight of early campus traditions, fostering camaraderie and friendly rivalry.

Two

Growth into a Modern University, 1927–1990s

In 1927, the University of New Mexico began a period of significant change with the appointment of James F. Zimmerman as president. This transformation was both architectural and academic, marking a shift from a regional institution to a nationally recognized university. One of Zimmerman's major achievements was the expansion of the campus, driven by his vision of a university that reflected the culture and history of New Mexico. Architect John Gaw Meem, who championed the Pueblo Revival style, was instrumental in reshaping the university's aesthetic. Meem's designs for iconic structures like Scholes Hall and Zimmerman Library became integral to the campus's identity, using local materials and architectural motifs that drew inspiration from the region's Native American and Spanish heritage. This era of growth continued throughout the Great Depression, during which several major buildings were constructed through federal New Deal programs. The Public Works Administration (PWA) helped fund these projects, ensuring that even in times of economic hardship, the university could continue to expand. These buildings, such as the Student Union Building (SUB) and Scholes Hall, not only provided much-needed infrastructure but also played a key role in employing local labor. The 1940s and 1950s saw UNM's infrastructure further expand as it responded to a surge in enrollment from returning World War II veterans, who took advantage of the GI bill. New facilities, such as the Pit—UNM's iconic basketball arena—were constructed, signaling the growing importance of athletics to campus life. Similarly, Popejoy Hall, a renowned venue for the performing arts, opened in 1966, solidifying the university's commitment to a diverse and thriving cultural environment.

Throughout the mid-20th century, UNM also evolved in its academic offerings. In response to national social movements, the university began emphasizing Southwestern history, Latin American studies, and minority inclusion. This shift in academic focus mirrored the broader changes on campus, with a growing emphasis on activism and student involvement in shaping the university's identity. By the mid-1980s, more than half of UNM students were women, and more than 38 percent were minorities. By the end of the 20th century, UNM had successfully blended its historical roots with modern architectural developments and a forward-thinking academic environment. The campus's physical layout and academic programs reflected the university's commitment to preserving its cultural heritage while advancing as a leading institution in the Southwest.

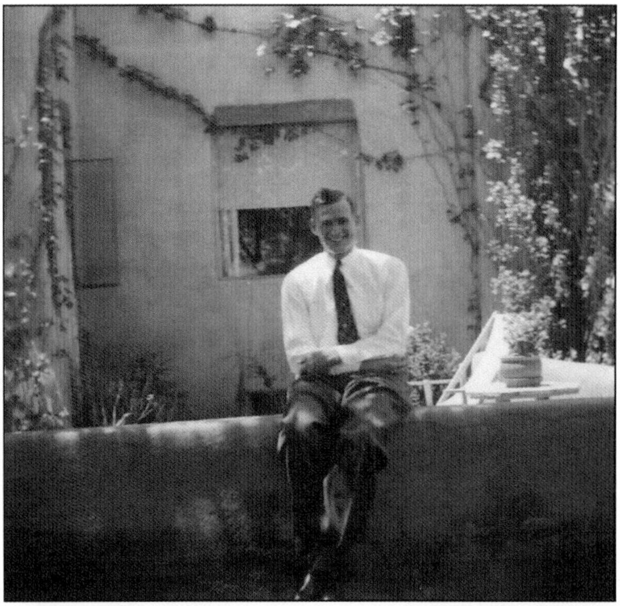

James F. Zimmerman served as president from 1927 to 1945, guiding the university through significant growth in enrollment and academics. His leadership saw the construction of Zimmerman Library and other campus New Deal projects. Despite challenges like the Great Depression and World War II, Zimmerman ensured UNM's development, fostering educational opportunities and resilience during a pivotal and transformative era in the university's history.

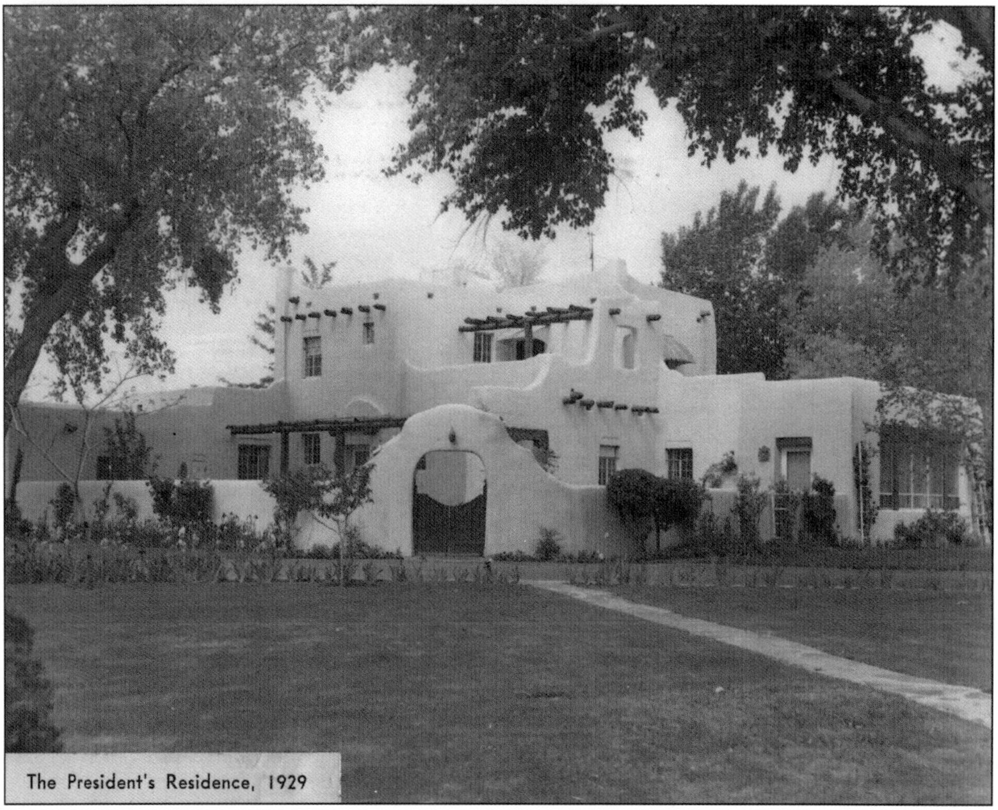

The Zimmerman family was the first to live in the President's House, now University House, an excellent example of residential Spanish-Pueblo Revival architecture. The house's design was considered so good that the building was used as a representative example of Spanish-Pueblo Revival–style architecture in a major survey of American building styles.

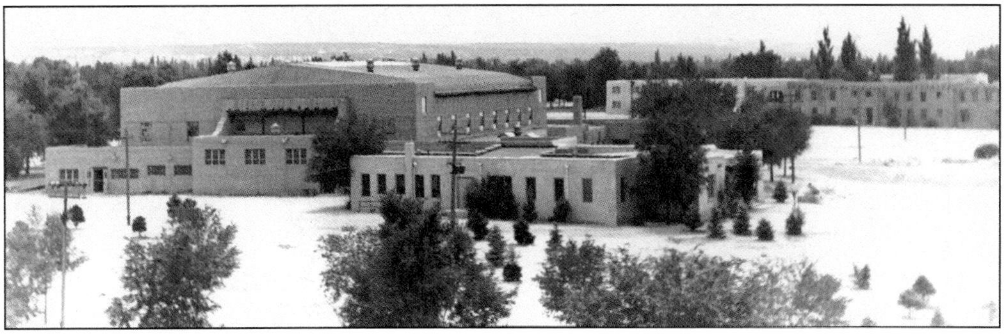

Carlisle Gym opened in 1928 and was the original venue of the New Mexico Symphony Orchestra. It was named after Hugh Carlisle, a UNM student who died in World War I. Carlisle Gym was added to the New Mexico State Register of Cultural Properties and the National Register of Historic Places in 1988. It is now the Elizabeth Waters Center for Dance.

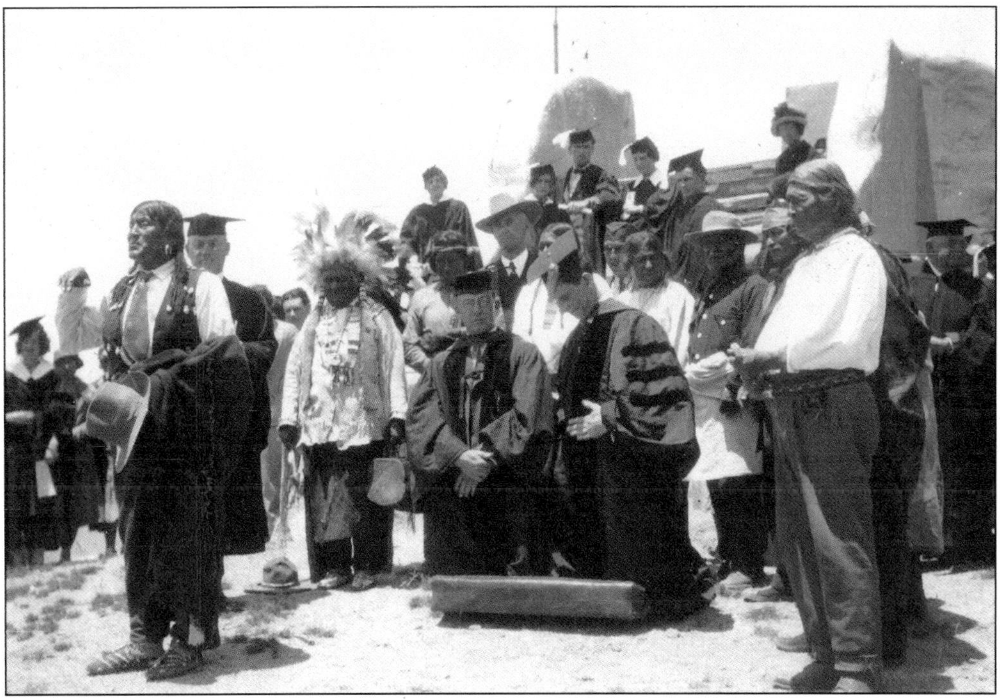

During Zimmerman's presidential inauguration on June 4, 1928, several new Pueblo-style buildings were celebrated, including a gymnasium, biology building, science lecture hall, and men's dormitory. It was celebrated by the presence of the governors of all the Pueblos in the state, all attired in their Native dress.

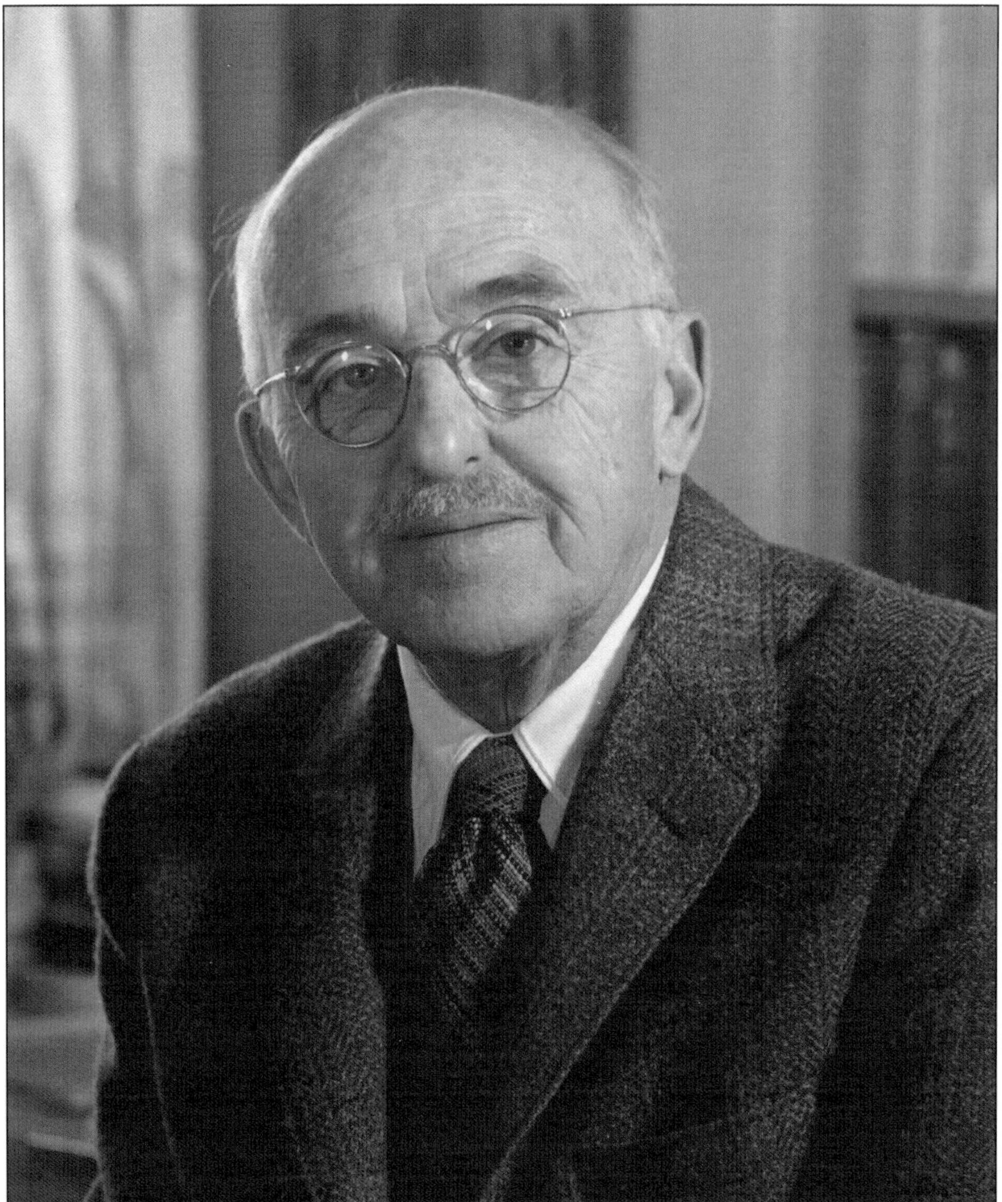

John Gaw Meem was a pivotal figure in the history of the university, serving as its official architect and shaping the campus with iconic buildings such as Zimmerman Library, Alumni Memorial Chapel, and Scholes Hall. In addition to these historically significant structures, Meem designed private homes for clients, many of which remain as million-dollar properties today. Throughout his extensive career, Meem perfected the Spanish-Pueblo Revival style, incorporating his unique elements into each design. One of his signature features was the use of twisted columns, often located near fireplaces, balconies, or doorways, which became a hallmark of his architectural style. Meem was also among the first architects associated with the Regionalism movement, which influenced American art, literature, and architecture during the 1920s and 1930s. His deep understanding of Pueblo and Spanish Colonial building techniques was rooted in his volunteer work with the Committee for the Preservation and Restoration of New Mexico Mission Churches during this period.

In May 1927, President Zimmerman convinced prominent archaeologist Edgar Lee Hewett to establish the Anthropology Department at the university, focusing on ancient and contemporary Southwestern cultures. Women have played a significant role in the program, particularly in the Chaco Field Schools from 1929 to 1942. The department has since achieved national recognition for its contributions to understanding the ancient and contemporary cultures of the region.

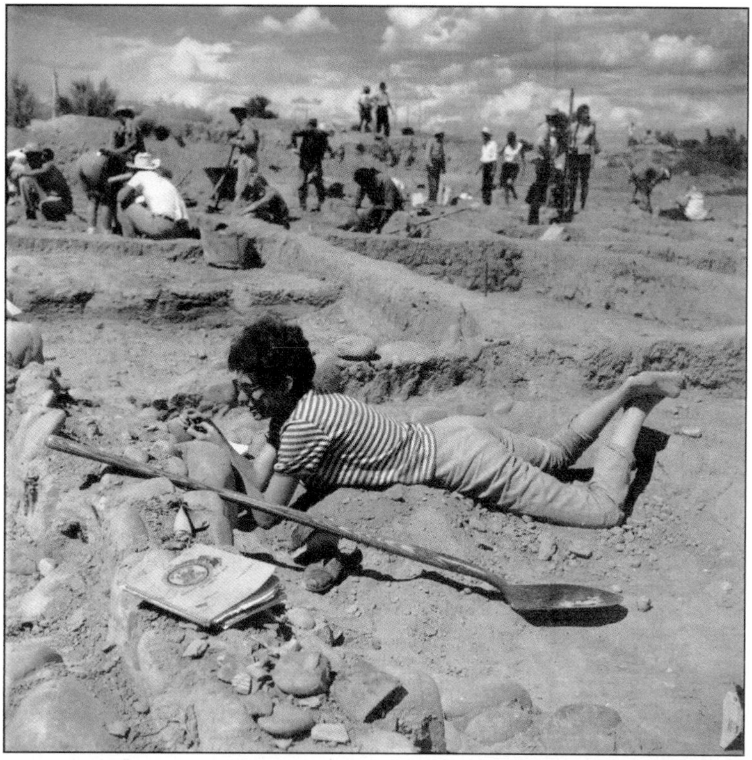

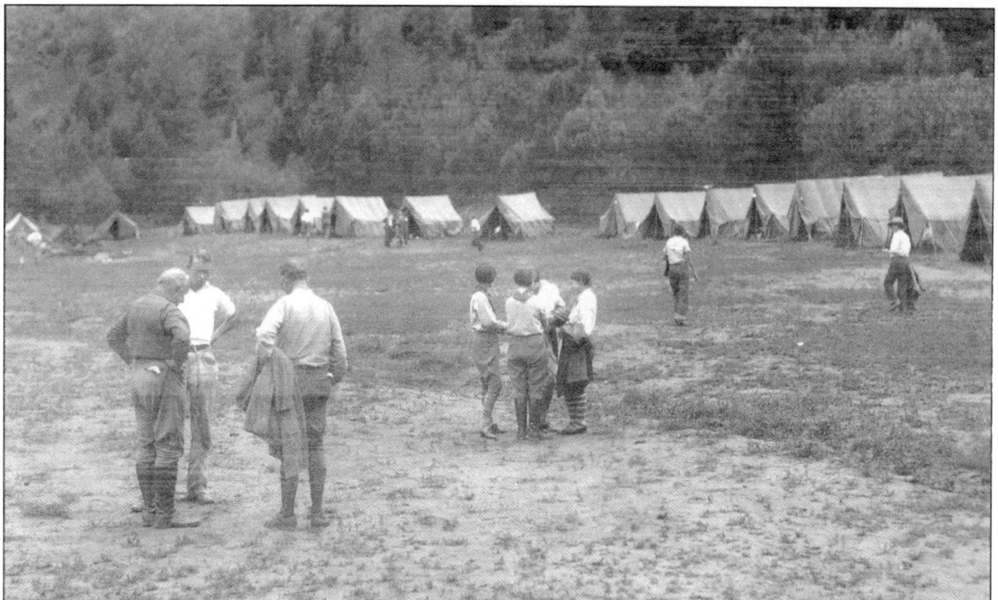

This photograph, taken in Jemez in 1929, captures the early field work at the Anthropology Department at UNM, which marked a focus on the Southwest's rich prehistory. President Zimmerman and Hewett established the department, affiliated with the School of American Research in Santa Fe. Zimmerman envisioned this regional emphasis as key to securing graduate program accreditation and elevating the department's national reputation.

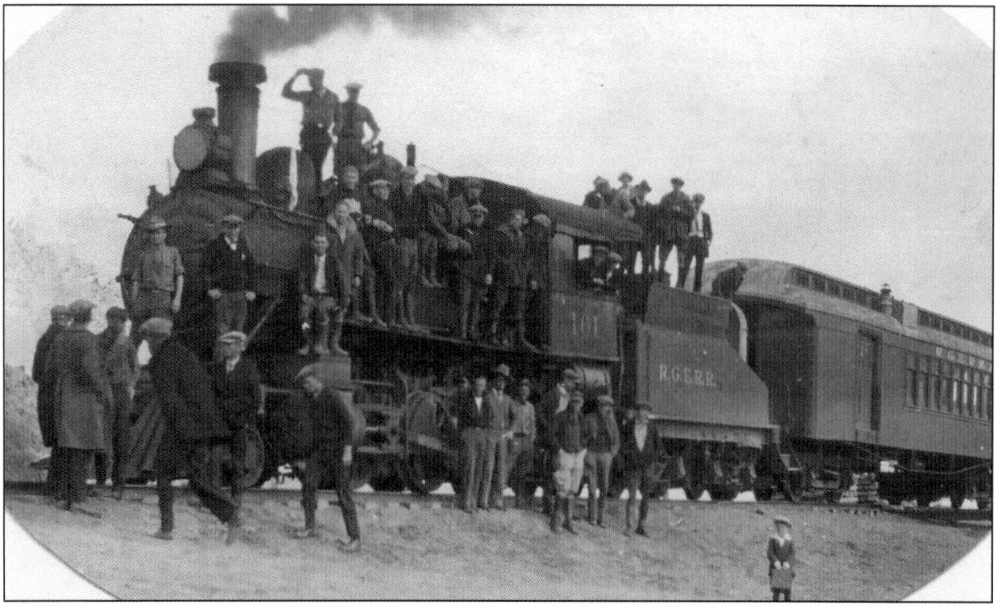

On March 28, 1925, about 45 engineering students spent the day at the Hagan coal mines in Colorado for a field trip. They drove to Santa Fe and continued by train operated by the mines. Invited by Dr. J.J. DePraslin, the mine manager, they descended into the mines for an in-depth inspection, gaining firsthand experience of mining operations and techniques.

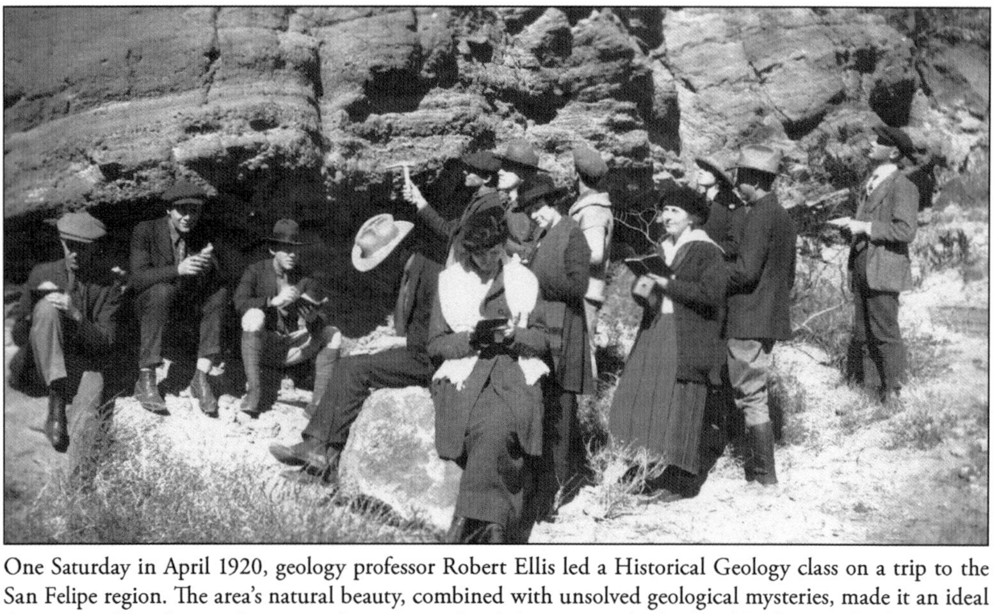

One Saturday in April 1920, geology professor Robert Ellis led a Historical Geology class on a trip to the San Felipe region. The area's natural beauty, combined with unsolved geological mysteries, made it an ideal destination. Traveling in three cars, the group explored the region, which offered both scenic landscapes and opportunities for geological investigation.

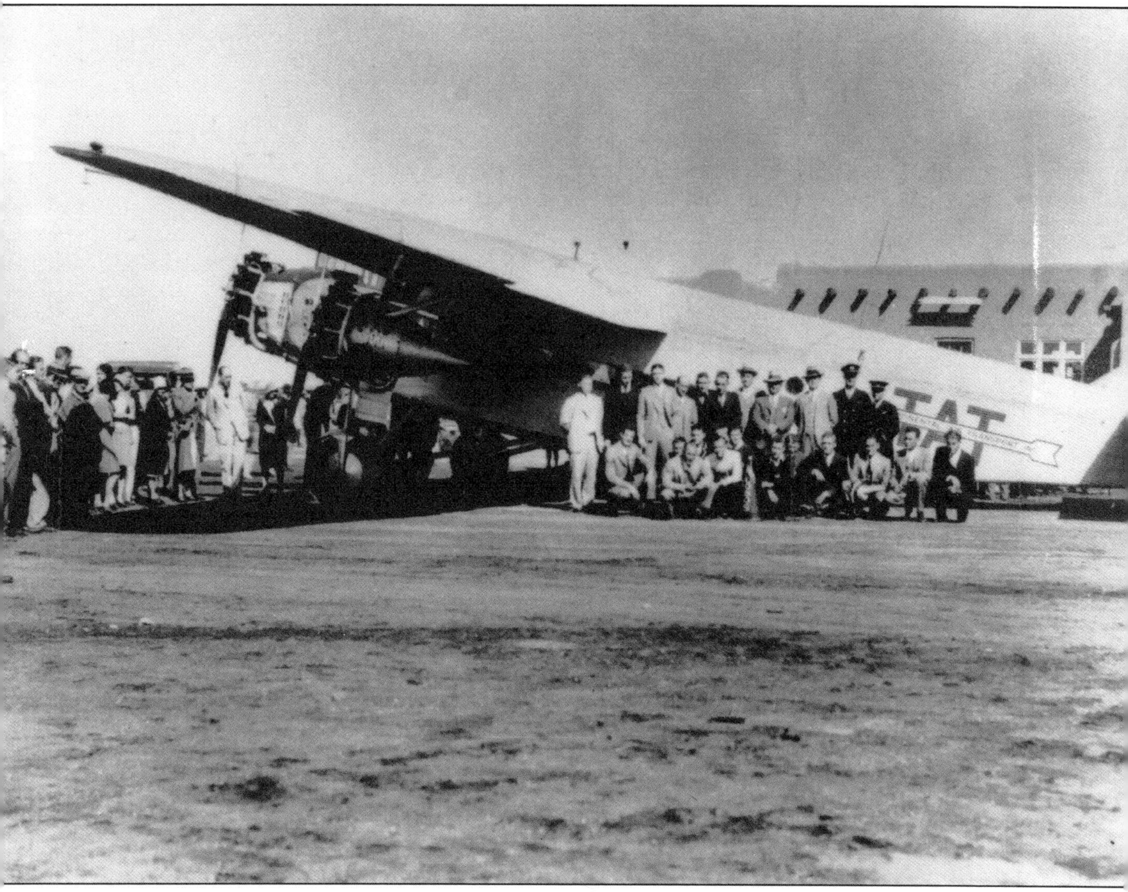

In 1929, the University of New Mexico football team made history as the first college football team to travel by airplane. The "Flying Lobos" journeyed to Pasadena, California, to play Occidental College at the iconic Rose Bowl Stadium, marking their first game outside the Southwest. Over 2,000 fans gathered to give them a spirited sendoff, showcasing the excitement surrounding this historic flight. The night game, played under floodlights, proved to be a challenging experience for the Lobos. Facing a stronger Occidental team, the Lobos suffered a 26-0 defeat. Coach Roy Johnson, who served as head coach for 11 seasons with a record of 41 wins, 32 losses, and 6 ties, later commented that the Lobos "did not play up to their usual standard." The team was overwhelmed by the grandeur of the Rose Bowl and a crowd of 17,000 spectators. Compounding their difficulties, they wore cleats designed for sand or dirt, struggling on the wet grass field. While the game was a loss, the event marked a milestone in collegiate sports history.

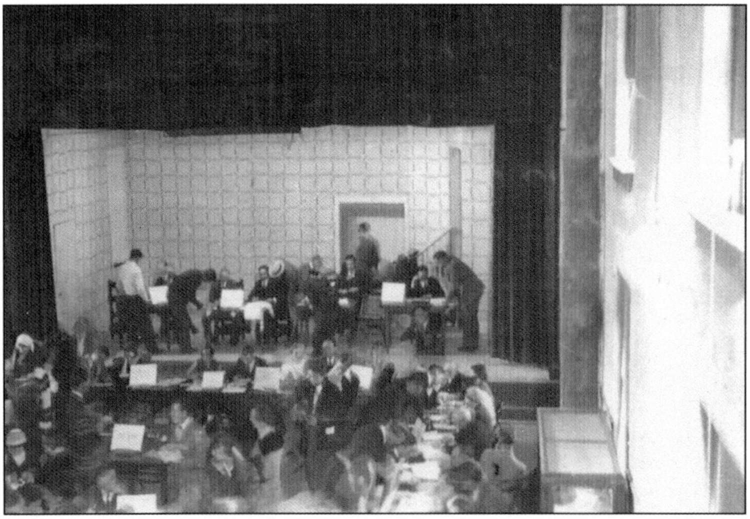

The 1932 midterm registration at UNM saw a rise in student enrollment compared to the previous semester, defying the challenges of the Great Depression. Despite widespread economic hardships, the increase in numbers highlighted the enduring value of education and students' determination to pursue their studies during uncertain times.

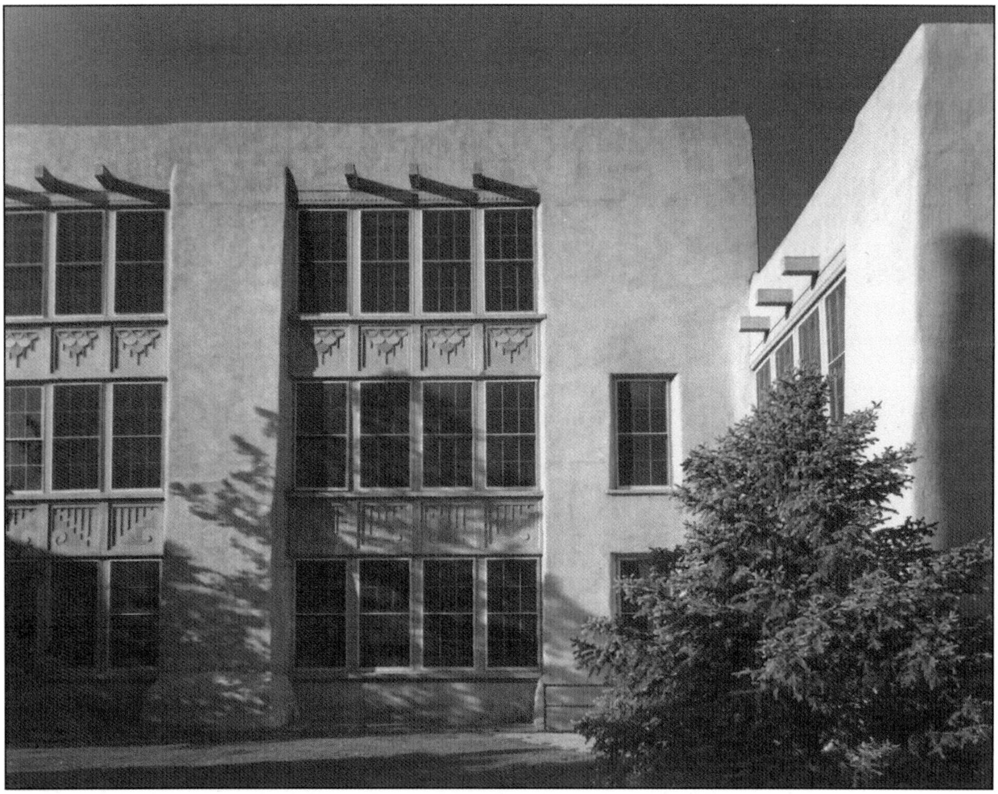

This detail of Scholes Hall, completed in 1934, highlights its Spanish Mission–style architecture, reflecting New Mexico's cultural heritage. Designed by John Gaw Meem as his first university project, it was part of a Public Works Administration initiative during the Great Depression. The building's traditional design elements, including Art Deco windows with stylized Indigenous symbols, represent both functionality and a tribute to the region's history, cementing its role in UNM's identity.

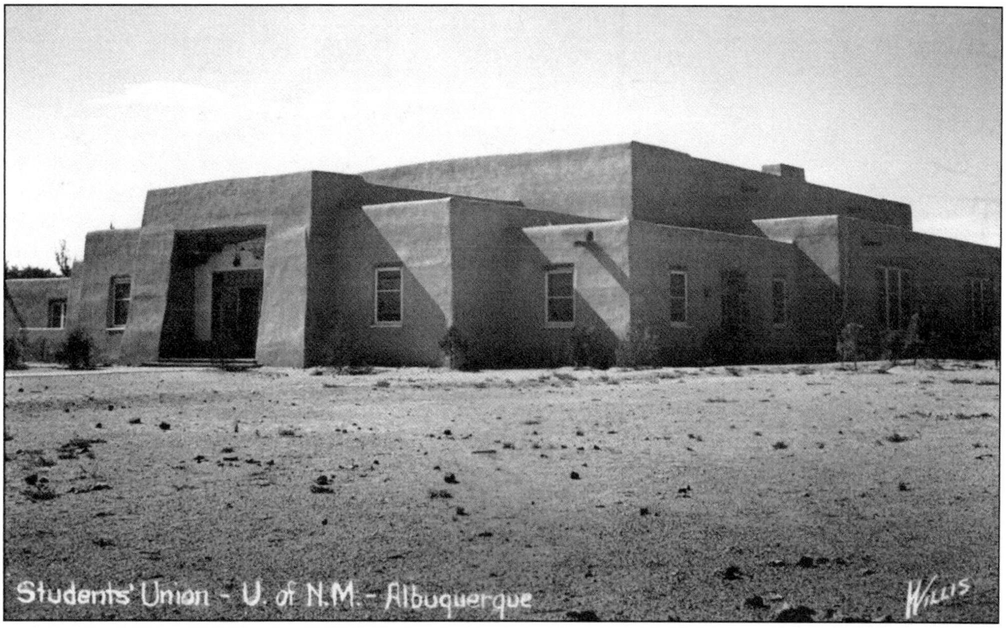

The Student Union Building opened in 1937 as a hub for campus activities. A contest was held to name the building, and SUB emerged as the popular choice. It housed the *Mirage* yearbook and Lobo offices, along with a lounge, meeting rooms, a barber shop, a bookstore, a fountain, a ballroom, and a playroom. The building now houses the Maxwell Museum of Anthropology.

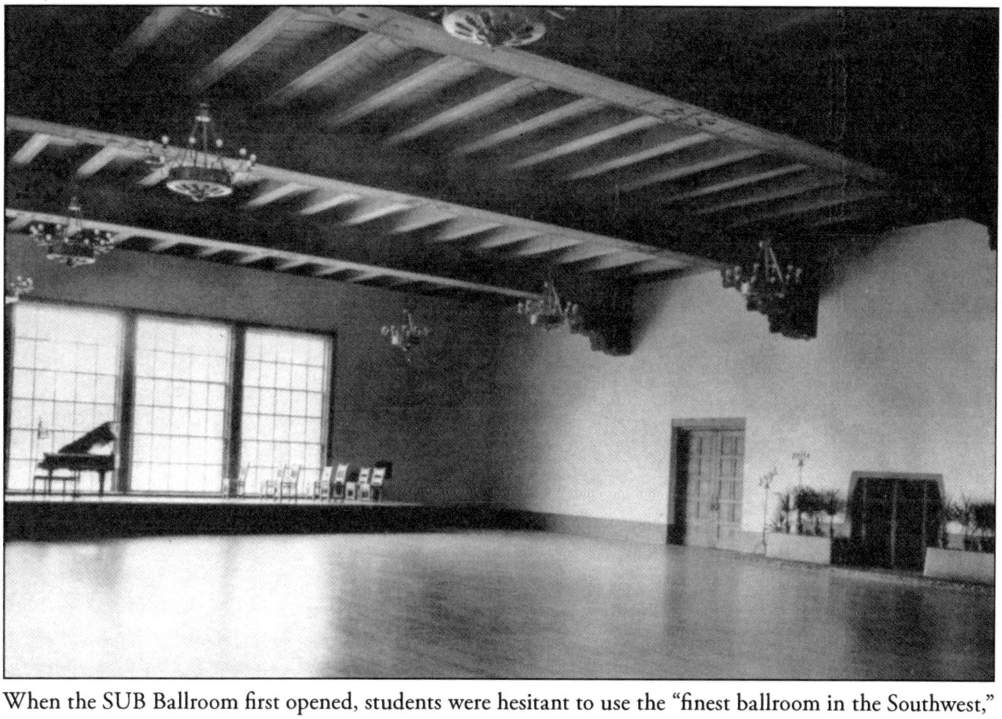

When the SUB Ballroom first opened, students were hesitant to use the "finest ballroom in the Southwest," opting instead for high school dances at the Legion Hall. Saturday night dances cost 75¢, covering orchestra fees, floor upkeep, lighting, and heating. The space eventually hosted various events, including the annual Hispanic Institute Ball, showcasing its role as a versatile hub for student and community gatherings.

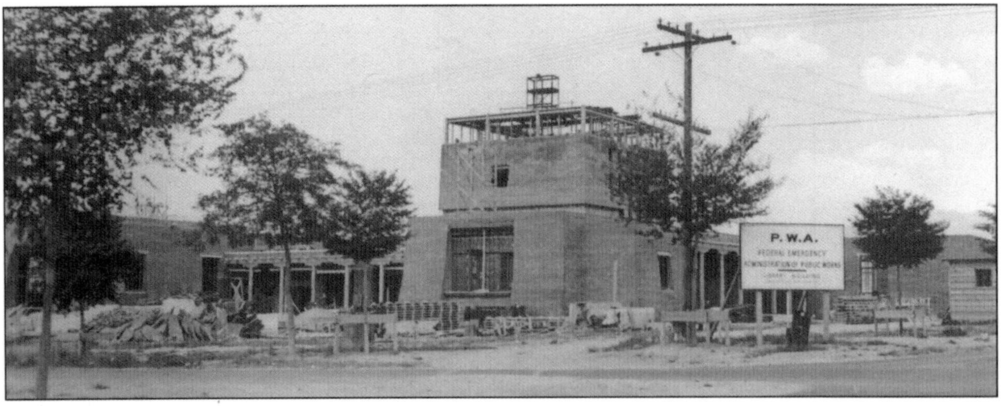

Despite the Great Depression, UNM's building program flourished through New Deal initiatives like the Public Works Administration. These projects funded significant campus structures, including Zimmerman Library, Scholes Hall, and Bandelier Hall-West, promoting PWA's basic principles of regionalism, cultural pluralism, and modernity. This photograph of Zimmerman Library under construction illustrates how PWA funding shaped the campus, blending cultural heritage with architectural innovation, and highlighting the era's emphasis on progress through public investment.

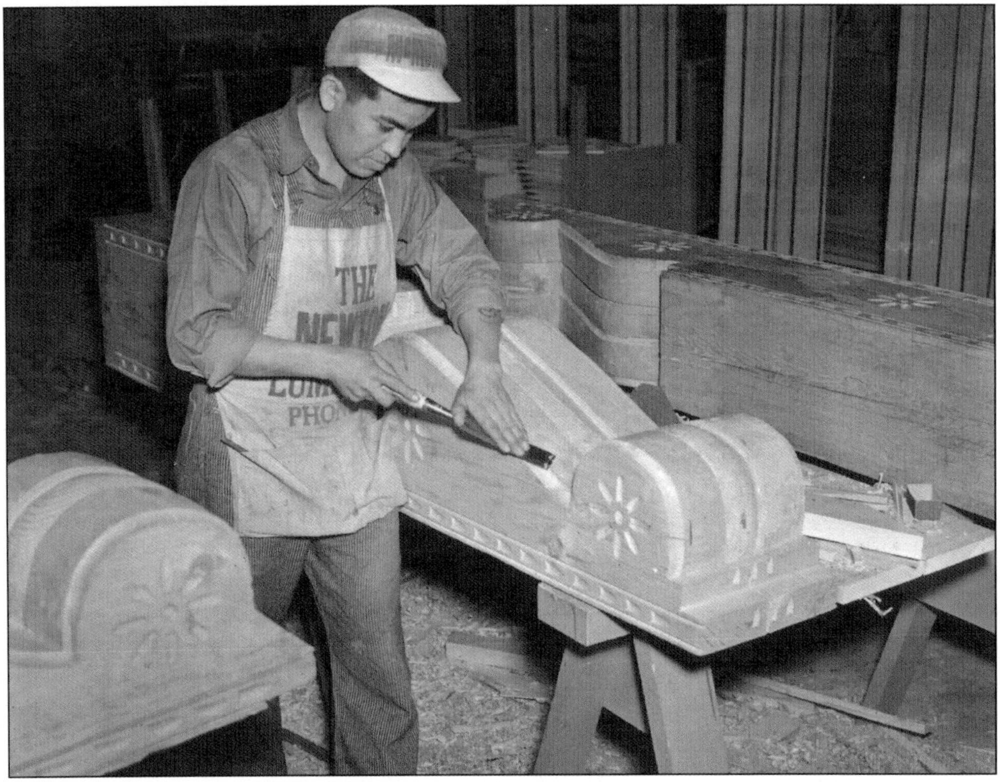

John Gaw Meem described the Spanish-Pueblo Revival style as a "regional expression of modern contemporary practice," emphasizing harmony between traditional aesthetics and modern techniques. This vision aligned with New Deal efforts to celebrate the "American scene" through diverse art forms, including architecture. Zimmerman Library embodies this ethos, utilizing innovative materials while employing Native and Hispano artisans. This image captures the meticulous detailing of the library, a testament to the craftsmanship behind its construction.

In 1938, the university dedicated its new library, designed by John Gaw Meem, who considered it his finest Pueblo-style work. The library's book storage tower became a campus focal point and iconic university symbol. Featuring high-ceilinged reading rooms and a lobby with carved beams and tin light fixtures, the interior reflected Meem's attention to detail. Furnishings were specially designed and handmade to complement the building's architectural elegance.

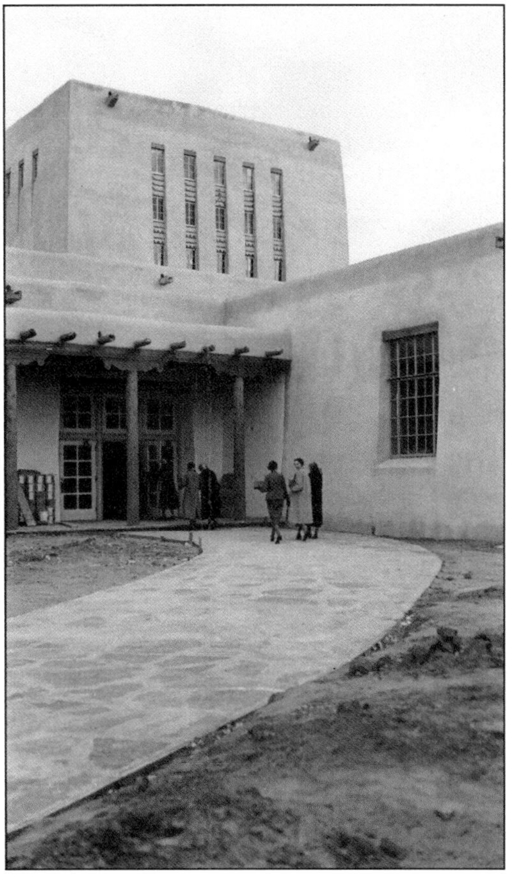

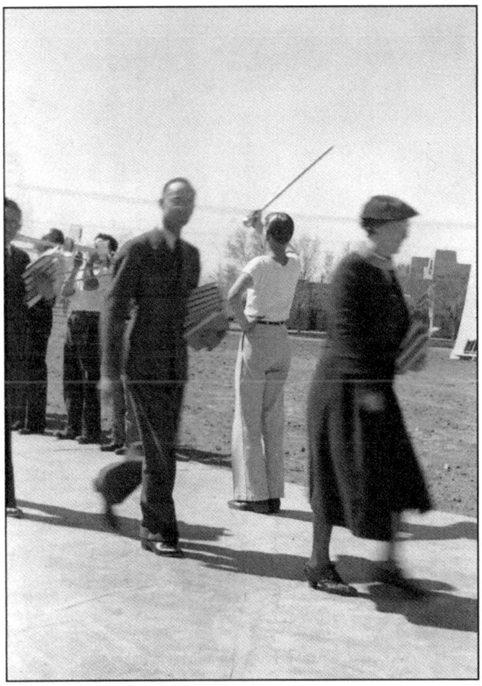

On March 5, 1938, students and faculty, led by Willa Zimmerman, Wilma Shelton, and Dean Hammond, moved some of the books to the new library. The university band led the procession.

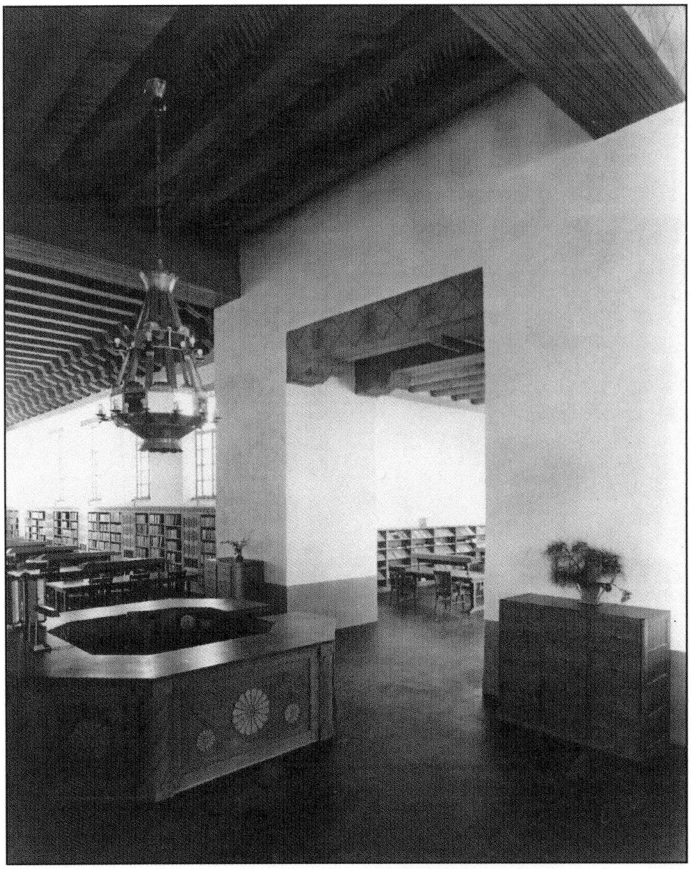

This photograph of the old reference desk in Zimmerman Library captures the craftsmanship and historical atmosphere that define this iconic space. Designed in the Pueblo Revival style, the library showcases intricate woodwork, hand-carved details, and traditional chandeliers, reflecting New Mexico's cultural heritage. The tin chandelier, crafted by Native artisans, is said to be the largest of its kind. The library remains a symbol of academic excellence and Southwestern history, now listed in the National Register of Historic Places.

Picnics at Supper Rock in Tijeras Canyon were a popular tradition among students. Freshman engineering students proudly maintained a painted "U" on the rock, a symbol of their school spirit that persisted until the 1950s.

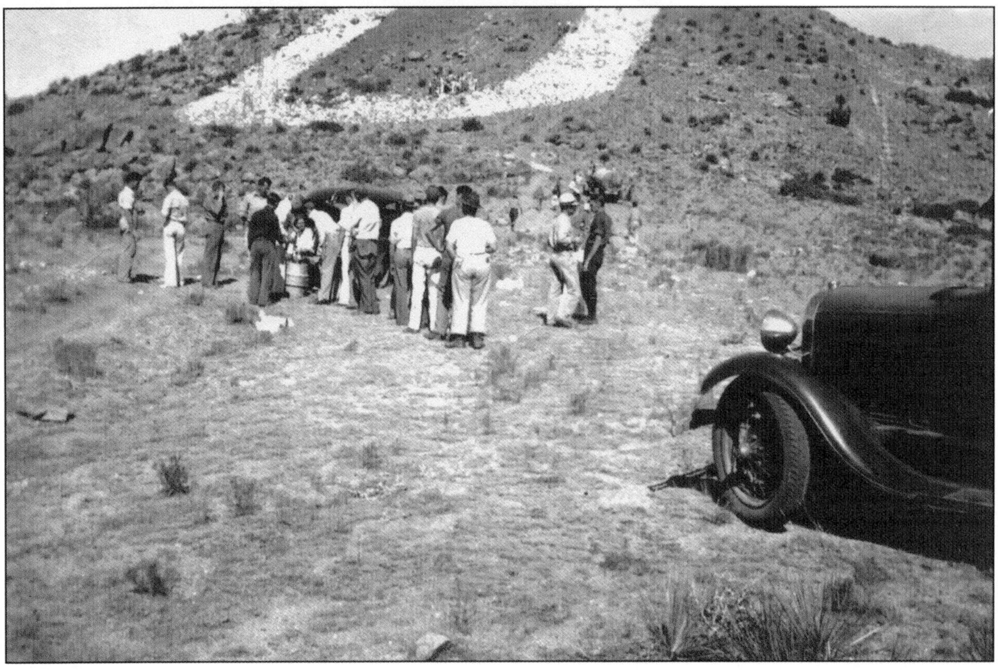

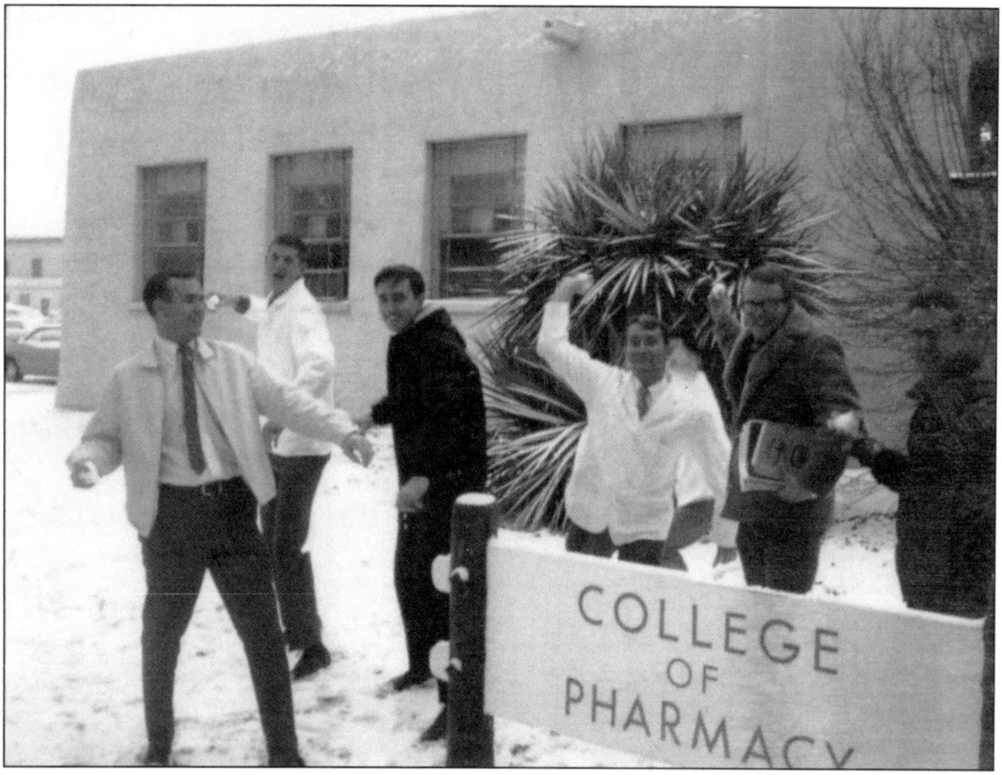

In this playful scene, pharmacy students engage in a snowball fight outside their building. Established in 1945, the College of Pharmacy was one of the younger programs on campus at the time. This photograph captures the early days of the program, reflecting the camaraderie and lively spirit of the first cohort, who would go on to make significant contributions to the state's healthcare system.

This photograph captures students from the College of Pharmacy working in a laboratory at a time when the program was rapidly expanding. Founded in 1945, it was one of the first buildings built on campus after World War II. The College of Pharmacy has since become a vital part of UNM's growing medical and research infrastructure.

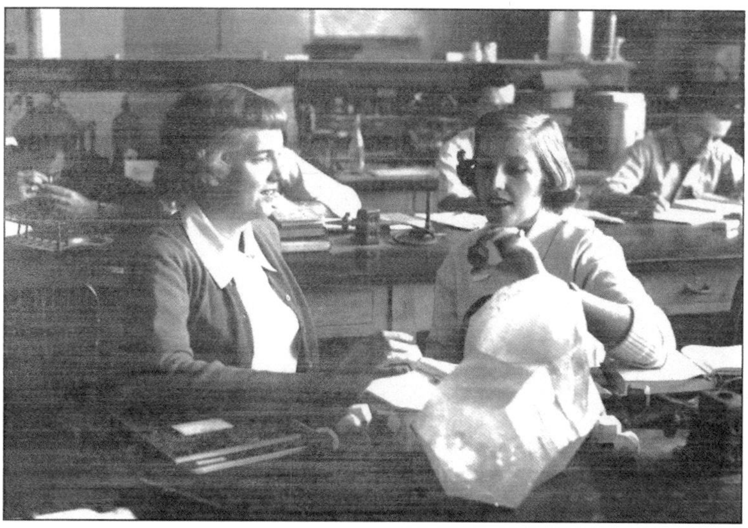

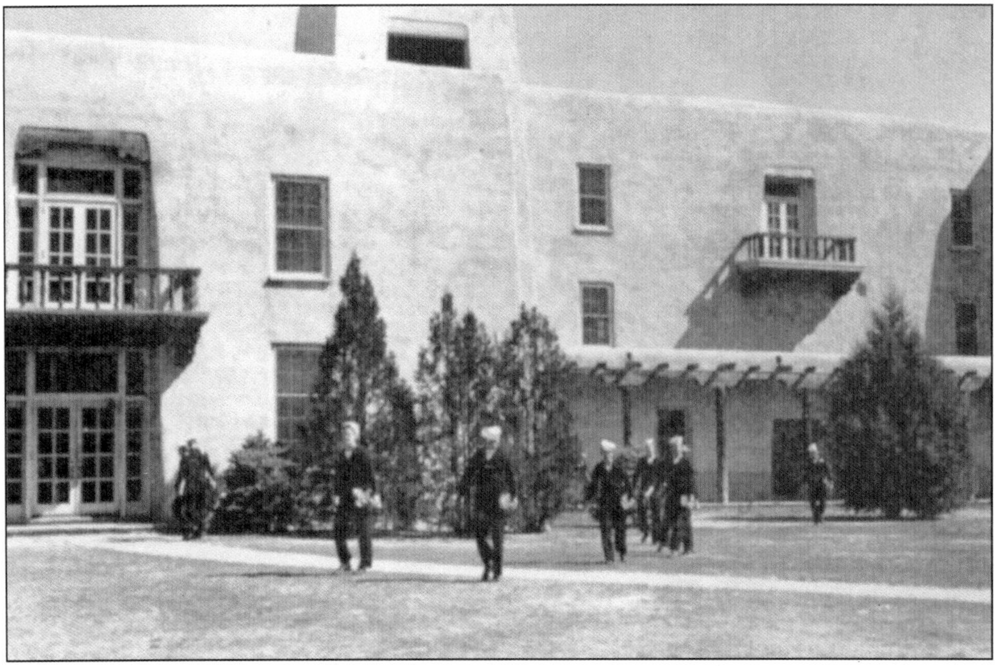

With the establishment of the V-12 unit on the university campus, half of the enrollment consisted of sailors sent by the Navy. These naval trainees occupied a unique position as both sailors and college students. They were essentially sailors, being subject to regular naval discipline and regulations while attending classes and participating in student activities with civilian students.

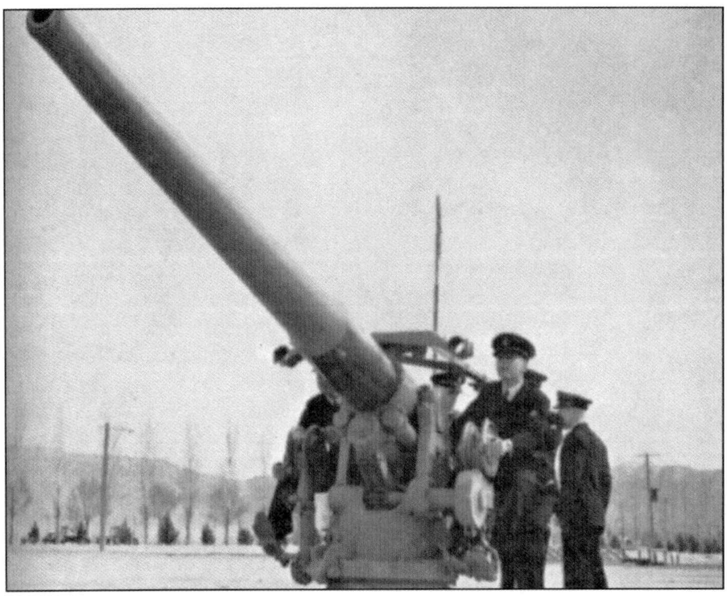

During World War II, the university became a key training ground for naval officers through its Naval Reserve Officer Training Corps (NROTC), established in 1941. As part of wartime preparations, gun turrets were installed on campus to support military efforts. Over 90 students enrolled in the program's first year, with physical training a key component. The NROTC continued until 1951, when it was dissolved due to decreased demand for officers.

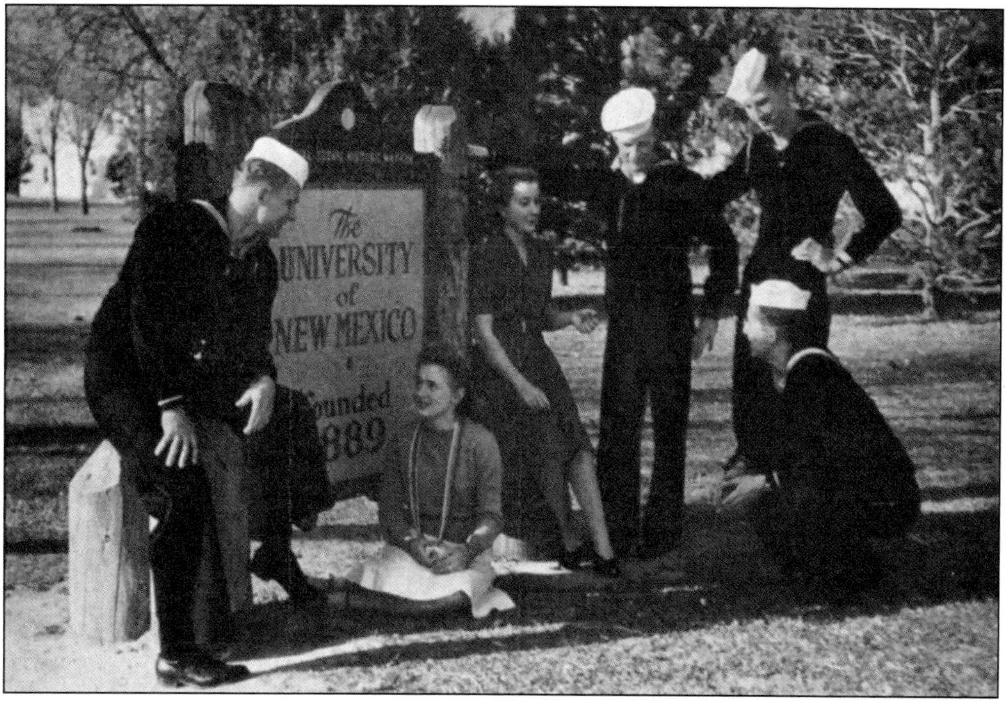

This 1944 photograph of UNM's campus reveals a pivotal moment in its history—wartime mobilization blurred the lines between military and civilian life. With approximately 500 Navy trainees in engineering, pre-med, and NROTC programs, uniforms became a common sight. Against the backdrop of the old university signage, students and servicemen crossed paths, sharing a quiet determination. The scene reflects a campus transformed by duty yet resilient in its pursuit of knowledge.

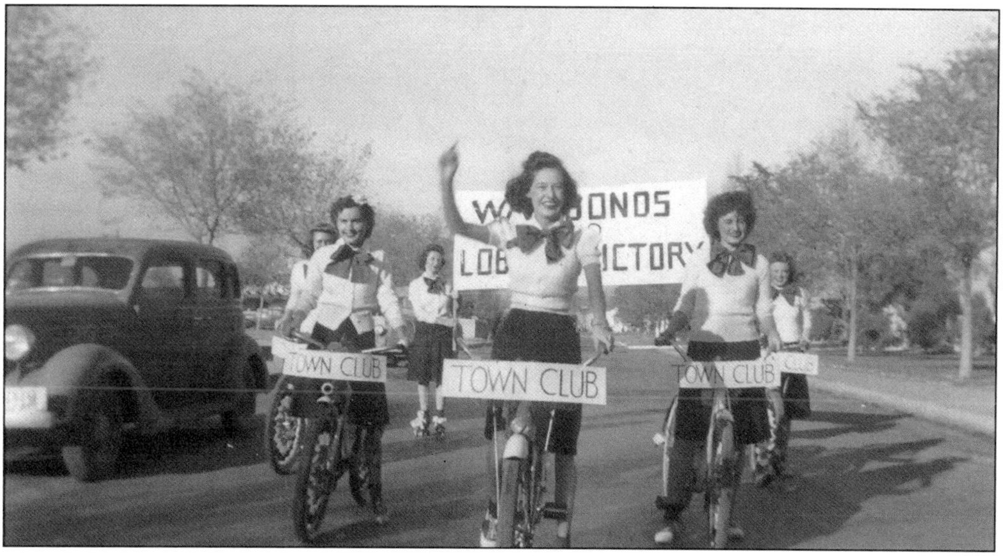

This photograph from 1942 shows members of the Town Club, a social organization for young women, promoting the sale of war bonds to support the Lobos and the national war effort. Founded in 1938, the Town Club aimed to cultivate a democratic spirit among female students and encourage their participation in campus life. Their involvement in the war bond drive reflects the broader mobilization of university communities during World War II.

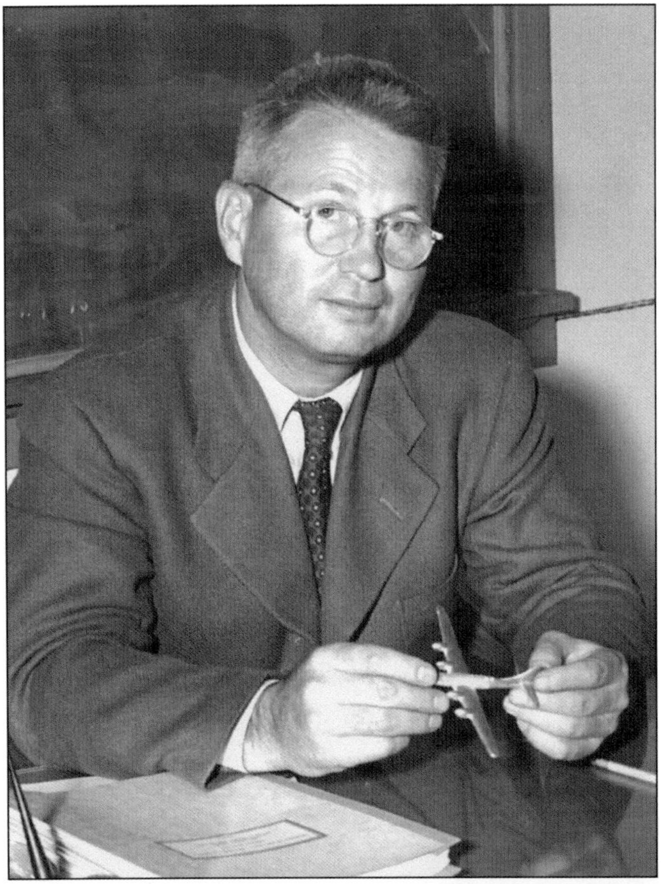

In 1942, President Zimmerman recommended E.J. Workman of the physics department to work for the National Academy of Sciences. Workman became the director of a special research project that developed the variable time (VT) proximity fuse, a weapon used by the Navy in World War II. The fuse played a crucial role in defending Britain against Nazi bombs, a fact revealed after the war.

The UNM Observatory, established in 1955 on the university golf course, began with a telescope purchased in 1951. Funded piece by piece through contributions from the Departments of Mathematics, Astronomy, and Meteoritics, along with university funds, it became a hub for public engagement and scientific discovery, reflecting UNM's commitment to expanding access to the wonders of the night sky.

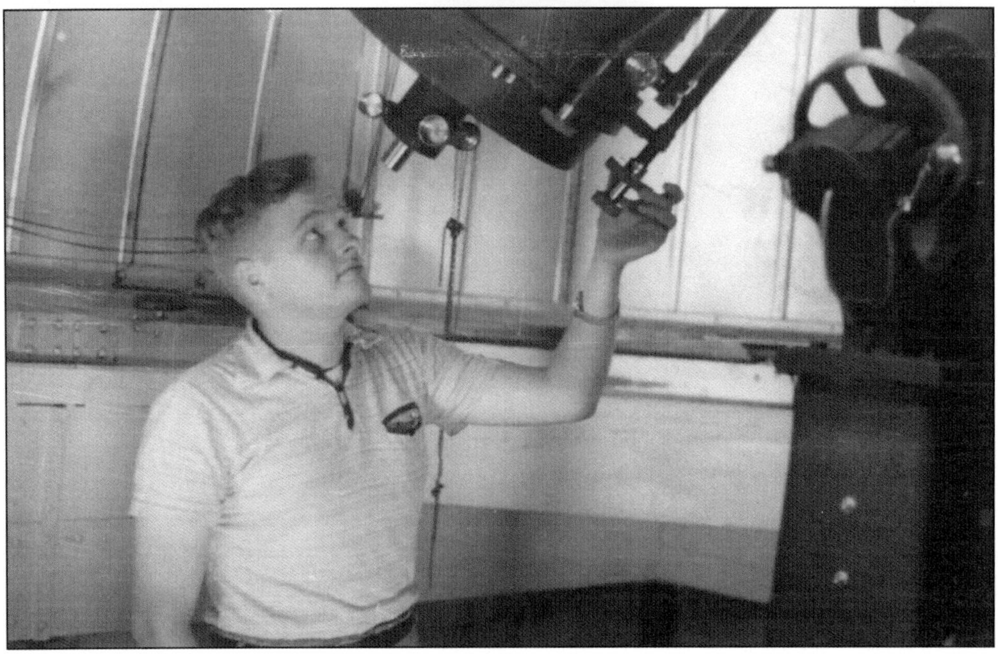

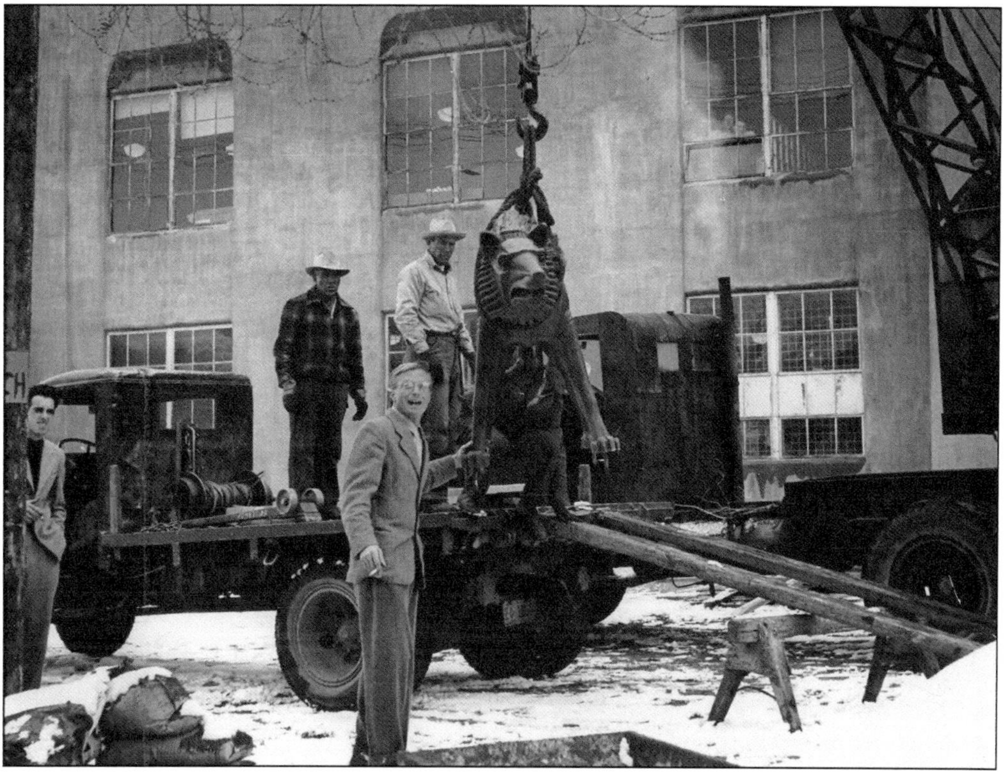

The Lobo statue, designed by John Tatschl in 1947, was installed in front of Zimmerman Stadium by the Physical Plant Department, based on a concept by art dean John Robb. Tatschl, who had previously earned national recognition by winning a prestigious sculpture competition, created and modeled the wolf. The project was funded through contributions from fraternities and sororities. Tatschl joined UNM as a professor of art in 1946 and remained a prominent figure on campus, teaching and producing various works of art. In 1960, the Lobo statue was relocated to the south side of Johnson Center.

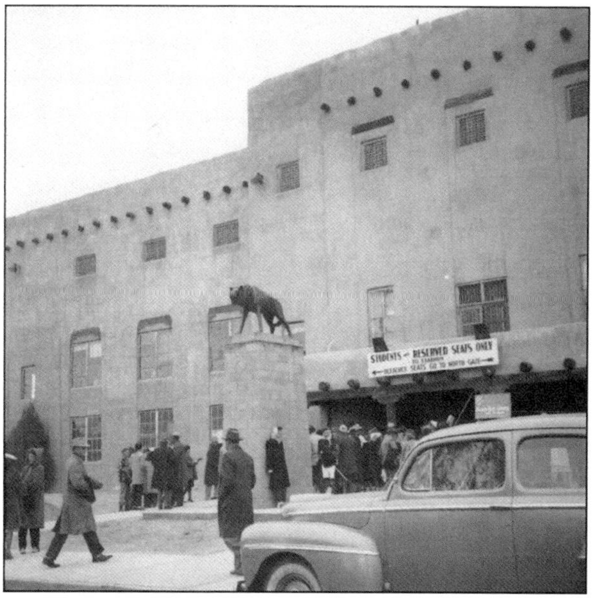

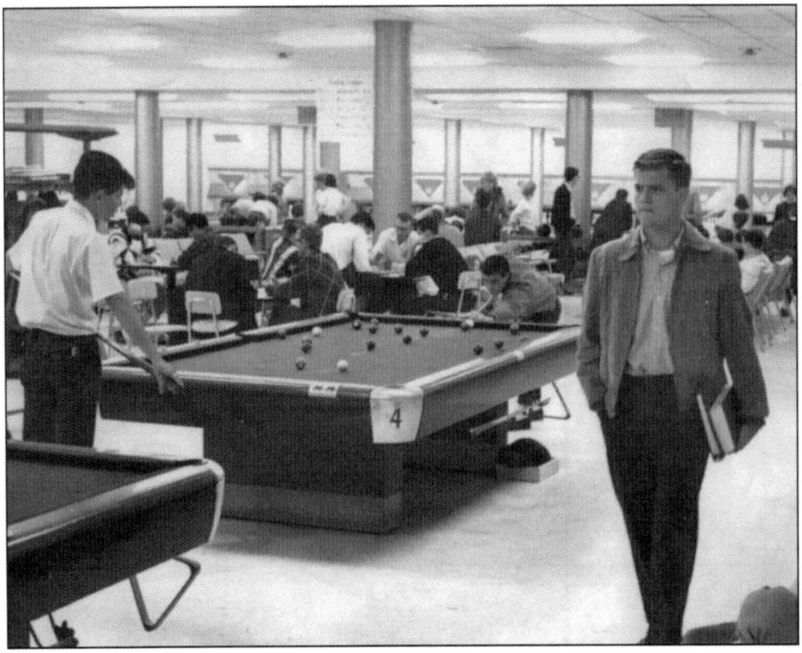

From 1937 to 1959, the old Student Union Building was the focal point of student social life. In 1959, however, the old SUB was shut down, and the New Mexico Union became the new student center, still called the SUB. It was funded by a bond issue backed by student fees.

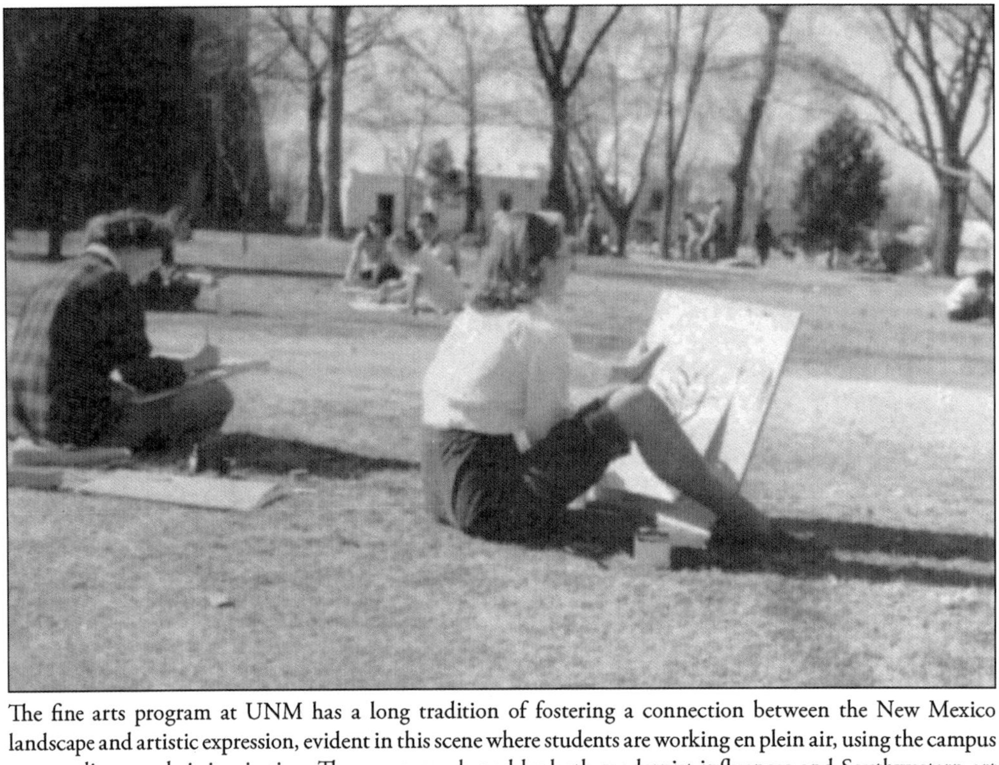

The fine arts program at UNM has a long tradition of fostering a connection between the New Mexico landscape and artistic expression, evident in this scene where students are working en plein air, using the campus surroundings as their inspiration. The program, shaped by both modernist influences and Southwestern art traditions, played a significant role in shaping UNM's cultural identity during the mid-20th century.

Founded in 1944 by Lincoln La Paz, the Institute of Meteoritics was the first in the Western world dedicated to meteoritical research. A notable achievement was recovering hundreds of specimens from the 1948 Norton-Furnas meteorite shower in Kansas. Its collection includes the one-ton Furnas County stone, the largest witnessed meteorite fall recorded at the time, which remains a centerpiece of its collection today.

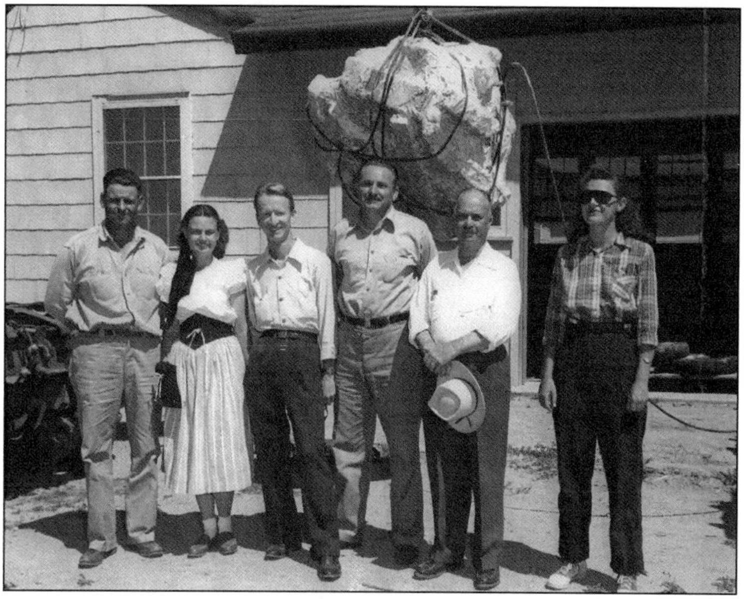

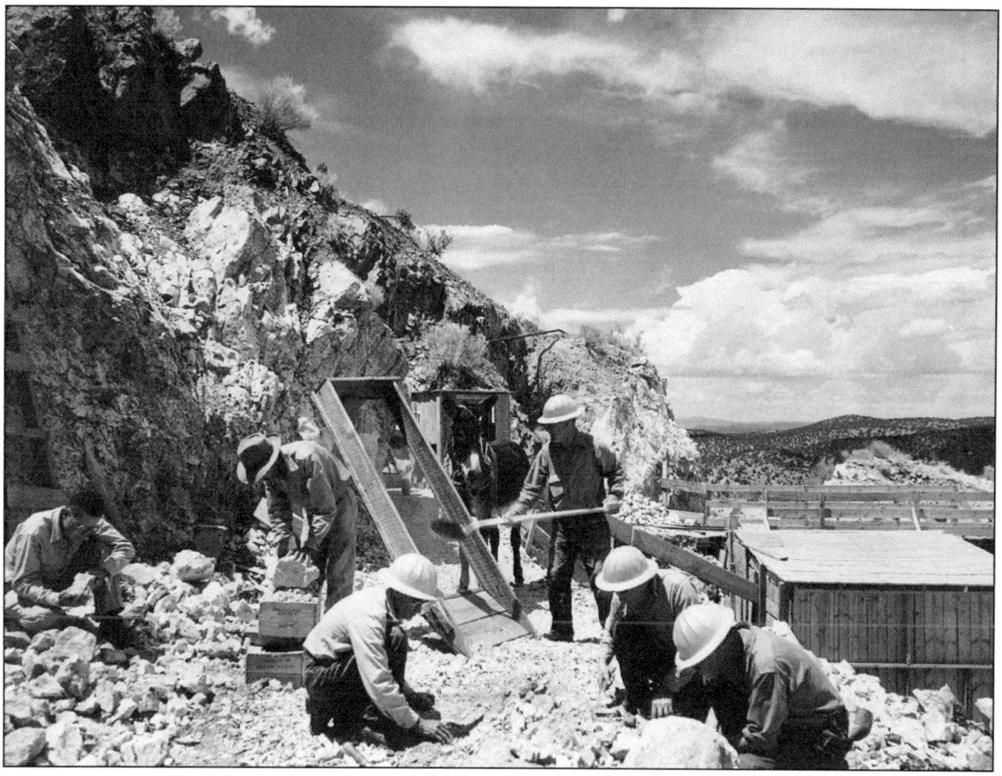

The Harding Pegmatite Mine, donated to the university by Dr. Arthur Montgomery (seated, far left), is a unique outdoor geological laboratory. Formerly an active site for mining lithium, tantalum, and beryllium, operations ceased in 1958. The property, acquired through a congressional act in 1974, now supports research, education, and controlled mineral collection, featuring walking tours and preserved geological features. The United States retains rights to strategic minerals for national security.

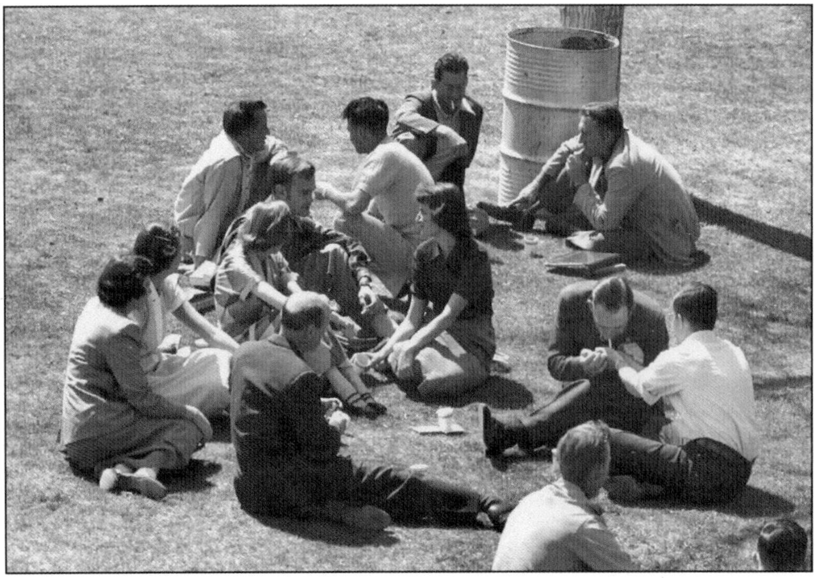

In the 1921 yearbook, a poem about the pleasures of youth goes as follows: "'Neath the shady trees / The couples sit upon the grass; / And all nature seems to invite / That awful deed, to 'cut' a class."

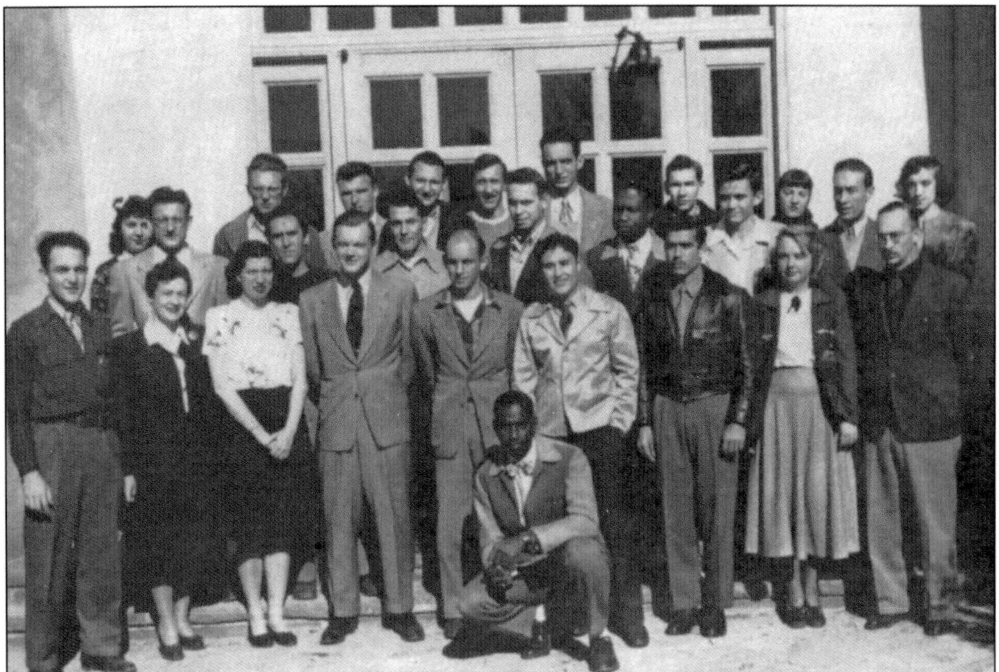

This photograph captures the founding members of UNM's NAACP student chapter, taken in 1948. These students were instrumental in advocating for civil rights following their leadership in a 1947 boycott against a local café that denied service to a Black student, George Long. The chapter, cofounded by Long and campus leader Herbert Wright, was key in securing Albuquerque's 1952 civil rights ordinance, a landmark legislation in the West.

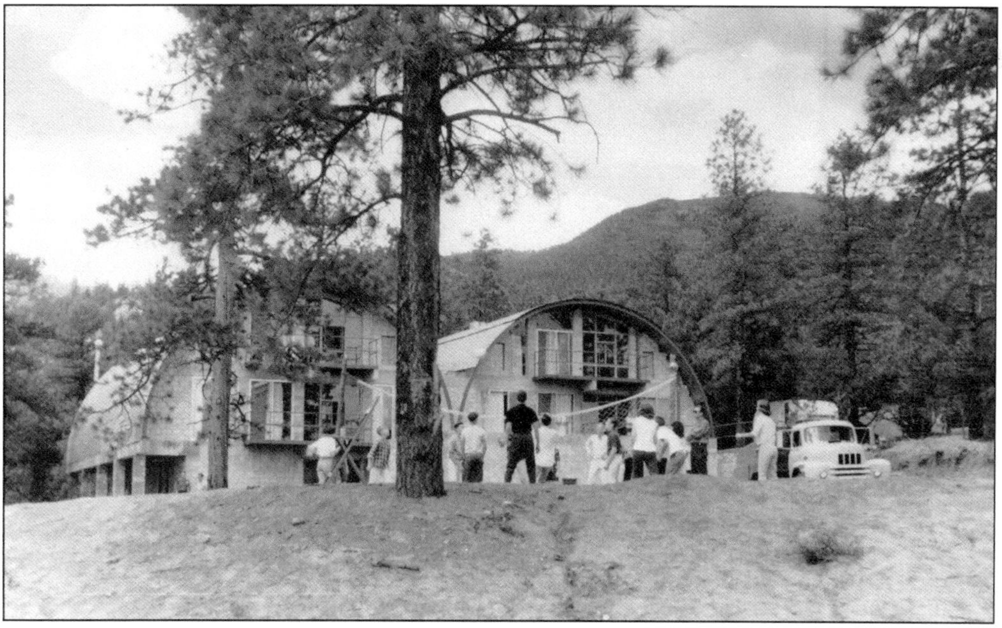

In 1955, Frieda Lawrence, widow of the famed writer D.H. Lawrence, gifted the D.H. Lawrence Ranch near Taos, New Mexico, to the university. The university has since worked to preserve the property, which serves as a historic and educational site. As per Frieda Lawrence's will, the ranch is maintained for "educational, cultural, charitable, and recreational purposes." Today, the site remains open to the public, ensuring the preservation of its natural and cultural heritage while providing educational opportunities for visitors.

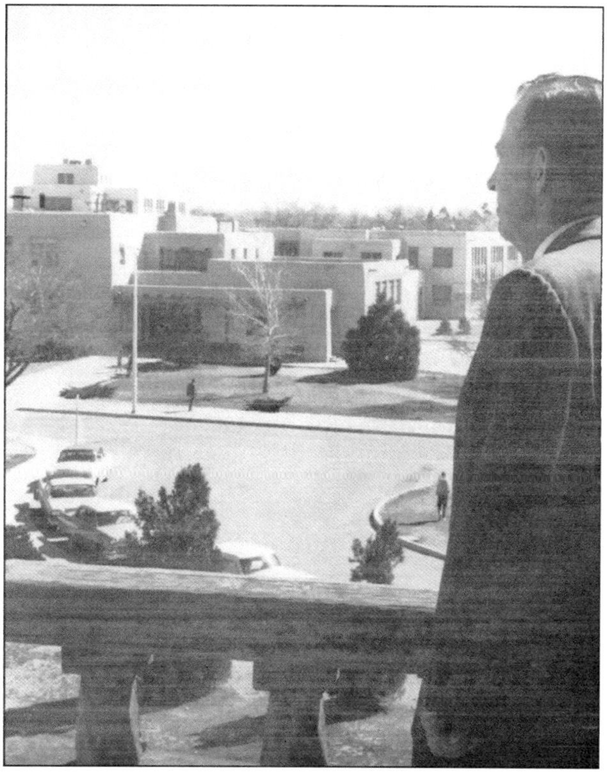

Pres. Tom Popejoy was the first native New Mexican to serve as the president of the university from 1948 to 1968. A distinguished alumnus and former football star, Popejoy exemplified the university's evolving identity during a time of significant change. Under his leadership, UNM expanded both its academic programs and its commitment to inclusivity, laying the foundation for future generations of students. His presidency marked an era of progress and innovation.

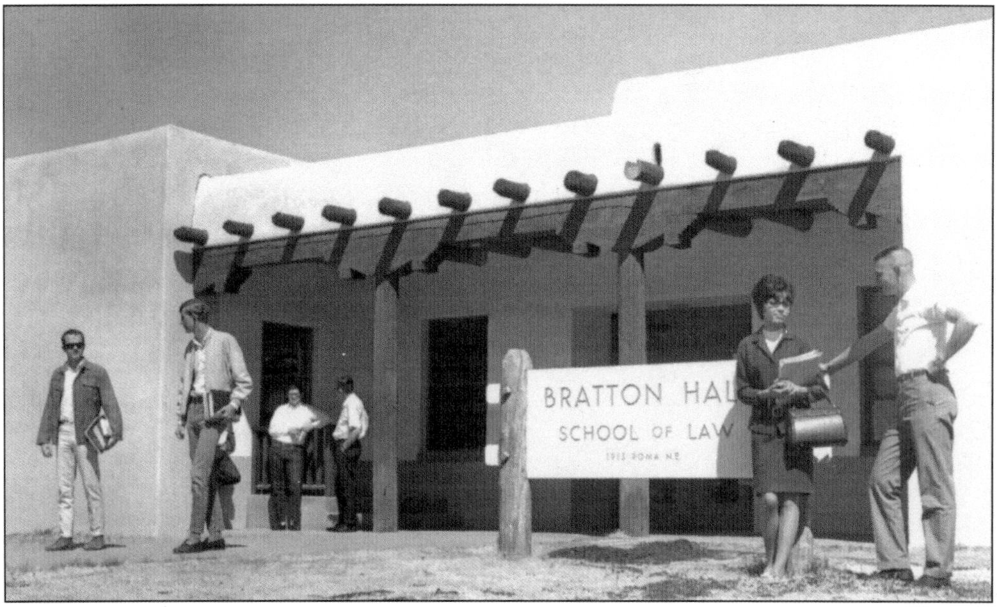

The first Law School building at the university was completed in October 1952 and later repurposed for the Department of Economics when the Law School relocated to the North Campus in 1971. In 1967, the Law School launched a preparatory program for Native American students, and Yvonne Knight of Ponca City, Oklahoma, became the first Native woman to graduate from the program.

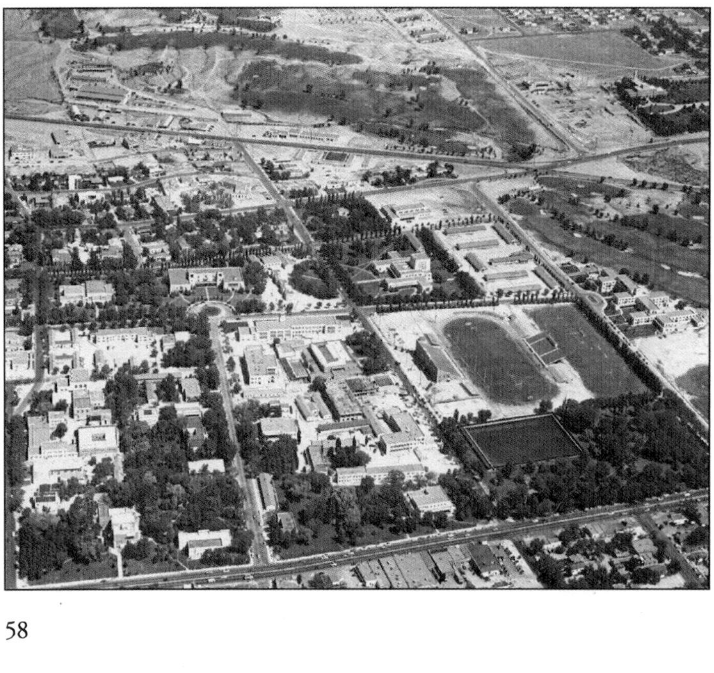

In the early 1950s, UNM faced rapid enrollment growth, prompting a building boom. With funding from student fees and revenue-generating facilities like housing and athletics, the university constructed the Biology and Chemistry Buildings. Student housing was in short supply, and attention turned to expanding campus facilities. Plans for a larger student union and new dormitories were prioritized to accommodate the growing student body.

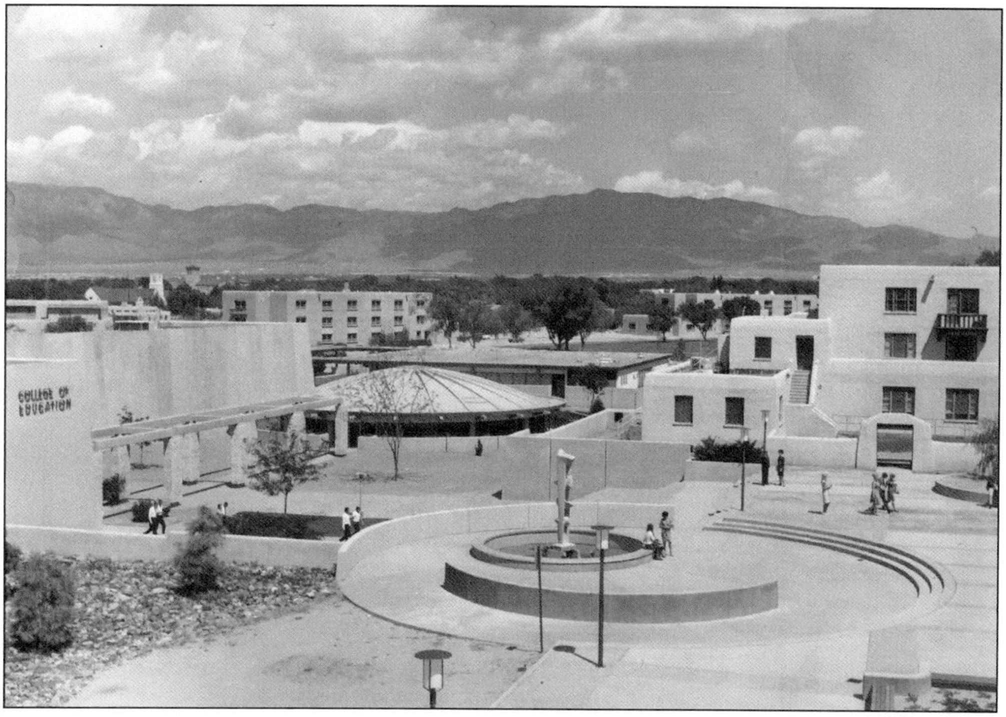

Opened in 1963, the Education Building's Kiva Auditorium, inspired by the ancient kivas of New Mexico's pueblos, blends cultural heritage with modernist architecture. This unique lecture hall embodies the fusion of traditional forms with contemporary design, creating a space that not only serves educational purposes but also pays homage to the region's Indigenous history. Its design opened the door for a regional modernism that respected traditional Spanish-Pueblo styling but allowed for innovative new forms and materials.

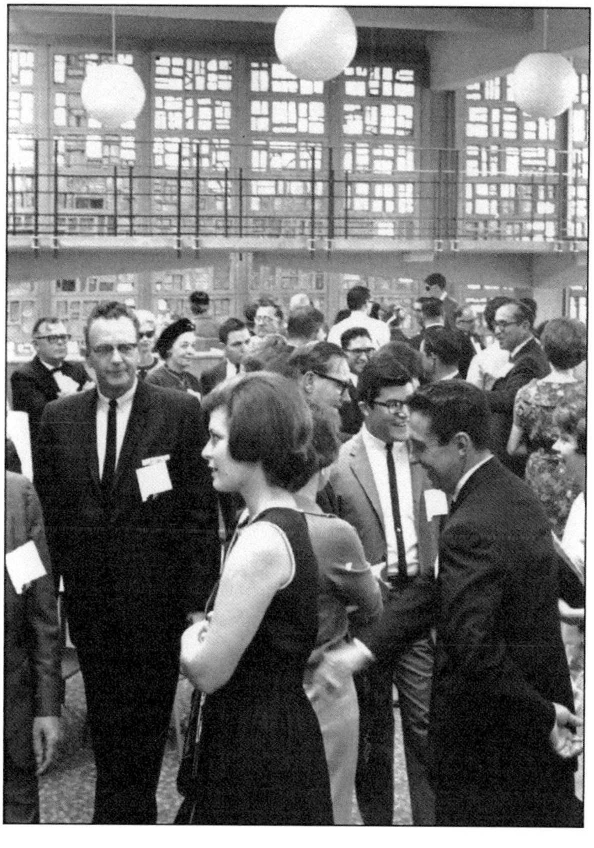

The Education Complex stemmed from Chester Travelstead, the College of Education's new dean, who proposed a modern facility to replace dilapidated buildings. In 1960, architect Max Flatow sought the opportunity to design the complex, marking a pivotal shift in architectural trends at UNM. Travelstead Hall exemplifies how Flatow's design revolutionized architectural norms in the region, with Travelstead Hall's influence on subsequent designs surpassing even John Gaw Meem's 1930s contributions.

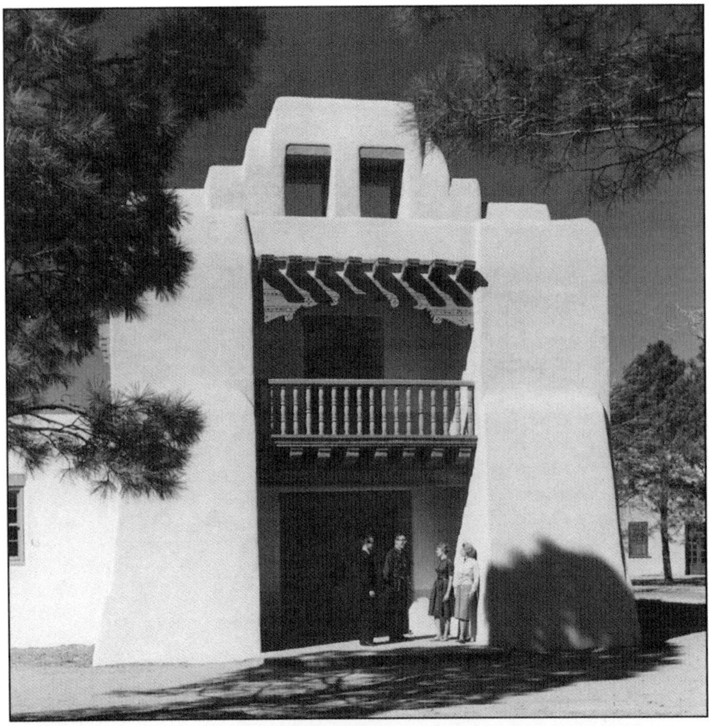

The Alumni Memorial Chapel, by Meem, was built and dedicated in the early 1960s to honor fallen soldiers and as a tribute to UNM alumni who have made significant contributions to the community. The venue also serves as a popular space for weddings and special ceremonies.

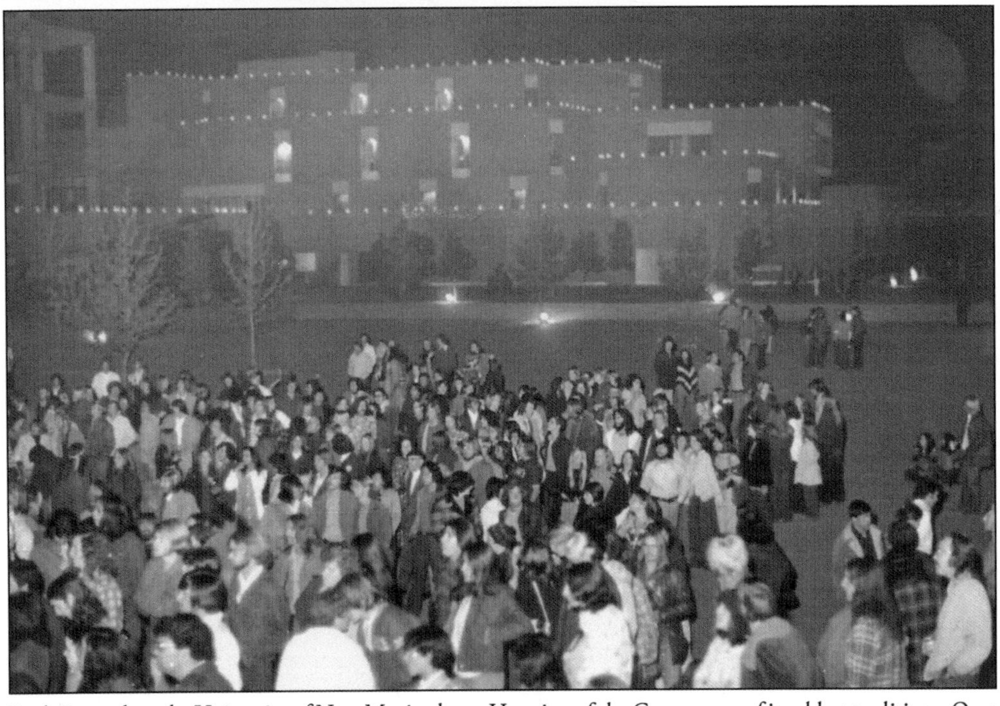

Each December, the University of New Mexico hosts Hanging of the Greens, one of its oldest traditions. Over 13,000 luminarias are set up by student organizations, creating one of New Mexico's largest public displays. Students and community members carol across campus, and as night falls, the luminarias are lit. This cherished event brings together hundreds to celebrate the holiday season in a warm and festive atmosphere.

This photograph highlights the university's Fine Arts Center, completed in 1966. Serving as a focal point for the university's art, music, and theater programs, the center embodies modernist architecture. With galleries, performance spaces, and classrooms, it fosters creativity and collaboration, offering students and faculty a space to engage in artistic expression and connect with the broader community.

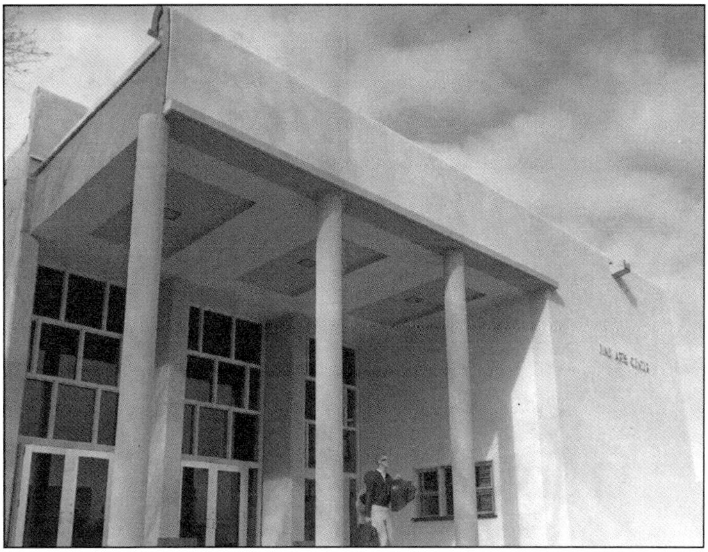

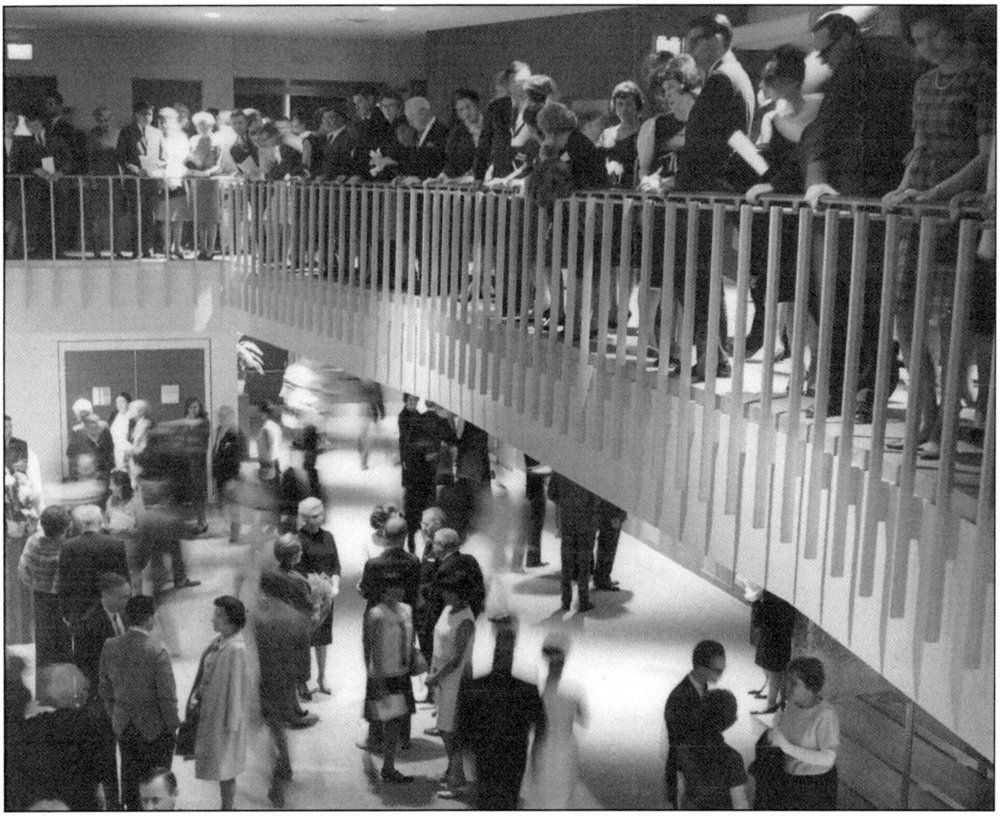

Popejoy Hall, named after Pres. Tom Popejoy, who spent 20 years advocating for its creation, officially opened on October 1, 1966. The largest performance venue of its kind in New Mexico, it seats nearly 2,000 people. Its founding marked a turning point for the university, bringing Broadway and first-rate theatrical productions to the state. The hall was dedicated with a performance by the Utah Symphony Orchestra.

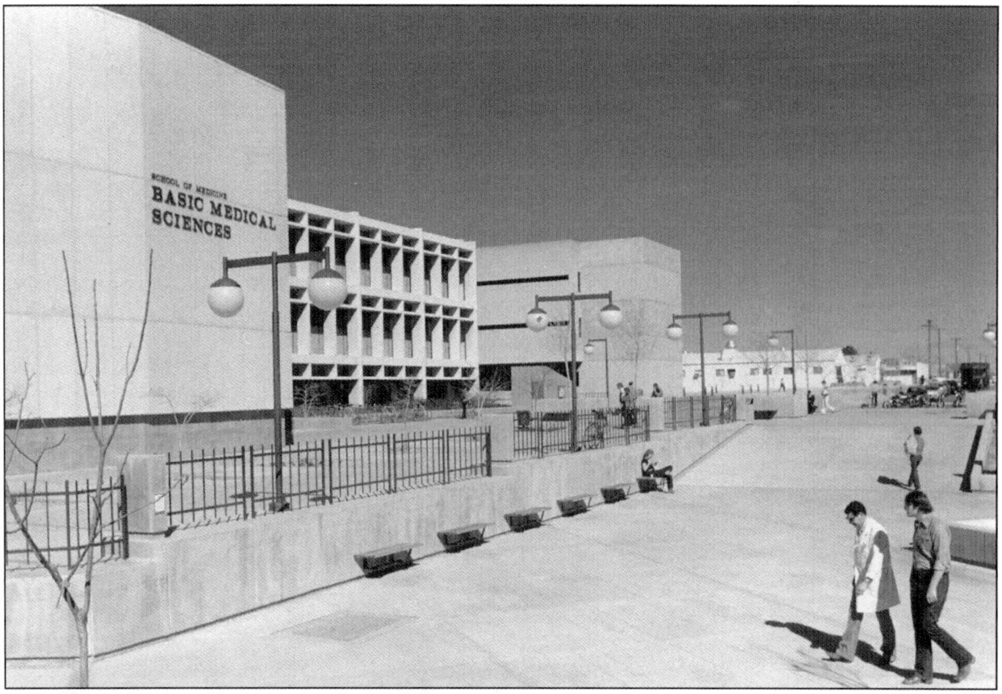

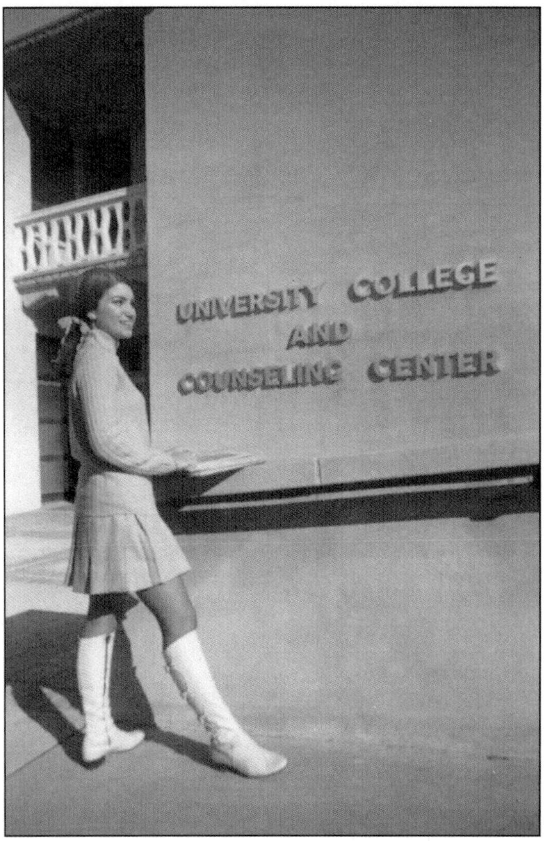

The university's School of Medicine admitted its first class in 1964 and was created to address the state's diverse healthcare needs, focusing on underserved and Native American communities. Consistently ranked among the best nationally, the school is known for its top-ranked programs in rural medicine and family and primary care.

The university established its Student Health Service in 1929 to prioritize student well-being, recognizing the importance of healthcare in education. Modeled after similar programs at other state universities, the service was funded by a dedicated health fee. After operating under the Division of Health, Physical Education, and Recreation from 1937 to 1939, the service moved to a new building in 1960, continuing to serve students today.

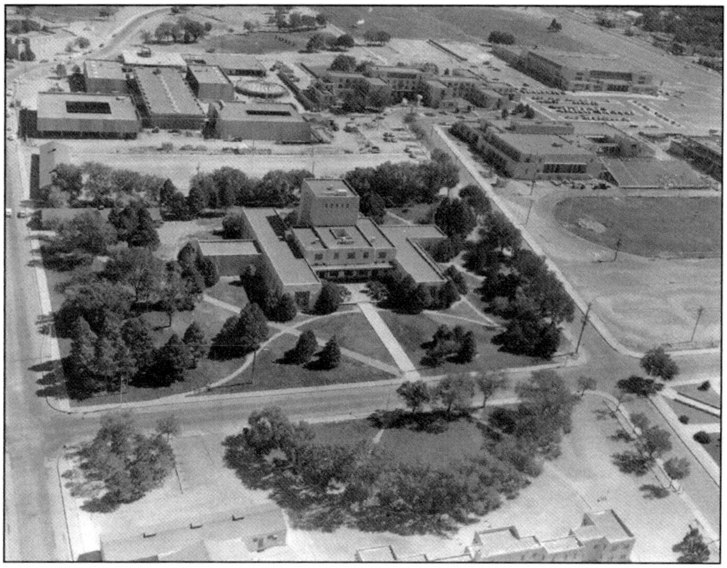

This aerial view highlights the early car-centric design of the campus, with roads encircling and cutting through the area. The library is positioned at the center, the education complex lies directly behind it, and the outdoor athletics facilities are visible to the right. By the 1970s, the campus design began to shift toward a more pedestrian-friendly approach, reflecting evolving priorities in urban planning and campus life.

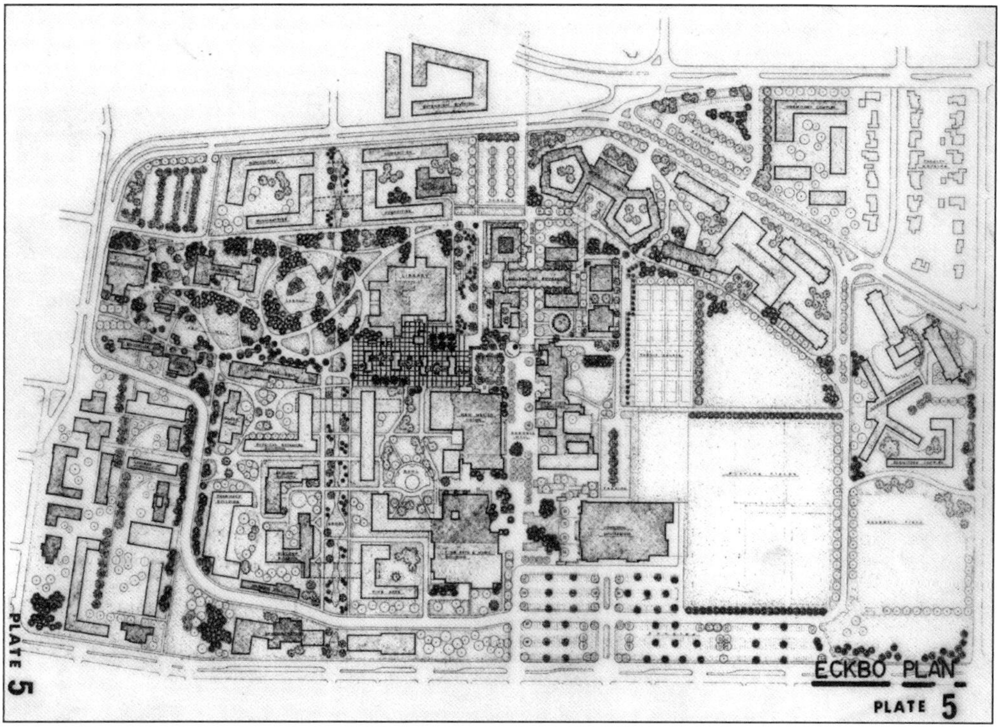

In 1962, to accommodate increasing campus enrollment and as part of the General Development Plan, a landscape design by Garrett Eckbo was proposed to create a more pedestrian-friendly campus. This plan envisioned a park-like pedestrian area with a pond between the administration building and Zimmerman Library, a concept later realized as Smith Plaza. The most notable feature, the Duck Pond, was completed in 1976, adding to the area's charm.

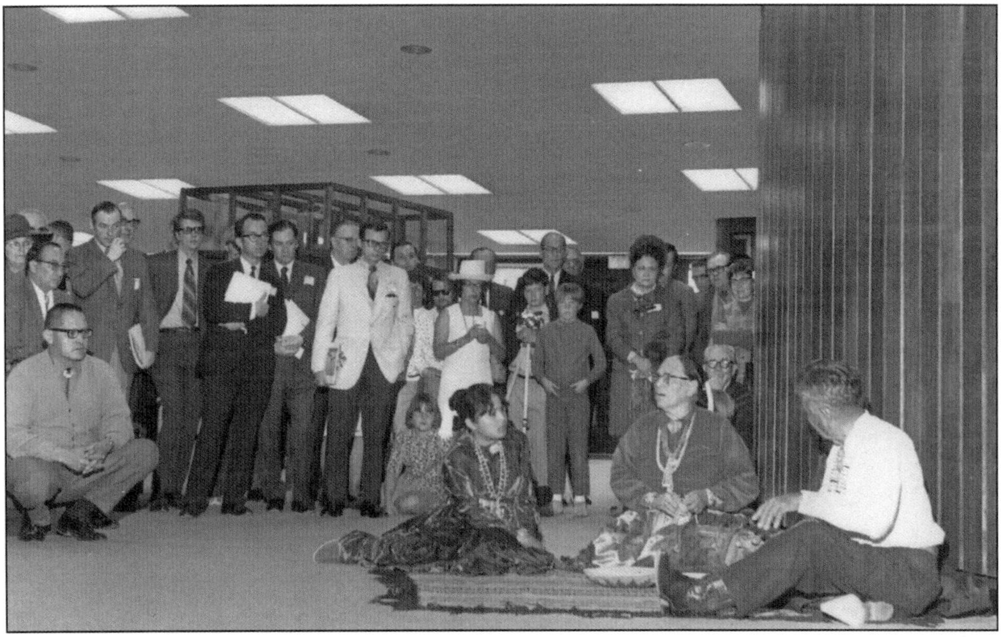

The new Bratton Hall for the UNM Law School was dedicated on April 17–18, 1971, with a series of celebratory events, including an address by US Supreme Court justice Byron R. White. The dedication featured an open house, a Southwest art and anthropology exhibition, and a special blessing ceremony by members of the Navajo tribe, marking the occasion with cultural significance for both the university and the broader community.

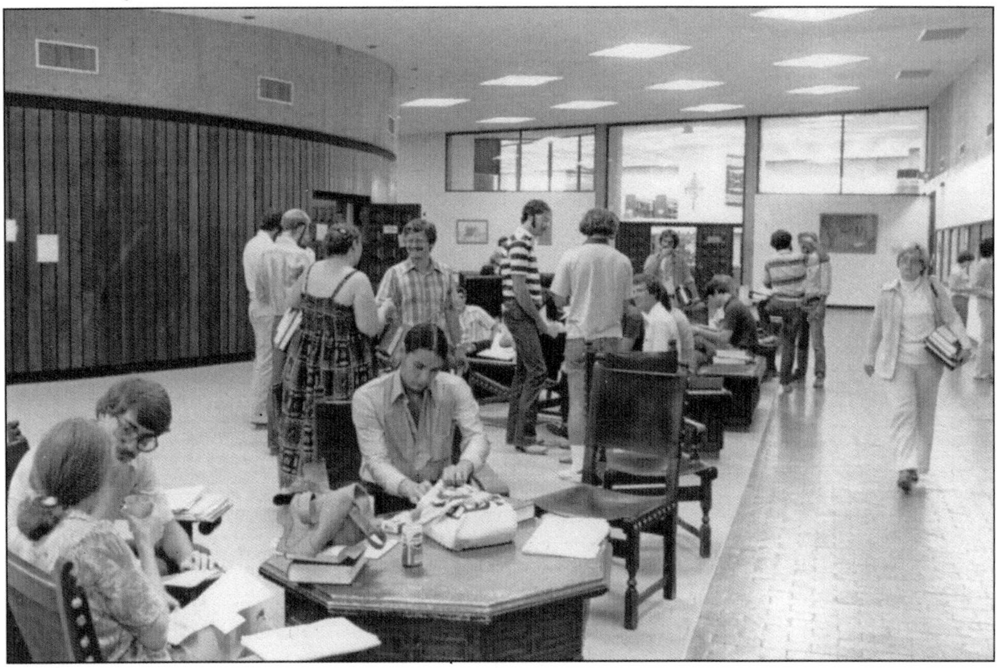

The School of Law and Native American Studies program has been a leader in advocating for Indigenous rights, particularly in relation to the Native American Graves Protection and Repatriation Act (NAGPRA). UNM has worked alongside tribal communities and legal scholars to ensure the respectful return of ancestral remains and sacred objects, underscoring the university's commitment to cultural preservation and Native American justice.

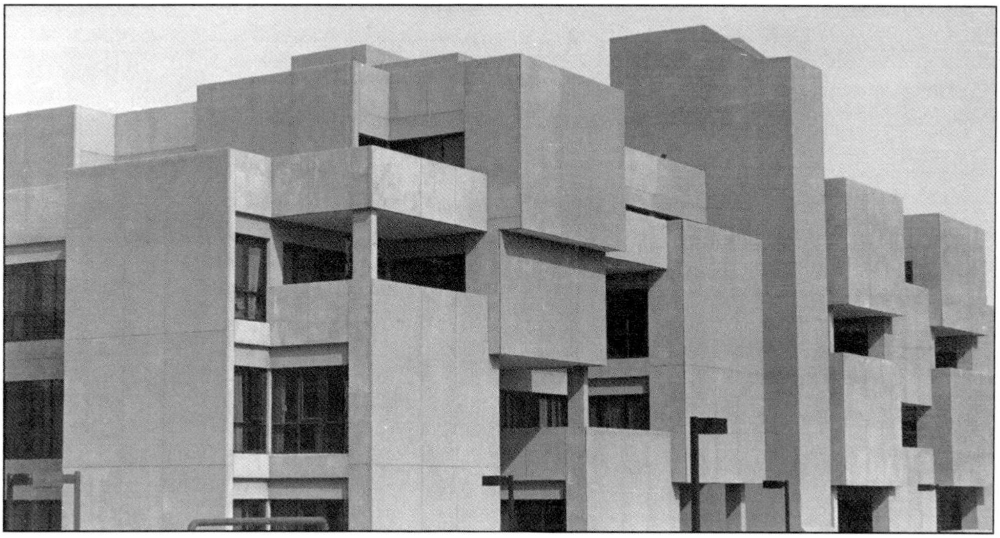

As humanities programs expanded, the need for additional space led to the 1972 approval of the Humanities Building's construction. While the design was rooted in brutalism, faculty expressed concerns over the lack of natural light and the building's fortress-like appearance, which they felt was not conducive to the collaborative and creative environment they envisioned. Despite these objections, the design was finalized, leading to a building that remains a controversial representation of 1970s architecture on campus. It is set to be demolished in 2025.

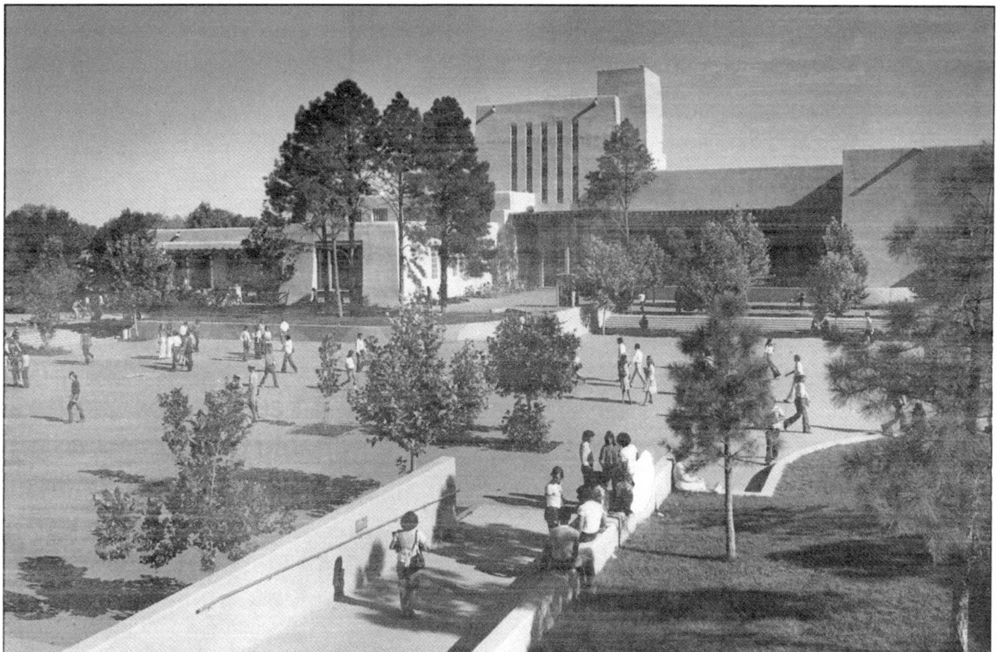

This photograph shows Zimmerman Library in the 1970s, showing the original structure alongside significant expansions completed in 1966 and 1973. Opened in 1938, Zimmerman Library became central to the university's academic community. By the 1970s, the library's expansion incorporated updated research facilities, study areas, and technology to meet the growing needs of students and faculty. The library remains a vital space for collaboration and learning.

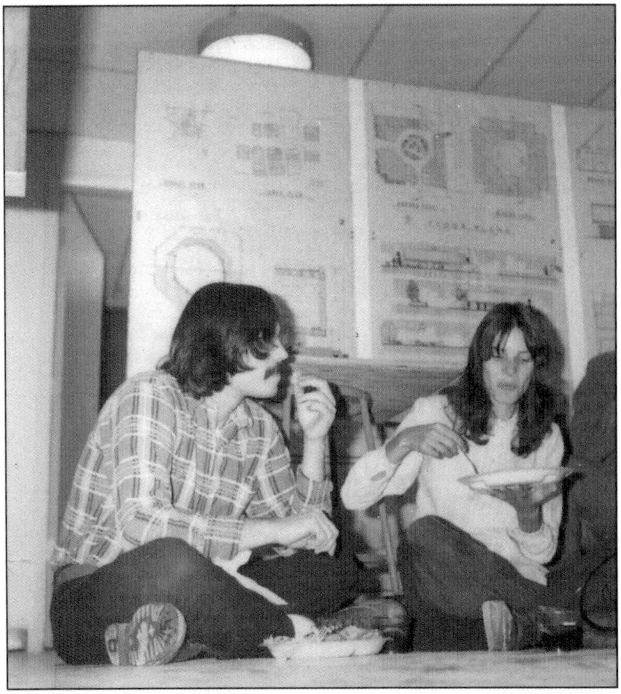

In 1971, the architecture program at UNM transitioned from the College of Fine Arts to become its own school. The university has had a significant role in designing and building settlements in the Rio Grande Valley since statehood in 1912. In 1936, the first architectural concentration was established within the College of Fine Arts. The program evolved into the independent School of Architecture and Planning in 1975. The school's new building, George Pearl Hall, which also includes the Fine Arts and Design Library, was completed and occupied in 2008.

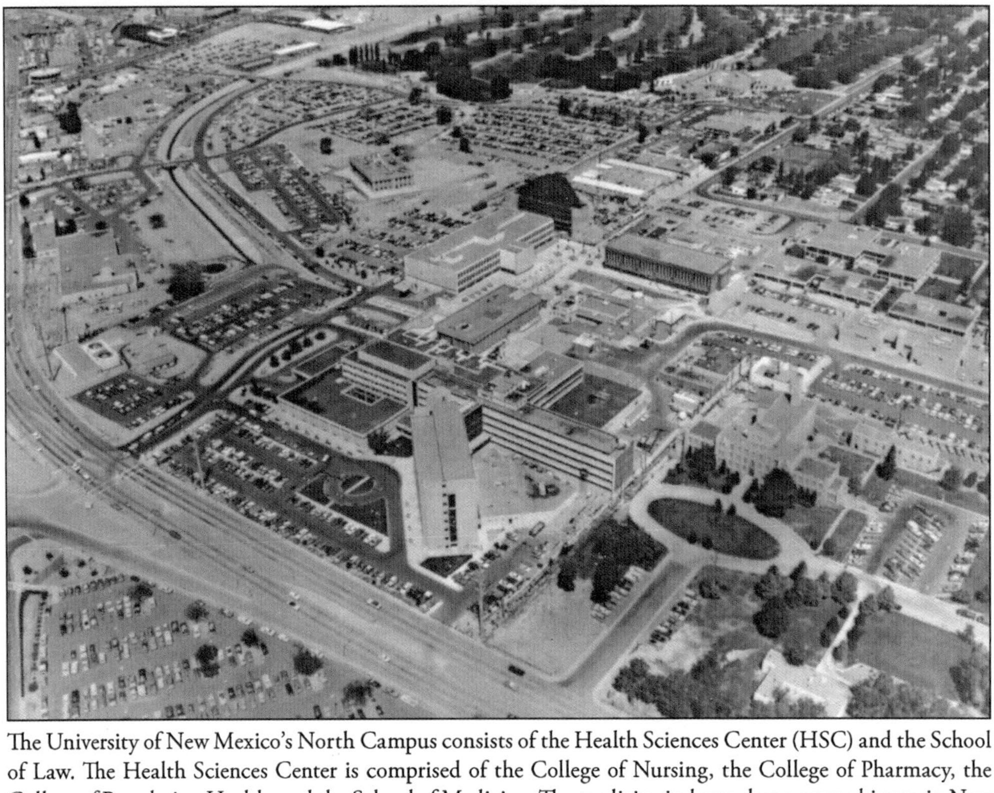

The University of New Mexico's North Campus consists of the Health Sciences Center (HSC) and the School of Law. The Health Sciences Center is comprised of the College of Nursing, the College of Pharmacy, the College of Population Health, and the School of Medicine. The medicine industry has a strong history in New Mexico because of all of the early sanatoriums established for tuberculosis.

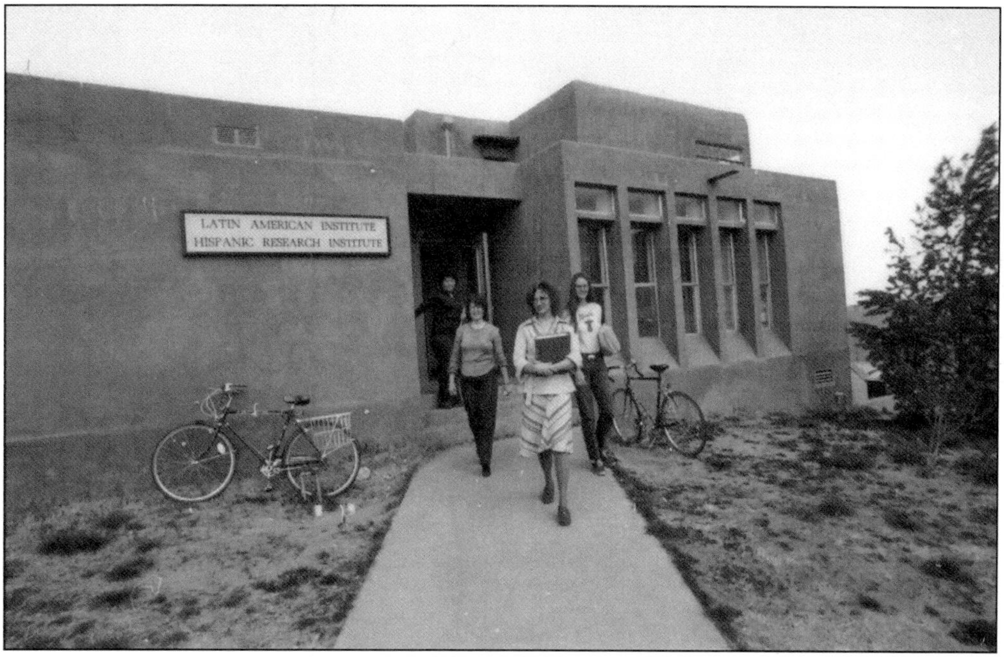

The Latin American and Iberian Institute (LAII) traces its origins to 1941 with the establishment of the School of Inter-American Affairs under Prof. Joaquin Ortega. UNM's Latin America initiatives have long emphasized community engagement locally and globally. LAII supports research on Latin America, Spain, Portugal, and beyond while producing educational resources like curriculum materials and literacy programs, including the *Vamos a Leer* book group, which incorporates books, films, and art exhibits.

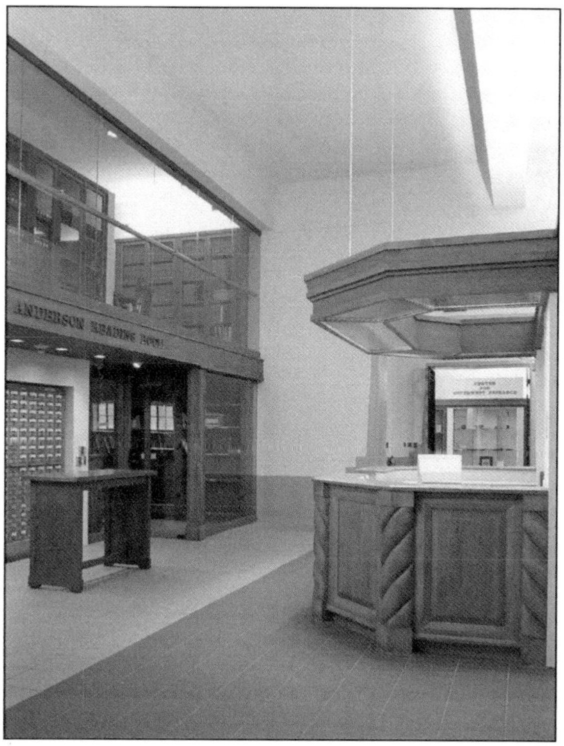

The Center for Southwest Research (CSWR) and the Center for Regional Studies (CRS) support university initiatives through student fellowships, research, and public programs, with a focus on the Southwest, Indigenous communities, and the United States–Mexico Borderlands. The CSWR's Pictorial Collections, established in 1986 as the Photo Archives and renamed in 1998, contain over 120,000 images that document the history and culture of the Southwest and Latin America, from historic daguerreotypes to contemporary digital images.

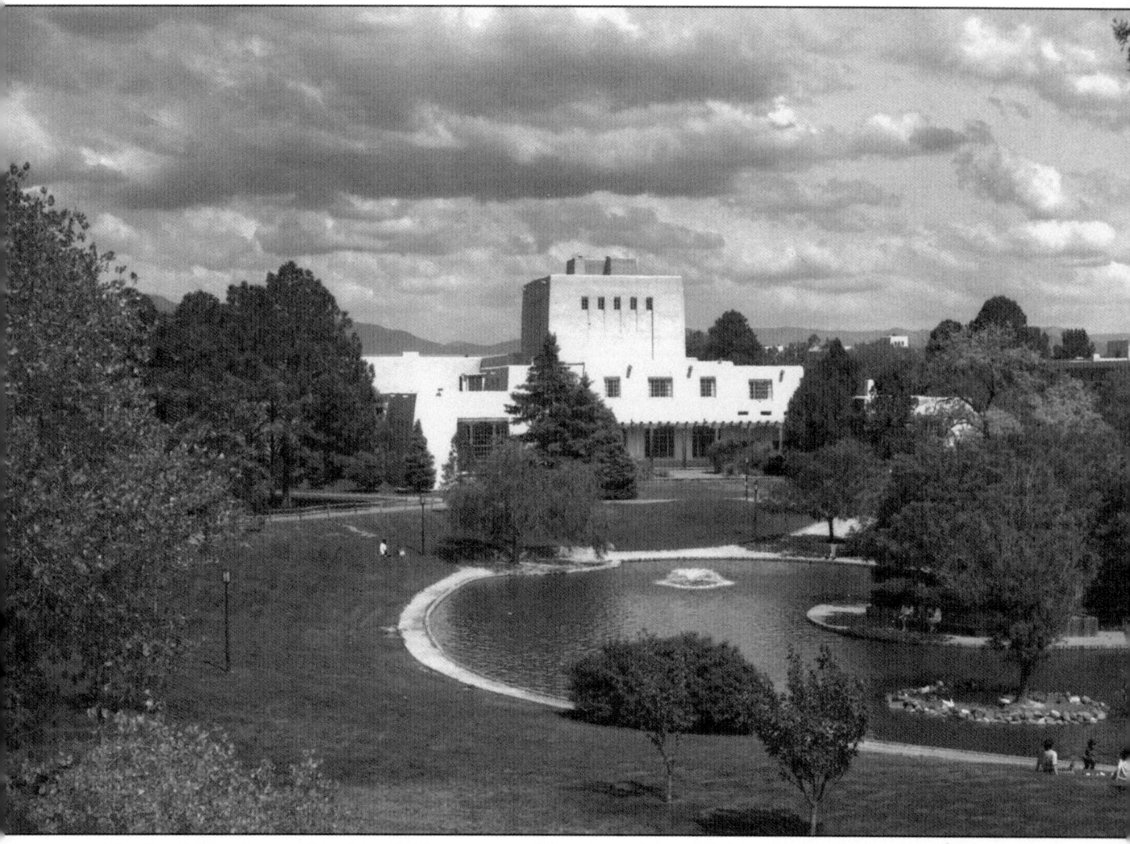

The Duck Pond, completed in 1976, is a central feature and one of the most significant enhancements of the campus, designed by the modernist landscape architect Garrett Eckbo. Originally conceived as the University Pond in the 1960s as part of the "Warnecke Plan" by John Carl Warnecke and Associates, the pond quickly became known as the Duck Pond after its popularity with local ducks. The pond was part of a larger vision to transform the campus into a more pedestrian-friendly environment, promoting ecological awareness and modernist design. Despite early criticisms of its aesthetic appeal, once described as the epitome of tackiness, and its impact on the surrounding landscape, including the removal of Yatoka Hall and a parking lot, the Duck Pond has since evolved into a beloved landmark. It became a place for relaxation, wildlife, and student gathering. However, the pond faced ecological challenges, such as overpopulation of ducks and conflict with domestic animals. In 2024, the university launched the Duck Pond Revitalization Project, aimed at enhancing water quality, improving safety, and maintaining the pond's environmental integrity for future generations.

Three

Student Activities and Traditions

The University of New Mexico has long been a cornerstone of academic excellence, cultural exchange, and community engagement. It reflects the rich diversity of New Mexico and provides a platform for students to grow intellectually and socially. The university has evolved alongside New Mexico, reflecting the state's diverse heritage and responding to the needs of its students. Over the years, the university has become a hub for progressive thought, activism, and achievement, producing generations of leaders across various fields. Athletics has been integral to UNM's identity, producing Olympians and Super Bowl stars. Legendary figures like Cathy Carr, Don Perkins, and Ira Harge have cemented their names in sports history. The establishment of the women's basketball team in 1898 was a significant milestone in the promotion of gender equality in collegiate athletics. More recently, in 2003, Katie Hnida made history as the first female to score in an FBS football game. Beyond athletics, UNM has continued to boast a rich array of student activities and traditions that foster creativity and engagement. Student organizations like the Kiva Club, which advocates for Native American rights, and the Photography Club, which nurtures artistic expression, have provided students with the opportunity to engage with their passions and make a difference on campus. Academically, UNM has been a leader in language programs in German; French; Navajo; New Mexican Spanish, a unique dialect; and others. These academic efforts enhance cross-cultural understanding and preserve the unique heritage of the region. UNM's impact extends to the literary world, having nurtured authors like Tony Hillerman, Rudolfo Anaya, Leslie Marmon Silko, and Lois Duncan. Their works, deeply rooted in the state's culture and history, have gained national recognition and further solidified UNM's reputation as a center for creativity and intellectual exploration. The university has also been deeply involved in social justice movements, from its participation in civil rights protests to its stand against the Vietnam War. One notable event in the 1970s was the strike led by Adolfo Padilla, which highlighted labor issues on campus. Through its diverse traditions, activism, and academic excellence, UNM remains an influential institution, continuing to shape the future of New Mexico's educational and cultural landscape.

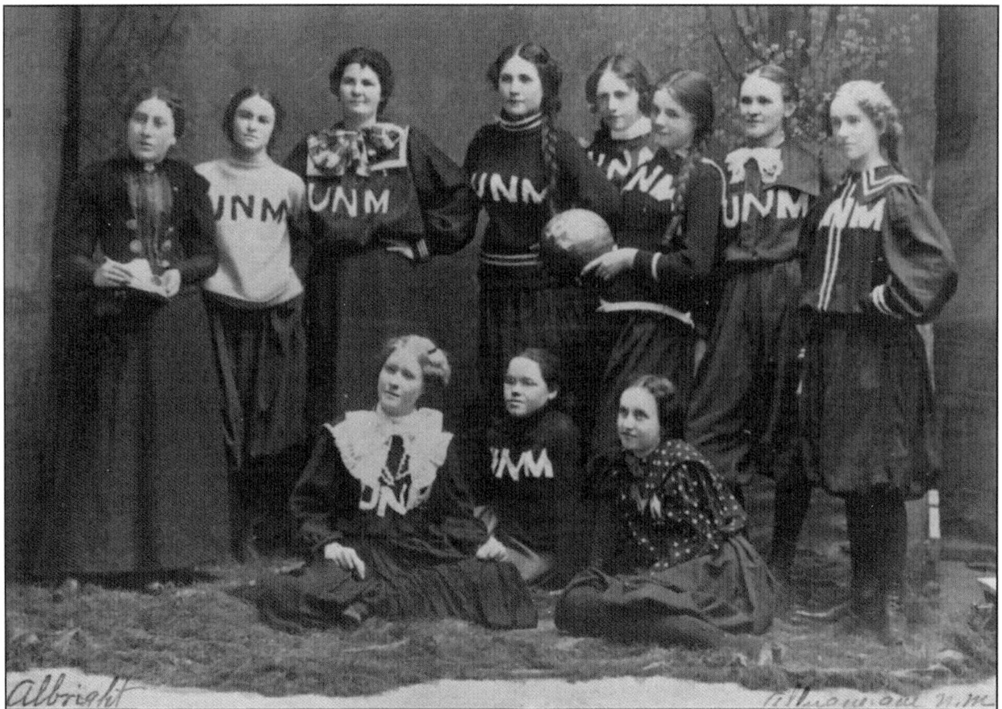

THE GLADIATORS

December 22, 1898, marked the beginning of UNM basketball history with an intramural game between two teams comprised entirely of UNM students: the Gladiators and the Olympians. The Gladiators wore green and gold, while the Olympians sported strawberry and cream. This historic match was the beginning of basketball at UNM, with both teams under the guidance of Myra Lukens, director of women's gymnasium work. The women played in high-button shoes and bloomers, setting a precedent for the future of sports at the university. This game represented both athleticism and the growing inclusion of women in university athletics, contributing to the foundation of basketball at UNM.

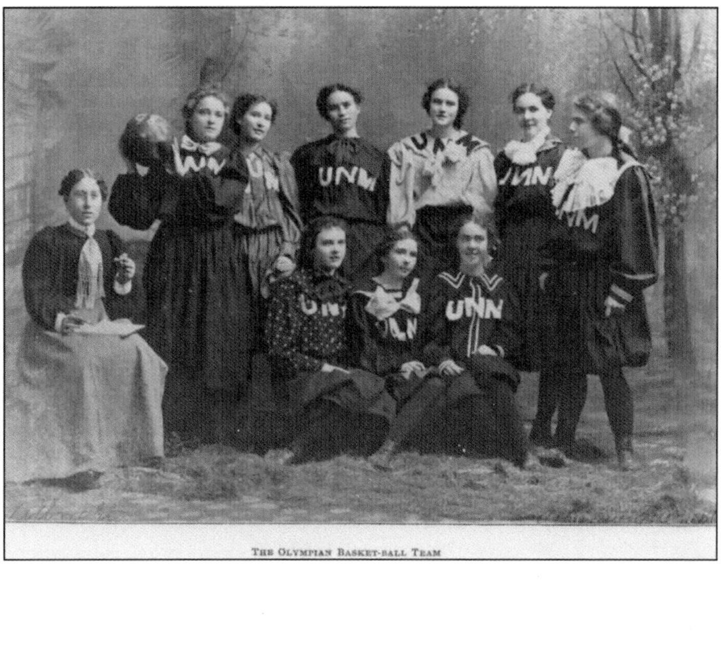

THE OLYMPIAN BASKET-BALL TEAM

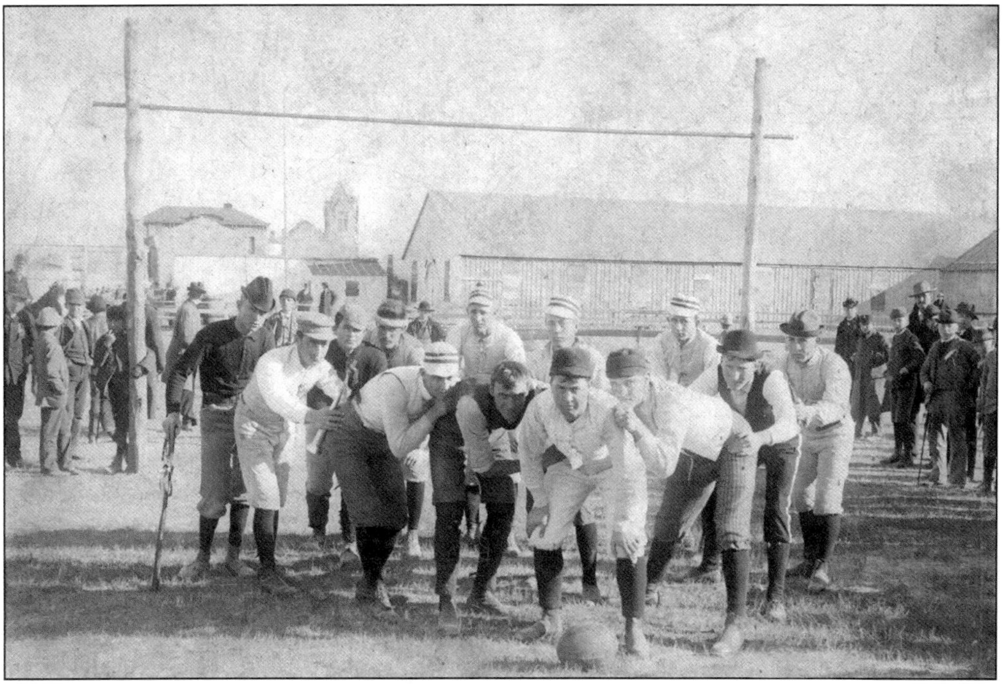

This 1896 men's varsity football photograph features Old Town's San Felipe de Neri Church in the background, showing some of Albuquerque's historical roots. Interestingly, UNM did not organize football from 1895 through the fall of 1898 due to low interest. The first recorded football game was against Albuquerque High School on October 27, 1892, played in a vacant lot. UNM lost 0-5.

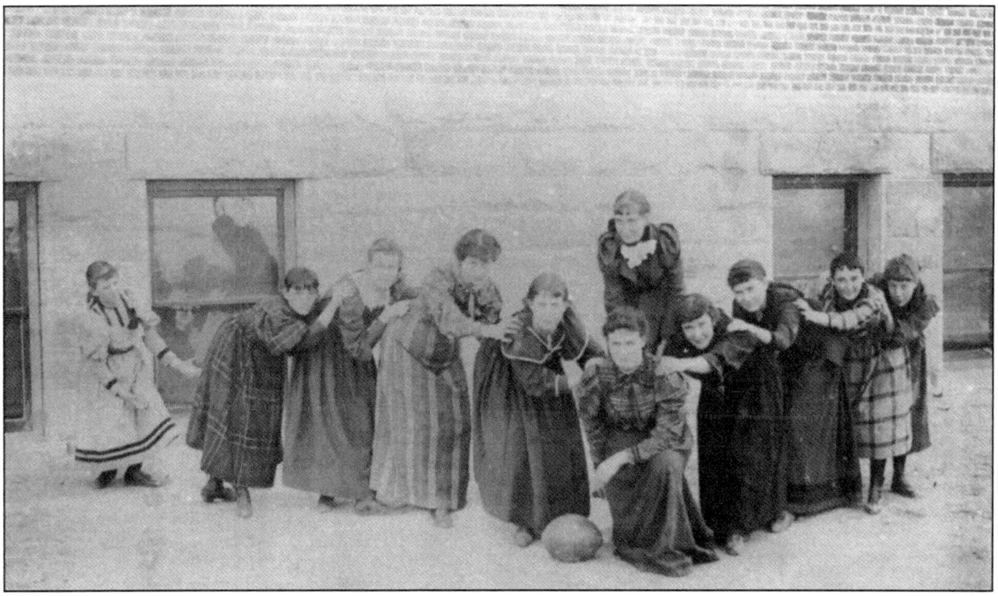

These UNM women in about 1896 playfully recreate the men's football team's iconic "flying V" formation. This humorous imitation reflects their engagement with campus culture and challenges to traditional gender roles. Though women's involvement in organized athletics at the turn of the century was often informal, this act symbolized their desire to engage with and comment on football's growing prominence in a playful way.

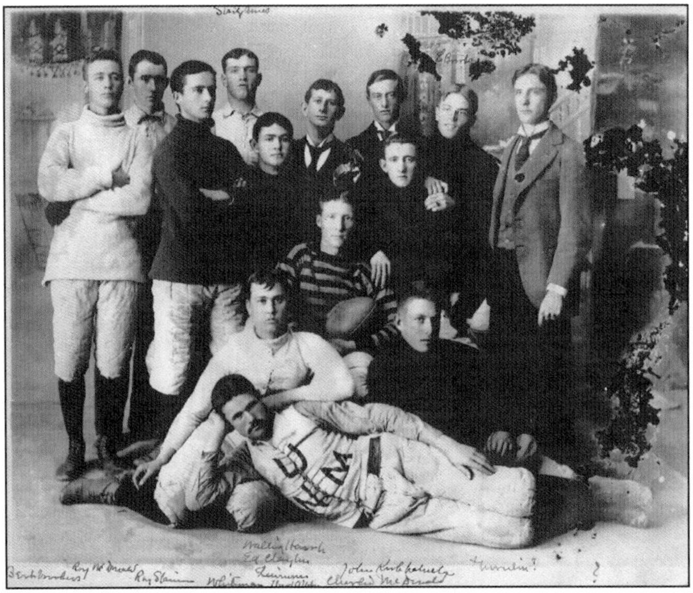

UNM's football history began in 1894 with the formation of the first Wolf Pack, marking the start of a strong athletic tradition. Coached by pharmacy professor W.A. Zimmer, the team played against the Indian School in three games, winning the final match in front of 1,500 fans after a loss and a tie. This early success sparked lasting enthusiasm for the sport at UNM.

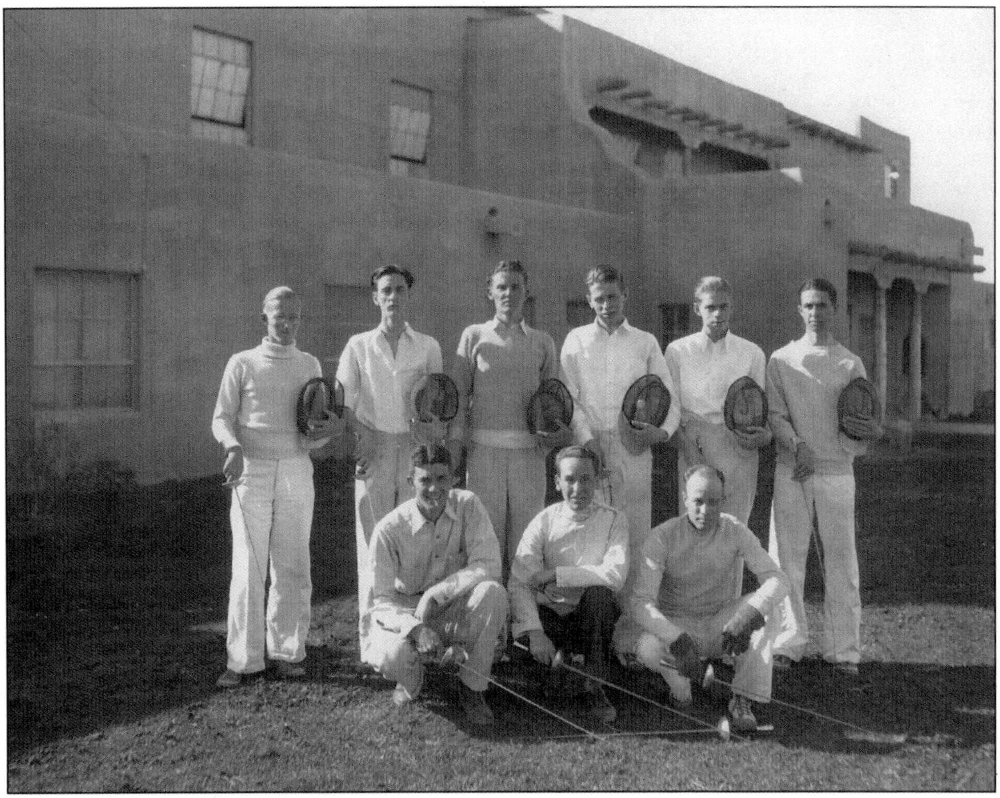

Before intramural sports became more common during the 1920s, few activities were offered for those uninterested in football or basketball. Fencing was a popular choice among young men, influenced by the tradition of dueling in Austria and Germany. These duels intended to leave a mark on the left cheek. Even those who disapproved of duels often felt compelled to engage in them to preserve their honor. The Fencing Association at UNM formed in 1967.

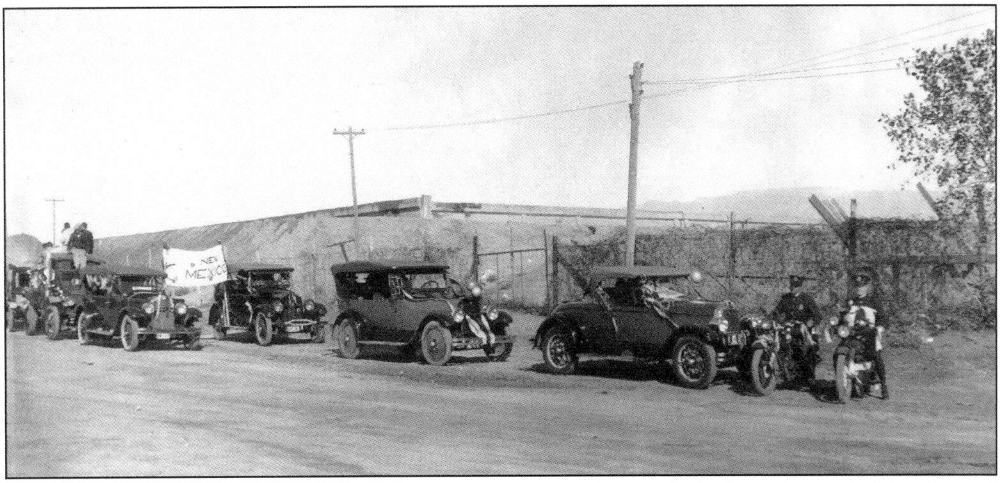

The first homecoming took place on November 7, 1925, coinciding with the big Lobo vs. Wildcat football game. The event was sparked by a growing alumni base. The Friday before the game featured a pep meeting and bonfire attended by several thousand, the largest at the time, with the slogan "Beat Arizona." A dance followed at Rodey Hall. Festivities included snake dances and parades. The Wildcats won 24-0.

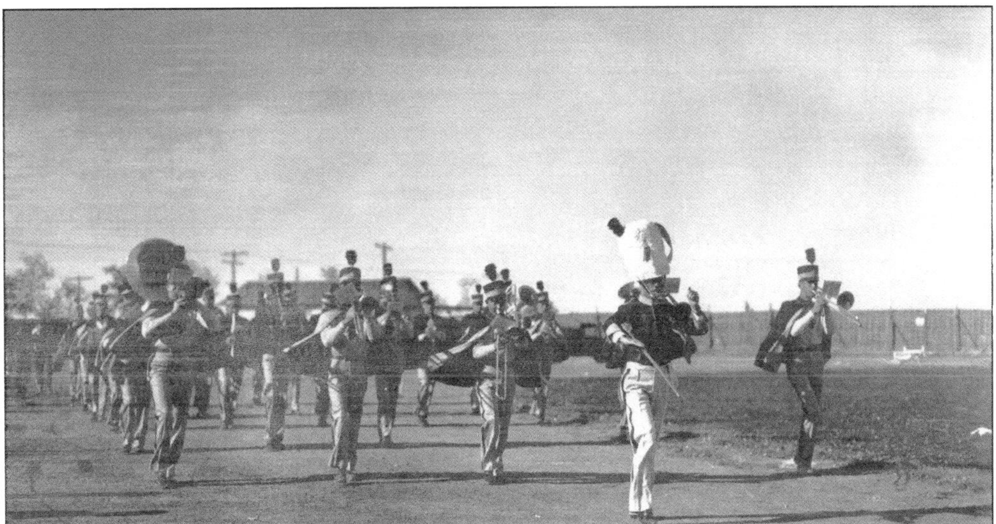

The University of New Mexico Marching Band was formed in 1930 and debuted new uniforms in 1931, ready for homecoming games. Descriptions of the uniforms were deliberately kept secret to build excitement for their premiere at the Flagstaff game. Before this, the team wore regular clothes, and funding was secured with 50¢ added student fees.

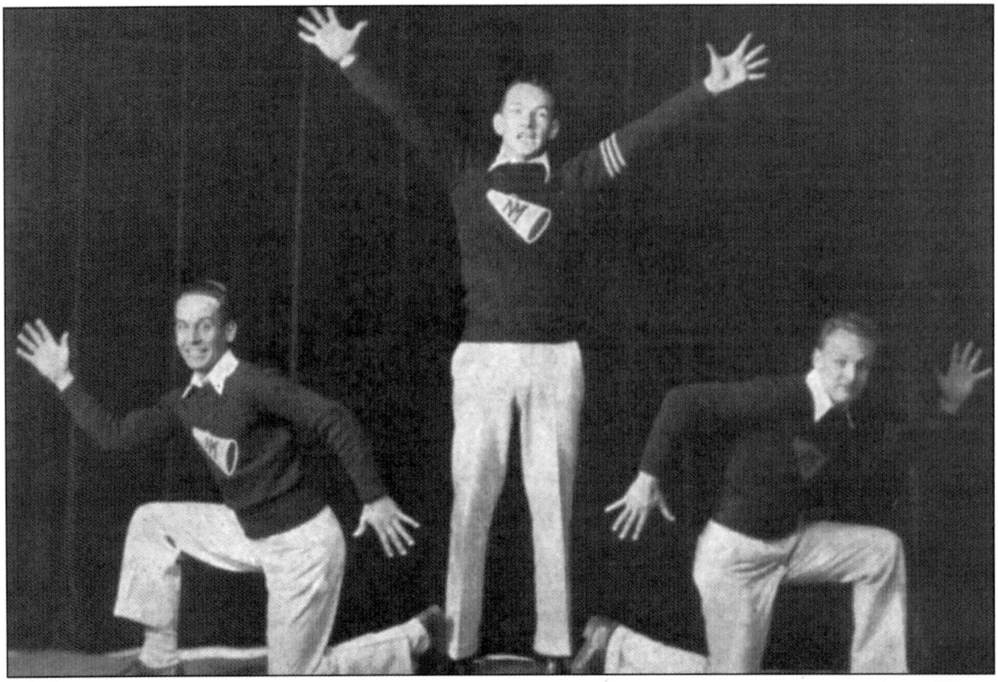

Cheerleading in the early 20th century was predominantly a male sport. These 1932 UNM cheerleaders showcase their energy with dynamic poses, proudly wearing the university's colors: crimson and silver. Chosen in 1897 from suggestions by Harriet Jenness, instructor in drawing, drama, music, and penmanship, crimson symbolizes the Sandia Mountains, while silver represents the ribbon-like flow of the Rio Grande.

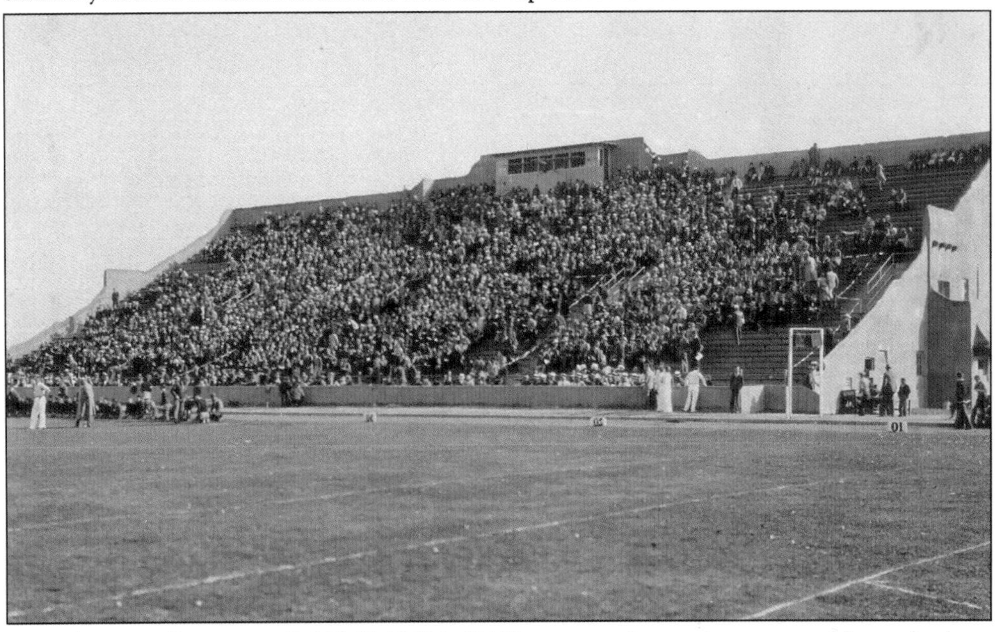

Opened in 1938, Zimmerman Field held 16,000–17,000 spectators for sporting events and featured a three-story Pueblo Revival–style grandstand designed by Meem. At the first postwar homecoming game, university president J.P. Wernette decided to name the stadium in honor of Dr. James F. Zimmerman. In 1959, the field was closed and repurposed into University Stadium.

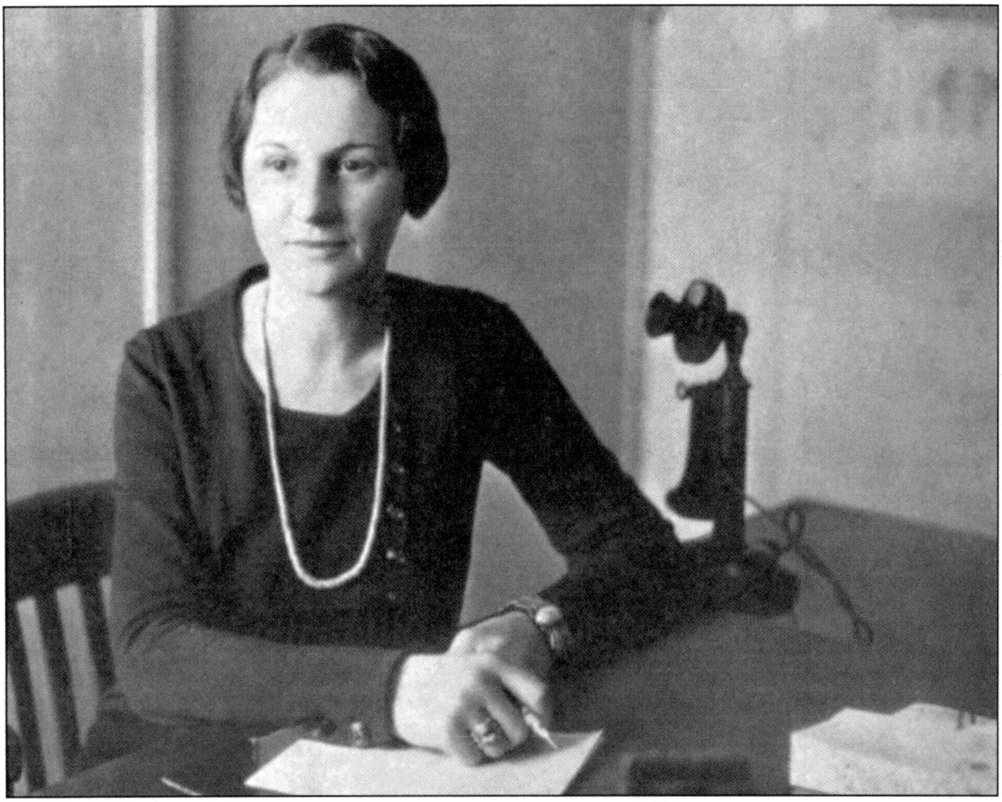

One of President Zimmerman's most significant appointments was Lena C. Clauve as dean of women, a post she held for 32 years, from 1929 to 1961. Dean Clauve was a 1925 graduate of UNM with a major in music.

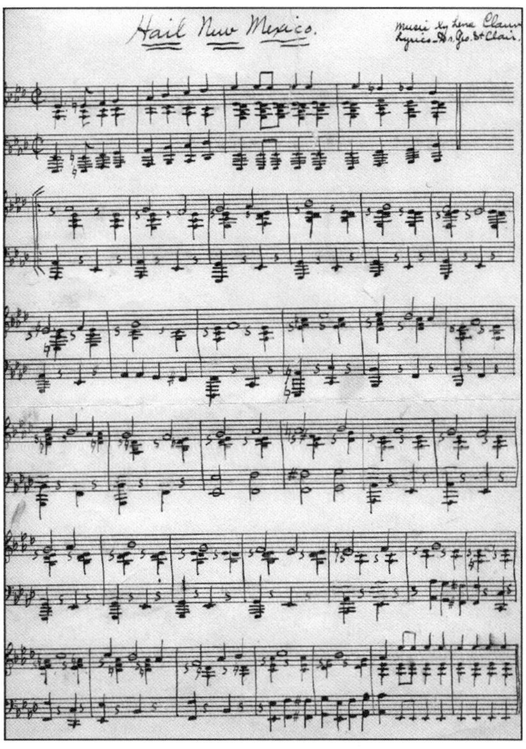

The UNM Fight Song was created in 1930 by Dean Lena Clauve, professor of music and dean of women, who composed the rhythm, and Dr. George St. Clair, a professor in the English Department, who wrote the lyrics. Originally intended as a fundraiser to clear the debt of the school newspaper, the song quickly became the university's official fight anthem.

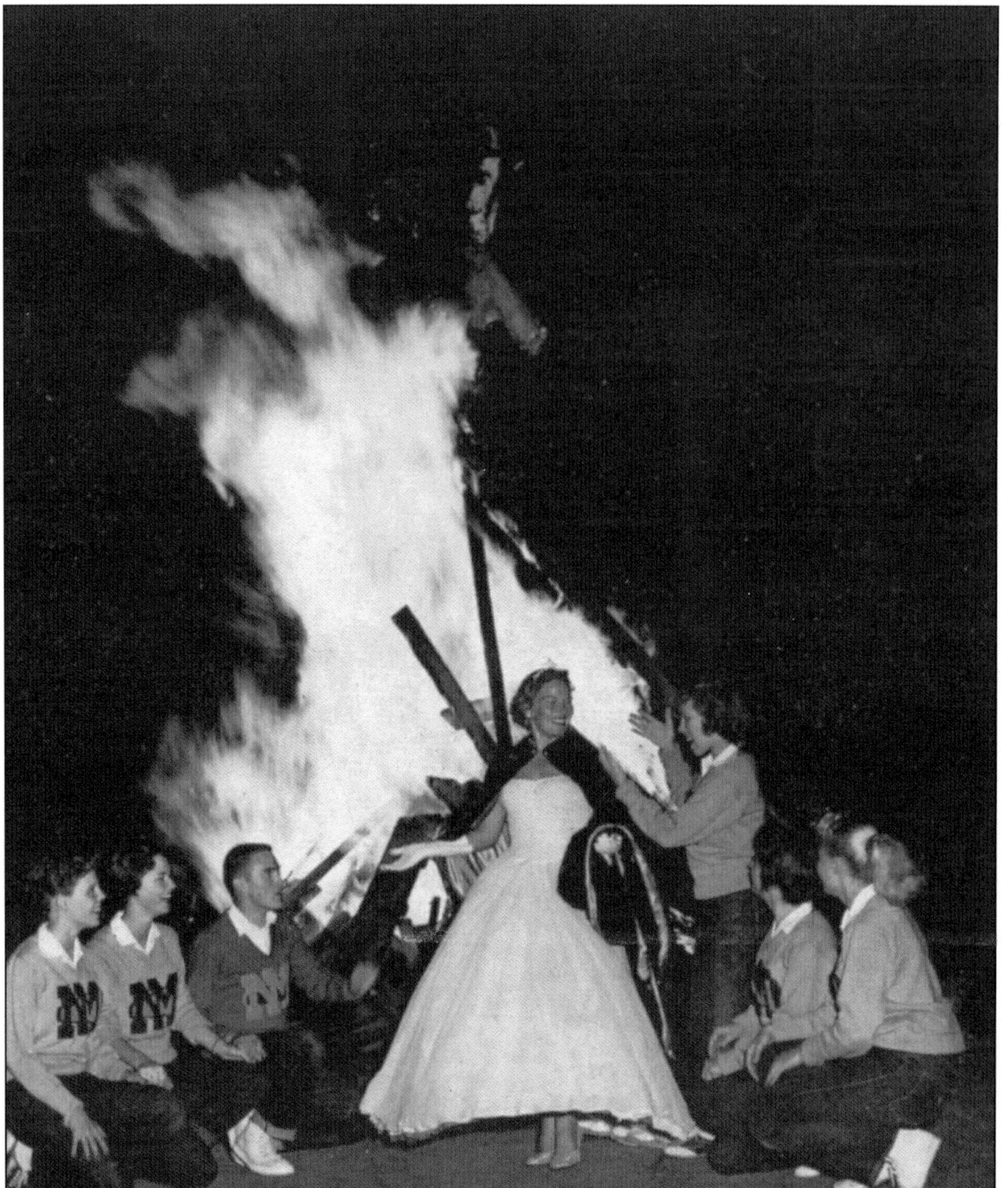

The 1958 homecoming celebration was a vibrant display of school spirit marked by the presence of the Homecoming queen in front of the traditional bonfire. Established in 1925 by UNM president David Spence Hill, the homecoming festivities included a pep rally, a parade of floats, and a football game, all culminating in a celebratory bonfire that became a beloved annual tradition. The bonfire served as a rallying point for students and alumni alike, symbolizing camaraderie and school pride. However, this cherished custom began to wane in the late 20th century due to safety concerns and changing campus dynamics, ultimately leading to the discontinuation of bonfires as part of the homecoming festivities.

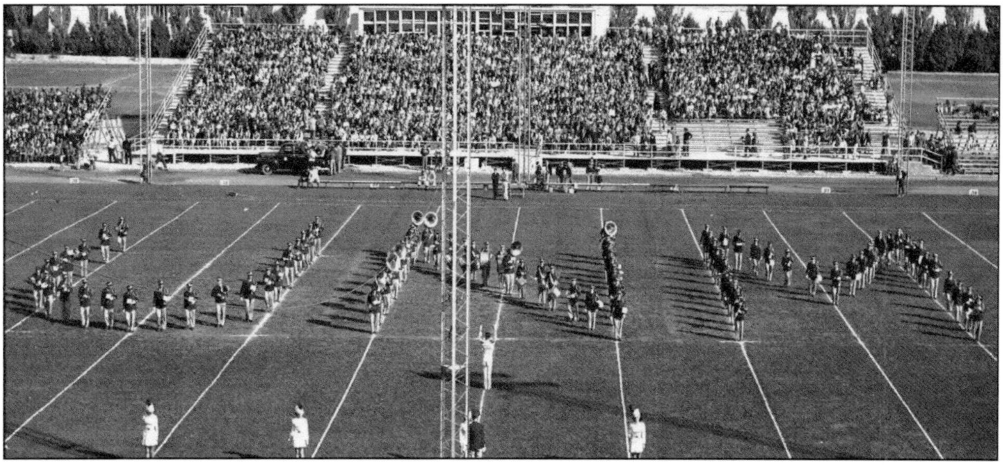

The university's marching band takes center stage in this 1955 photograph, forming the letters "UNM" on the field. The marching band, now the Spirit Marching Band, has been the university's most visible ensemble, continuing to regularly perform for spectators at all home football games and to represent the university at games across the country since its inception in 1930.

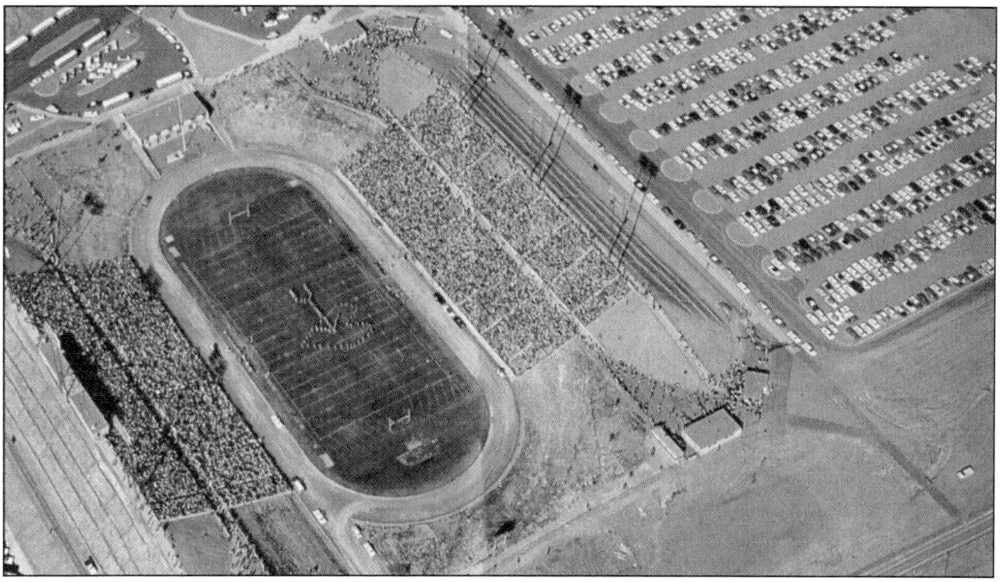

This aerial from 1963 captures a moment in time when the stadium was a vibrant backdrop for UNM's spirited events. University Stadium saw its first game on September 17, 1960. Prior to 1960, UNM played its home games at Zimmerman Field (1938–1959) and University Field (1892–1937), where Ortega Hall, the Humanities Building, and Woodward Hall presently stand. This new stadium had a capacity of 30,000 and room for expansion if needed.

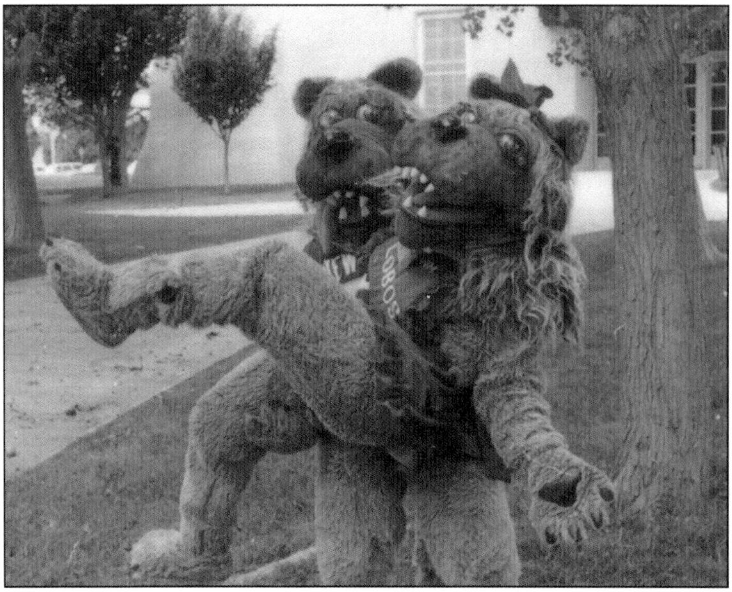

The Lobo mascot, having represented the university since 1920, embodies the cunning leadership and prowess associated with the wolf. The idea of adopting a wolf as the football team's mascot was first proposed in 1920, with alumnus Bruno Dieckmann allegedly capturing a wild wolf to donate to the university. The 1960s saw the introduction of the human mascot Lobo Louie, and by the 1980s, Lobo Lucy was introduced as a comascot.

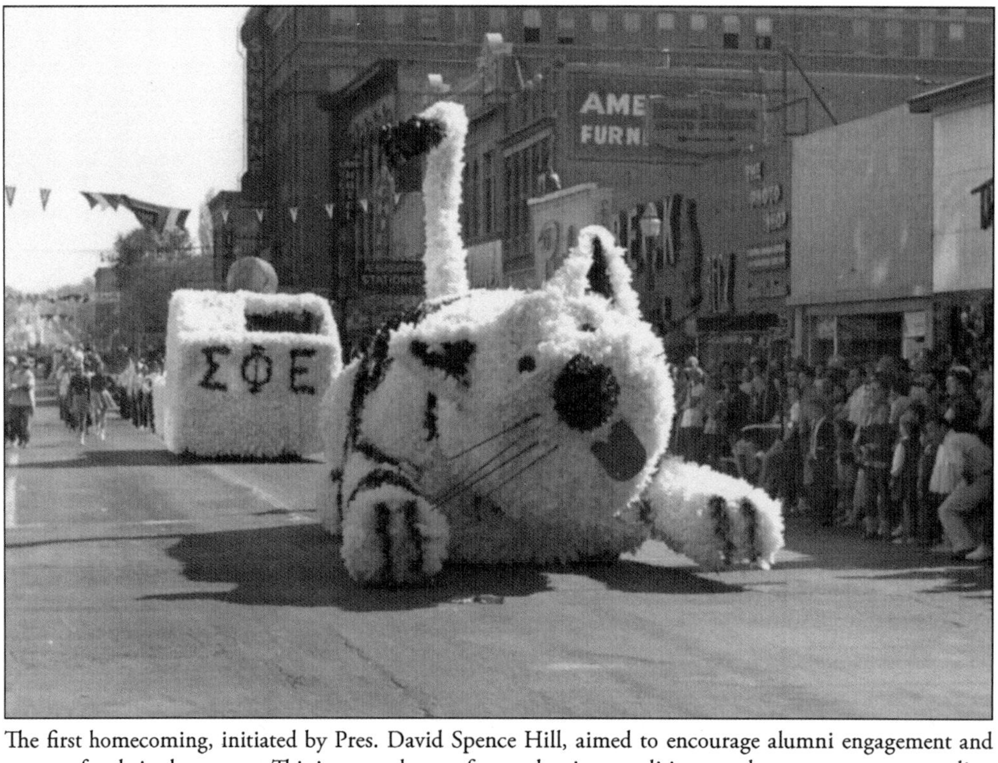

The first homecoming, initiated by Pres. David Spence Hill, aimed to encourage alumni engagement and support for their alma mater. This inaugural event featured unique traditions, such as campus men parading downtown in pajamas and freshmen women wearing mismatched attire. Over time, homecoming has evolved to include reunions, tours, luncheons, decorations, and parades downtown, though the spirit of the event remains the same.

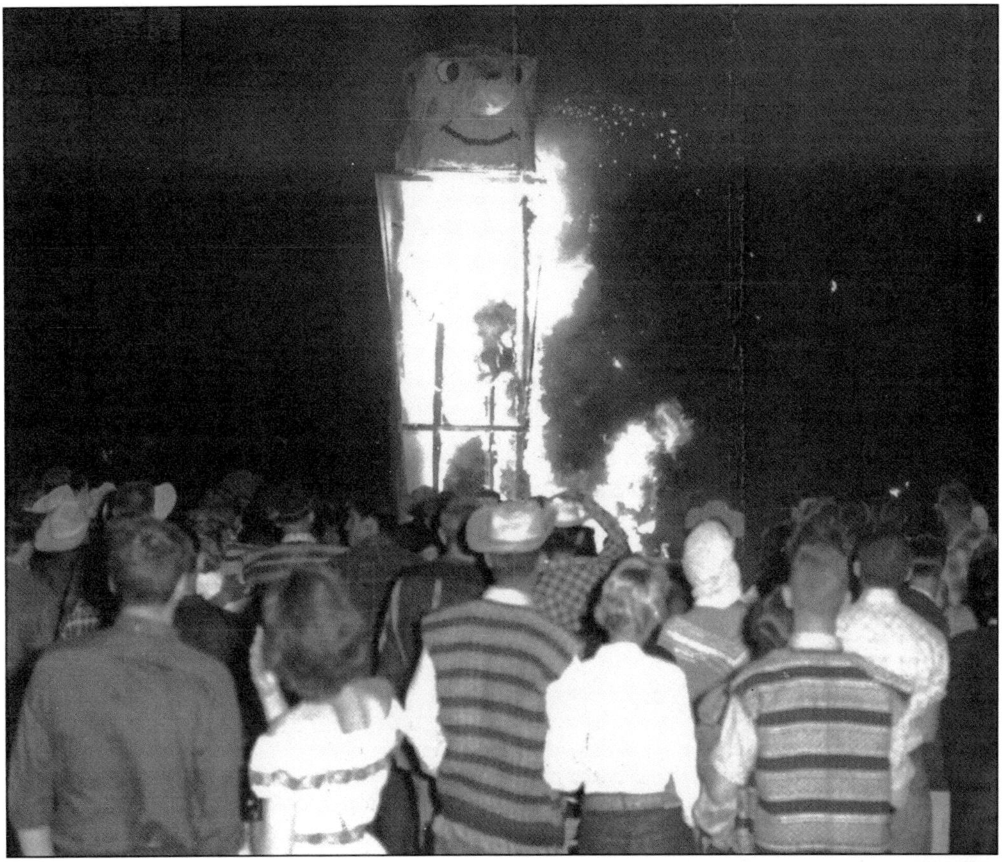

In 1946, Richard N. Bibler created "The Little Man on Campus" comic for the *University Daily Kansan*. The comic, featuring student Worthal and his nemesis, Professor Snarf, became syndicated across college newspapers in the 1950s. The university adopted the burning of Professor Snarf, or El Espíritu del Mal Estudio, as a central Fiesta Day ceremony, symbolizing the release of academic woes. Once the gloom had gone up in smoke, students gathered in front of the administration building, where dancing began and the Fiesta Reina was crowned. The ritual continued until it was discontinued in 1965. The first Fiesta Day in 1948 featured luminarias, colorful costumes, and a lively celebration. However, the event turned tragic when Fiesta King George de Shurley was injured while lighting the bonfire, which exploded, sending him to the infirmary. The festivities typically continued with the Fiesta Parade the next day, led by the crowned Rodeo Queen, nominated by the Boots and Saddle Club rodeo, alongside the Fiesta King. The day concluded with a lively Fiesta dance in the evening.

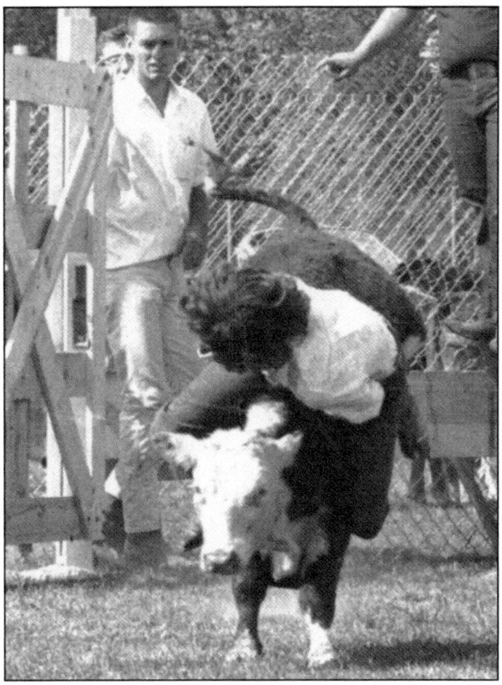

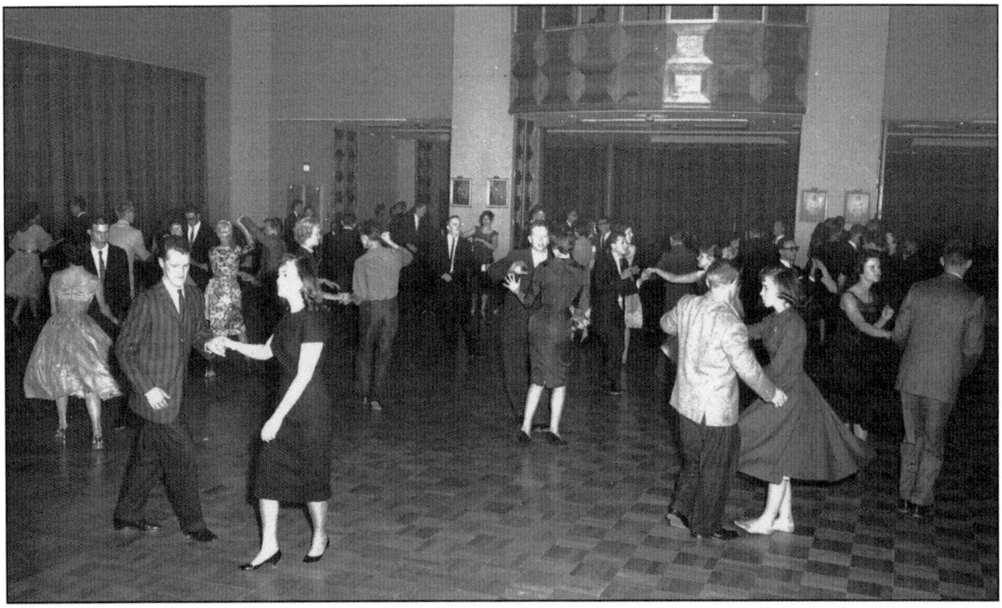

While college is primarily for studying, there is no shortage of social events. Teas, parties, informal dances, dinners, and dates gave students plenty of opportunities to have fun and stay up to date on the latest happenings.

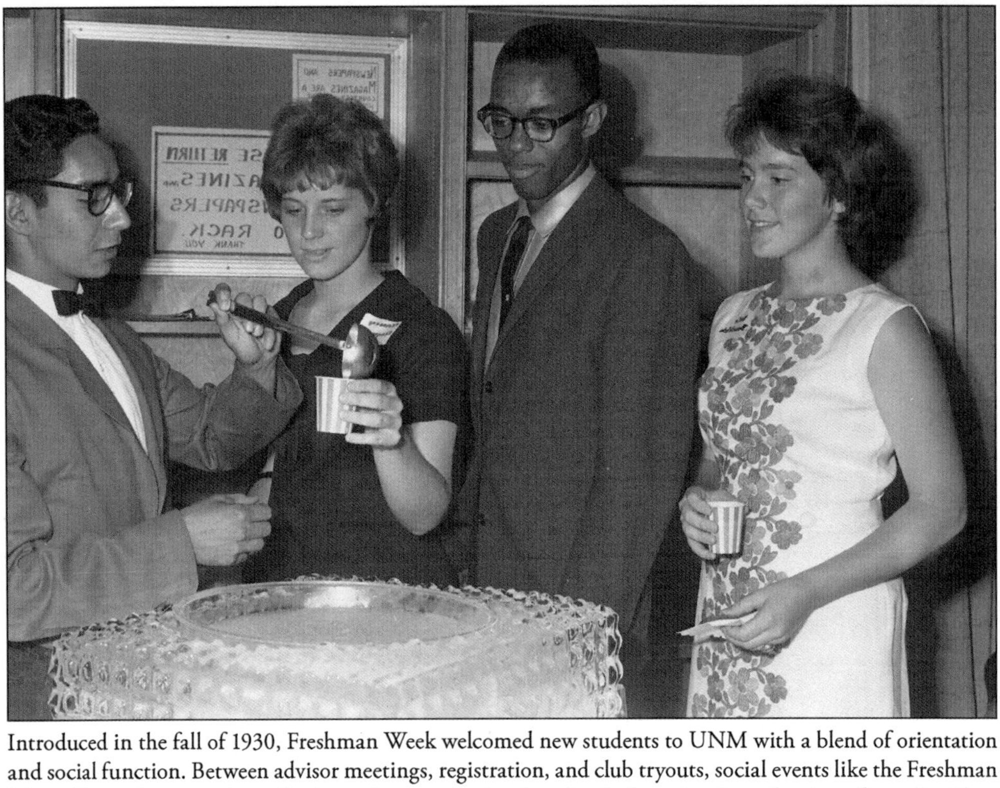

Introduced in the fall of 1930, Freshman Week welcomed new students to UNM with a blend of orientation and social function. Between advisor meetings, registration, and club tryouts, social events like the Freshman Mixer fostered connections. Each student received a handbook featuring introductions from President Zimmerman and Dean Clauve, a university history, and strict rules: no high school insignia, mandatory school songs, and cheers to learn. The tradition eased transitions, turning strangers into proud Lobos.

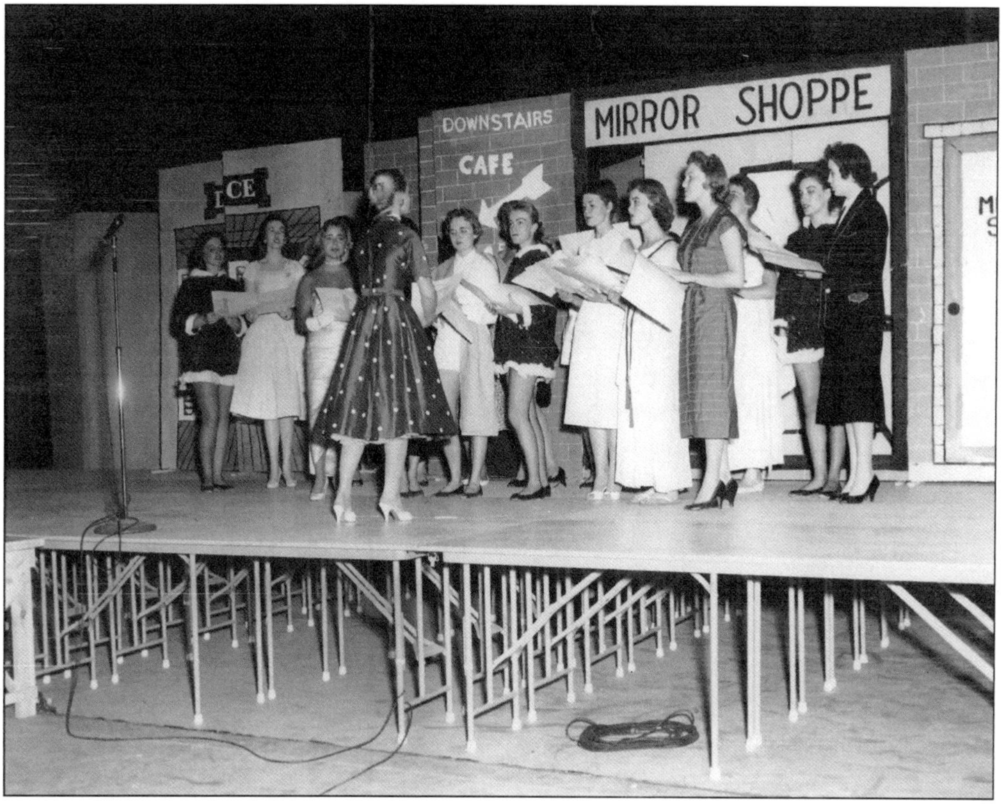

Early traditions, such as stunt night, were a collective effort to have a fun party. There was singing, costumes, and dancing, and the party usually stuck to a theme. The dance was usually held in Carlisle Gym.

The De Anza Club, founded in 1951, aimed to promote Spanish culture in the Southwest. The club organized meetings featuring guest speakers and lecturers as well as social functions to foster community engagement. By offering a space for dialogue and cultural exchange, the club contributed to raising awareness of Spanish heritage and its influence in the region.

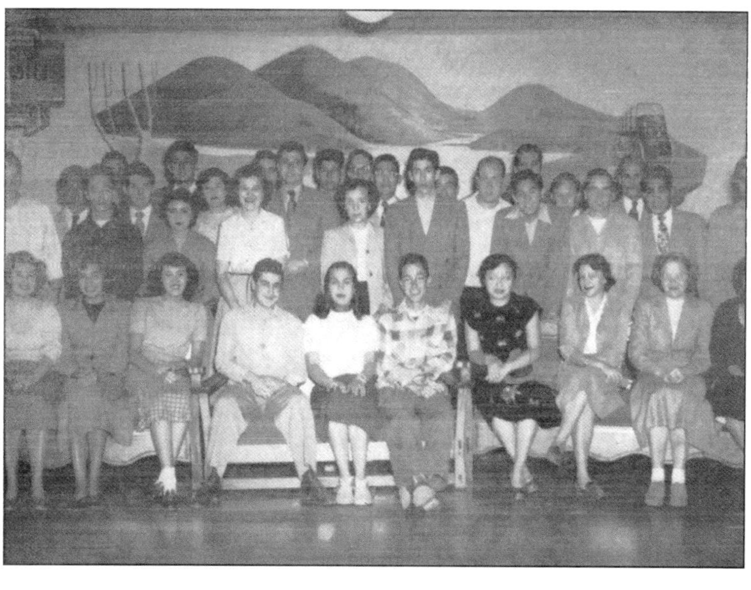

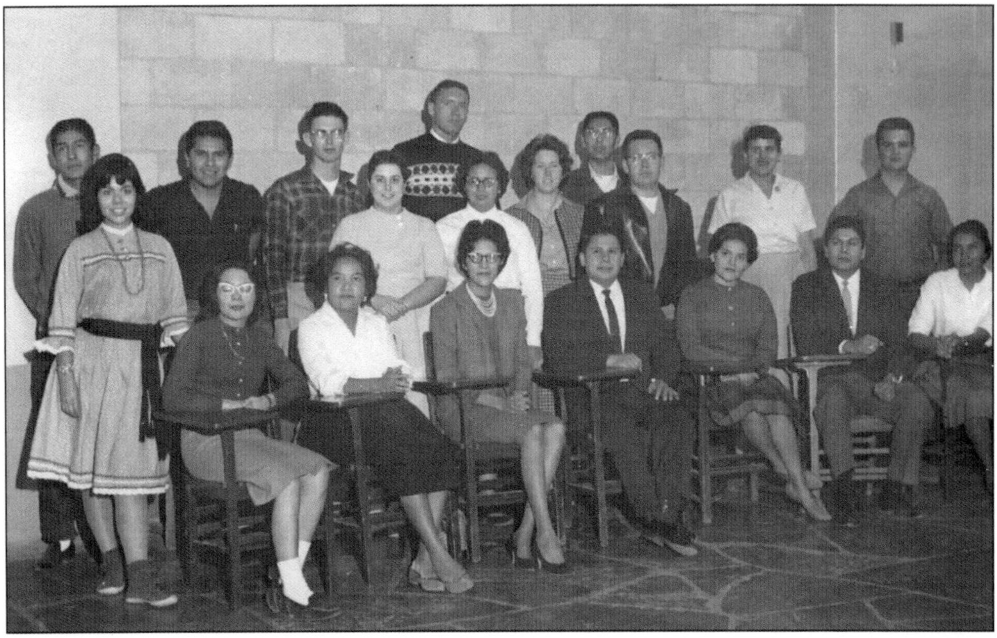

Founded in 1952, the Kiva Club was the first student organization dedicated to Native American students at the University of New Mexico. Its mission focused on giving Native students a platform to voice their concerns and perspectives, especially regarding issues that impacted Native communities and education. Drawing members from diverse Native groups, the Kiva Club has played a critical role in supporting its members and advocating for higher education among Native Americans. As the oldest and largest Native American student organization at UNM, the Kiva Club organized cultural events such as the Nizhoni dances each April. These dances raised funds for scholarships, promoting both cultural awareness and academic achievement, solidifying the club's legacy as a vital institution for Native students at the university.

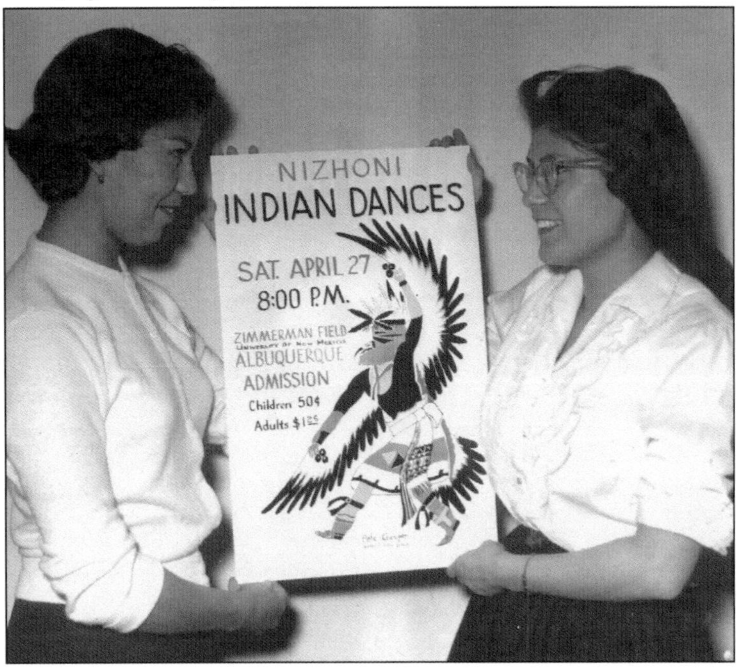

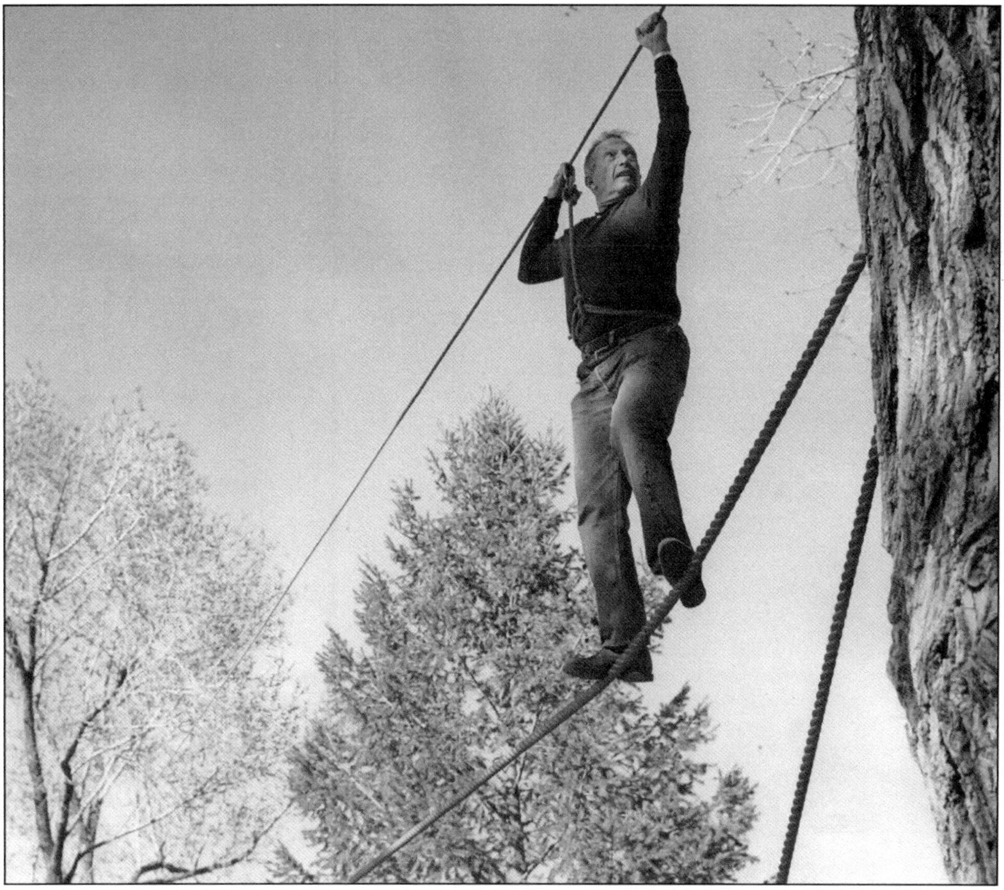

In 1962, the University of New Mexico became a key Peace Corps training center for Latin American countries, training over 18,000 volunteers by 1966. Chosen as the first year-round Peace Corps training site in the United States, UNM's strong focus on languages, Latin American studies, and cultural understanding made it the ideal institution for the program. The training emphasized community development, public health, and education, combining Spanish language immersion with practical exercises. Volunteers participated in challenging Outward Bound activities, including rappelling, swimming for extended periods, and walking across ropes. The program's success was rooted in UNM's ability to blend academic expertise with hands-on experience, equipping Peace Corps volunteers with the necessary skills for their impactful roles abroad.

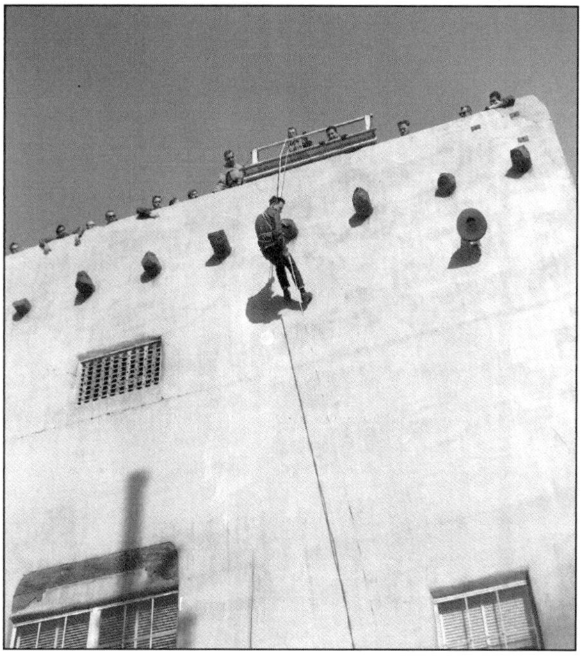

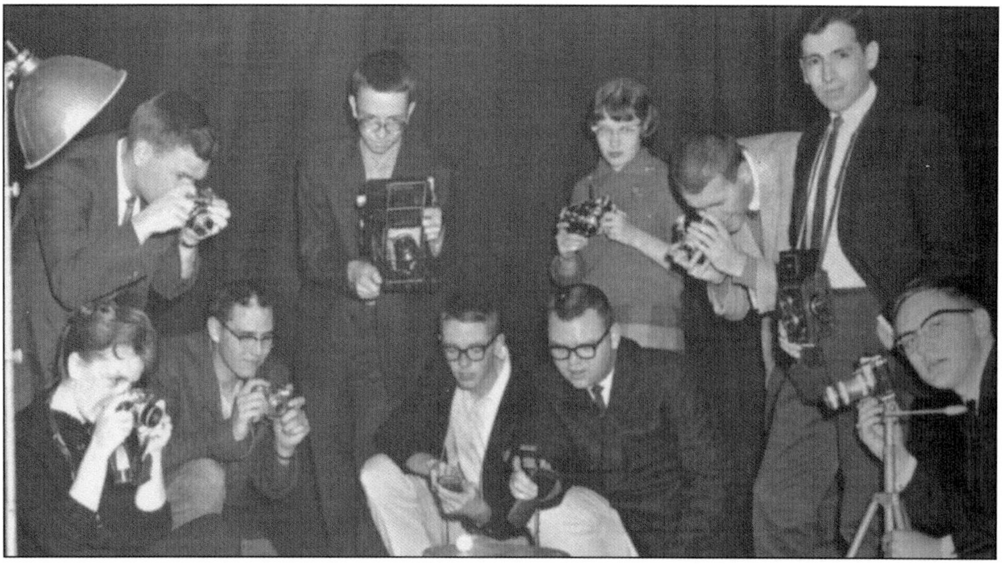

Created and operated in order to promote interest and further skills in the multi-phased area of photography, the Photography Club was open to any student who wished to participate. The club's activities included demonstrations, contests, field trips, models, and guest lecturers, and it maintained a darkroom for students to develop their own pictures. It was founded in the fall of 1959.

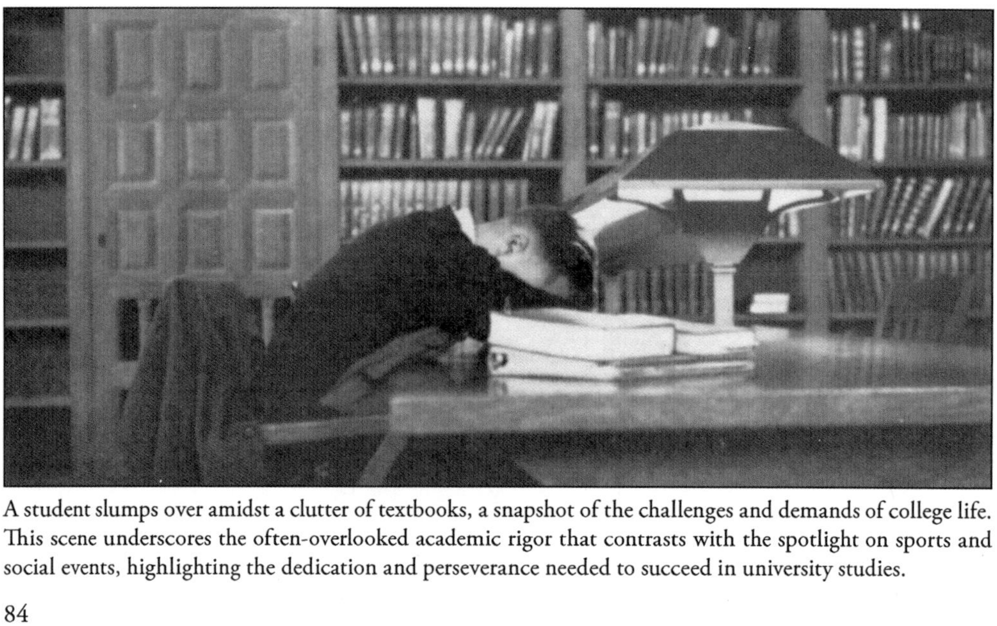

A student slumps over amidst a clutter of textbooks, a snapshot of the challenges and demands of college life. This scene underscores the often-overlooked academic rigor that contrasts with the spotlight on sports and social events, highlighting the dedication and perseverance needed to succeed in university studies.

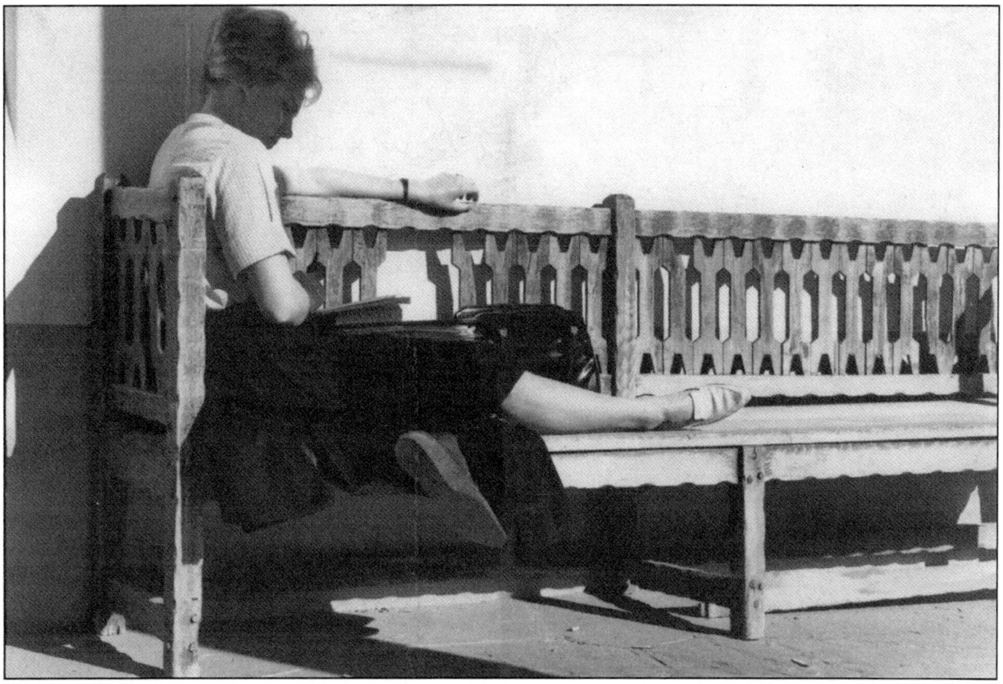

In the 1950s, UNM embraced innovation with educational TV courses reaching rural communities and advanced language labs for French, German, and Russian instruction. The university expanded its academic offerings with new doctoral programs, while enrollment reached record numbers. Research addressed critical needs like water conservation. Beyond academics, UNM served as a cultural center through museums, libraries, and public programs, fulfilling its mission to educate and enrich New Mexico.

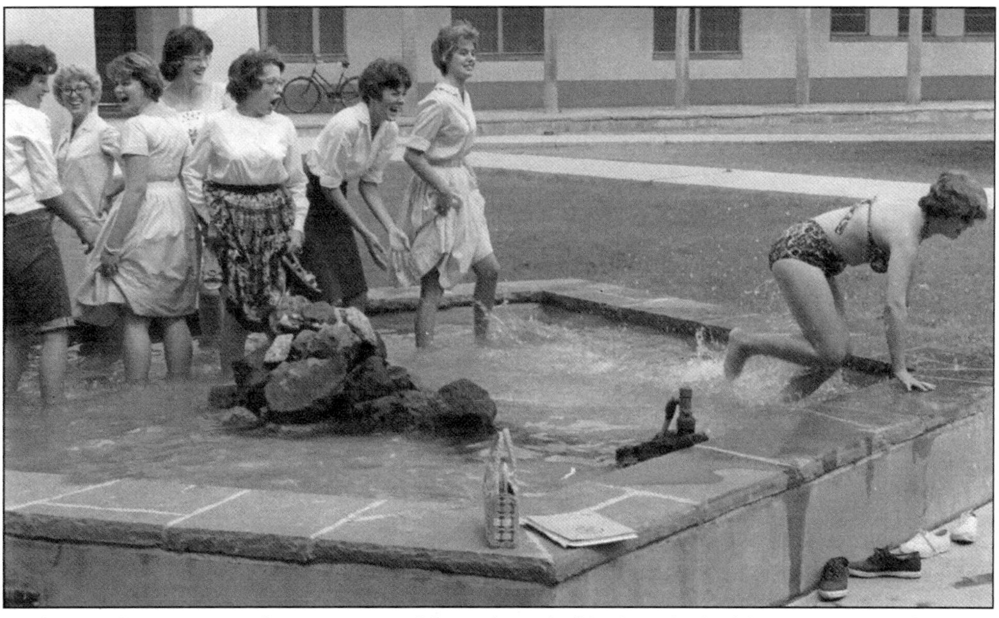

Students at the University of New Mexico celebrate the end of finals with playful moments in the fountain, capturing the relief and joy that mark this time of year. These traditions highlight the vibrant campus life and the balance between academic dedication and moments of fun and celebration.

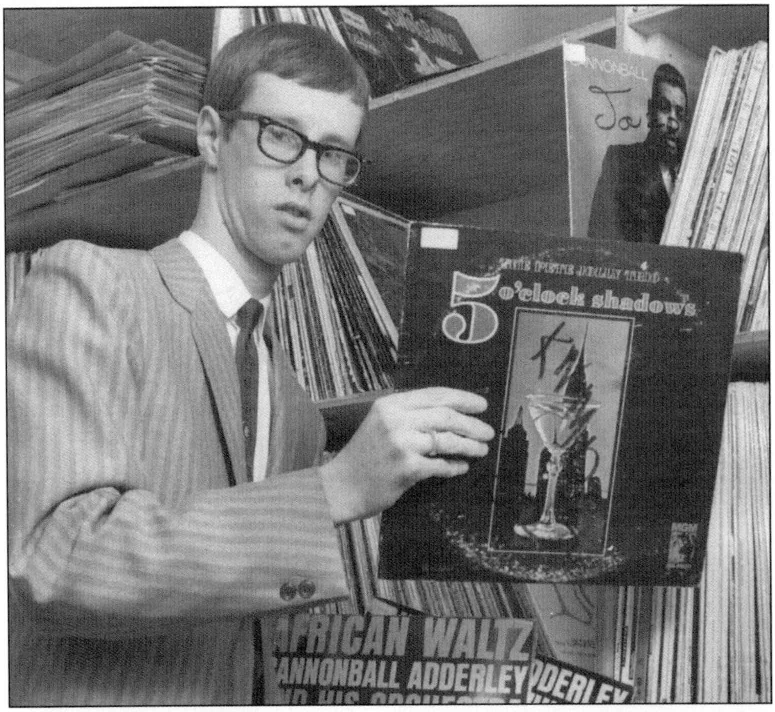

KUNM-FM is owned and operated by the university and is one of two National Public Radio stations in Albuquerque. It began on April 30, 1960. Originally only AM, it broadcast primarily classical and jazz music, but by 1969, its emphasis had shifted to "underground" rock music in a free-form radio style.

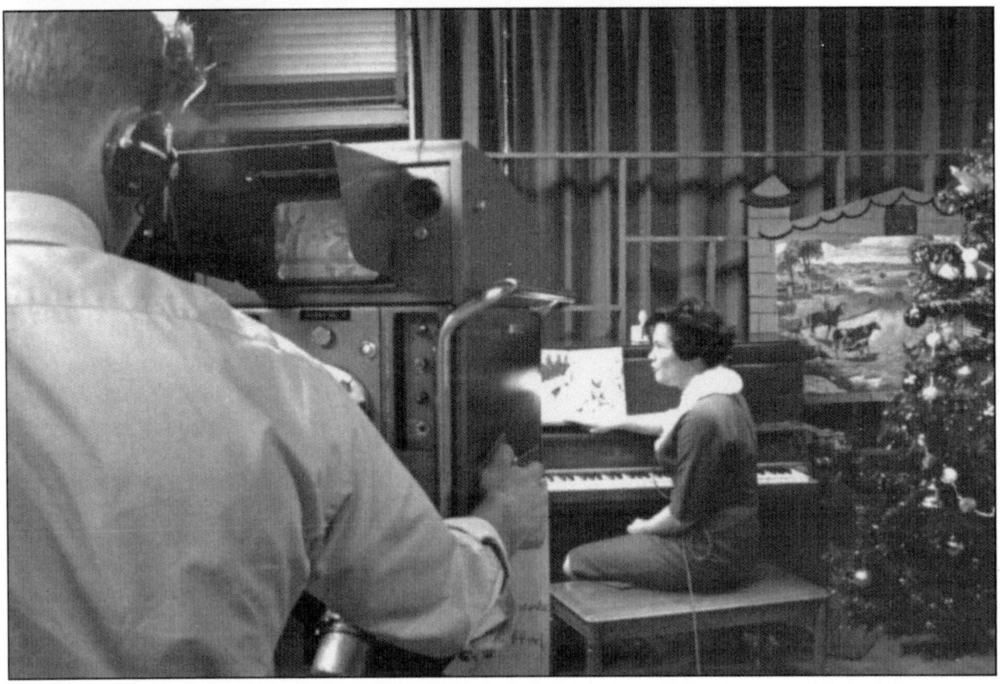

In 1958, KNME-TV became New Mexico's first public educational television station, created in collaboration with Albuquerque Public Schools and the Department of Education. It began broadcasting on May 1, 1958, with a mission to "further [one's] right to knowledge." Additionally, KNME's radio counterpart, established in 1957 by student Bill Retz, was the only US station fully managed by students, funded by state appropriations for public interest and education.

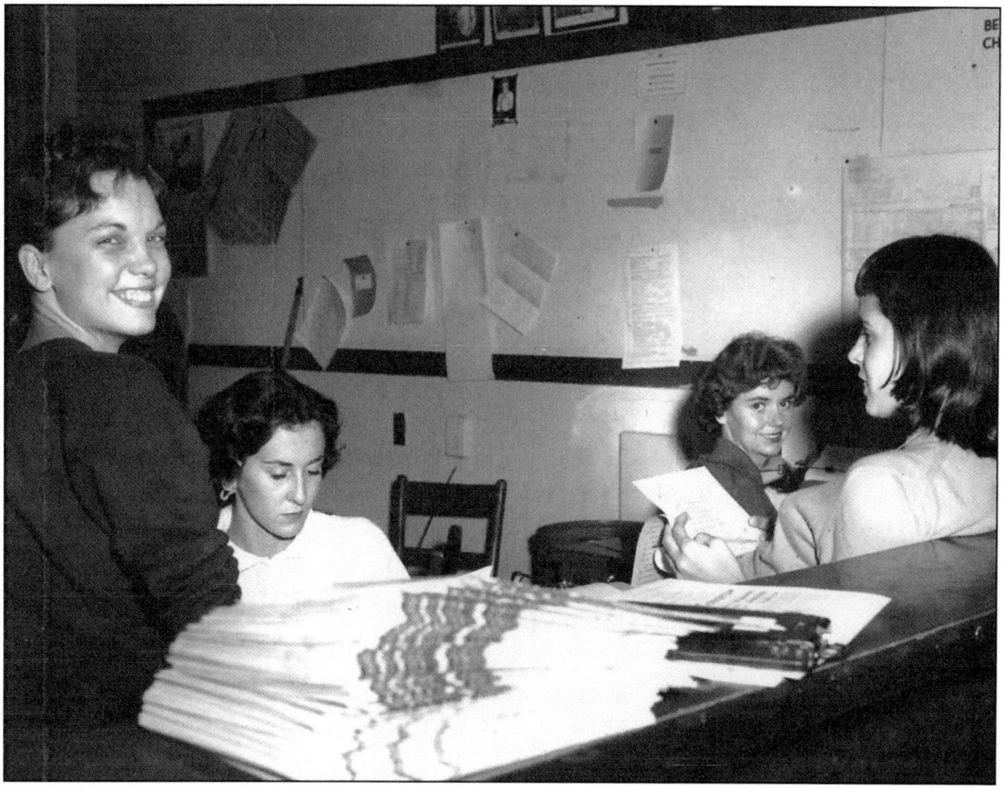

The UNM student newspaper has a rich history, tracing its origins to the *Cactus*, published in 1895 as the first student-run campus publication. In 1898, the *Mirage* was launched as a monthly paper, later becoming weekly in 1902. Initially managed like a magazine, it featured student essays, profiles, and feature stories, emphasizing higher education, literary excellence, and UNM standards. Renamed *UNM Weekly* in 1903 or 1904 in a weekly format at President Tight's suggestion, it evolved into the *New Mexico Lobo* in 1923. By 1950, it became the *New Mexico Daily Lobo*, retaining that name since 1971. With over 125 years of history, the *Daily Lobo* remains a vital resource for students, documenting university life and milestones across its many iterations. Today, it holds the distinction of being the third-largest newspaper by distribution in New Mexico.

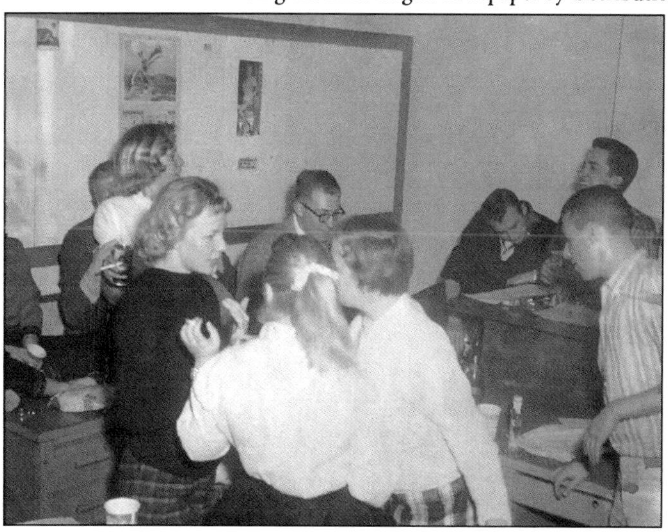

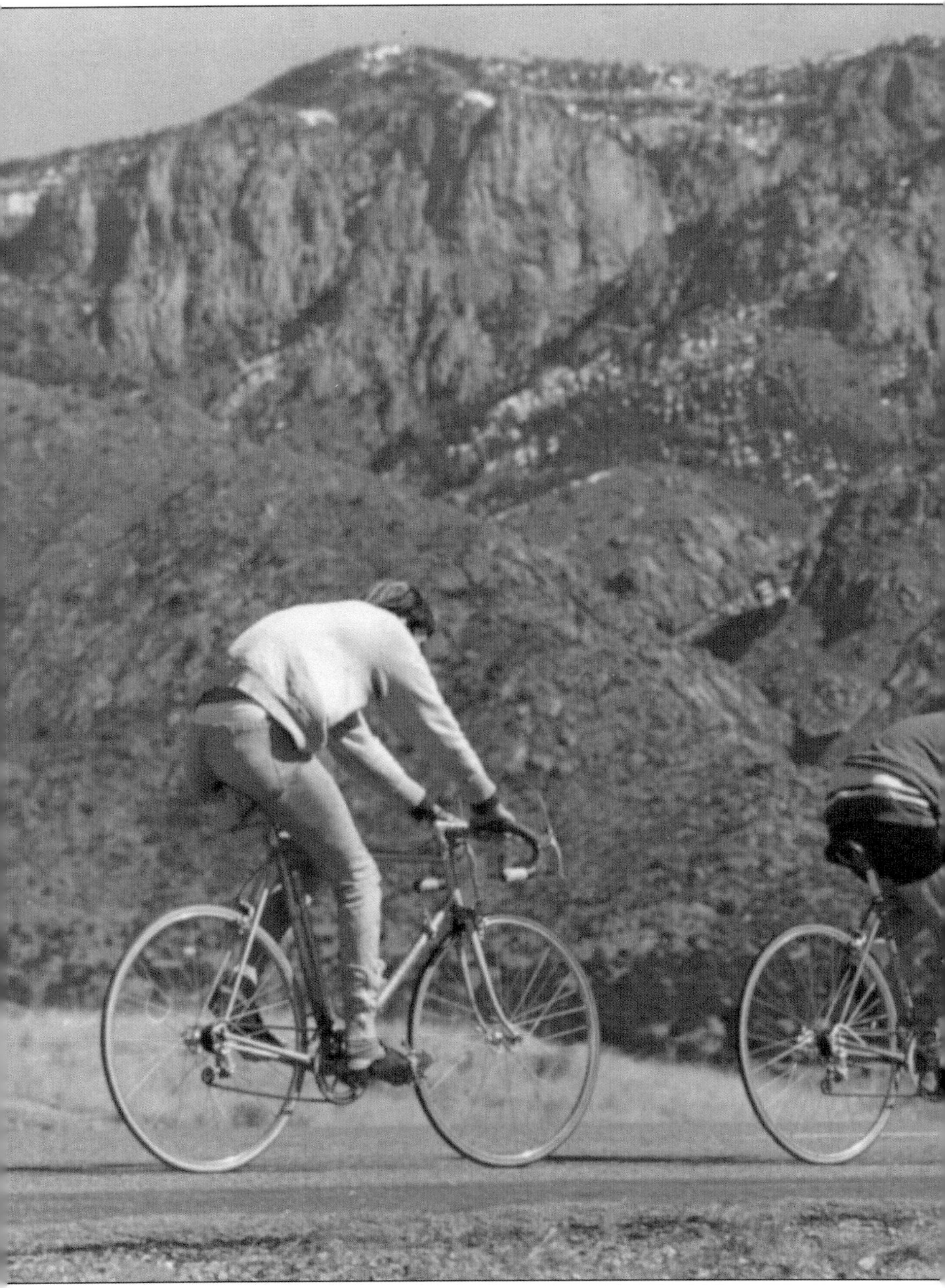

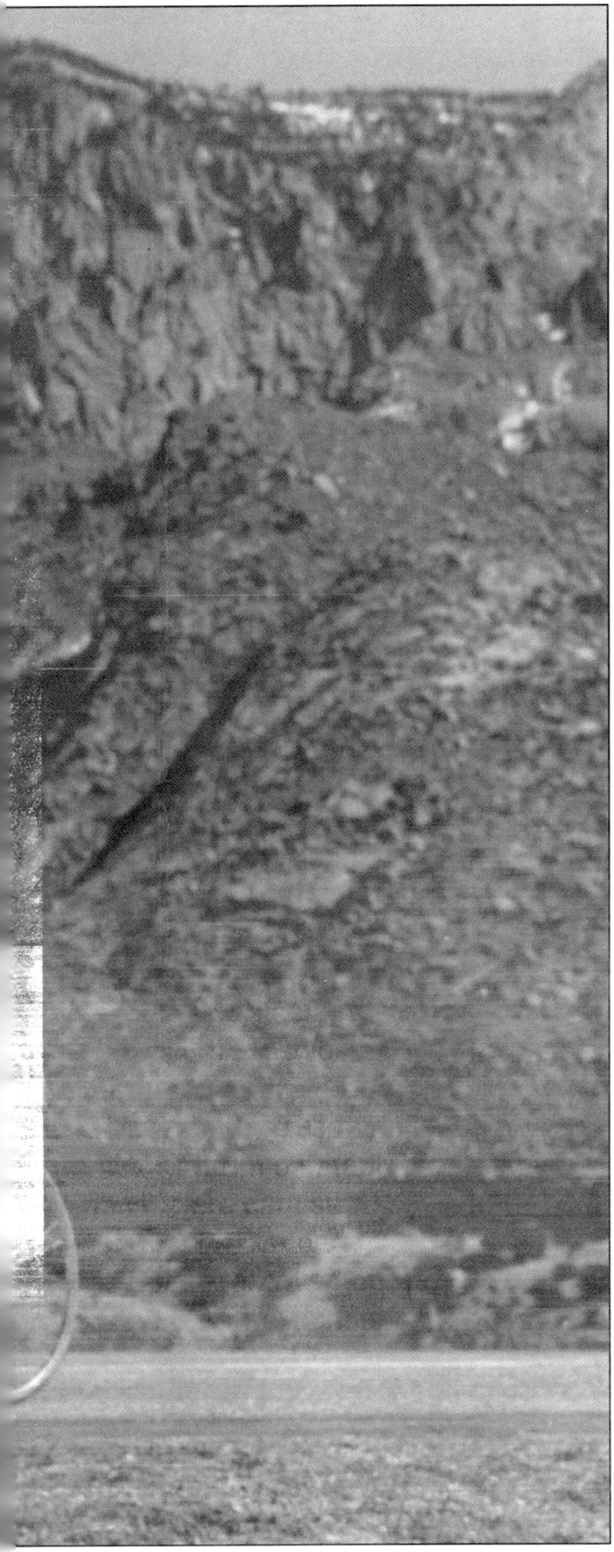

Cycling gained popularity in 19th-century New Mexico despite the lack of paved roads. Dirt paths, compacted by generations of wagons and burros, were surprisingly smooth, leading a newspaper to proclaim New Mexico to be a "cycler's paradise." Albuquerque formed a cycling club in 1890, and members rode to destinations like Tijeras Canyon. By 1892, the city boasted at least two bicycle dealers, and clubs became venues for group rides, socializing, and fostering a broader cycling culture. At UNM, cycling had historical significance. UNM's third president, William Tight, was an avid cyclist. The university later formed a bike club in the mid-20th century to promote both recreational and competitive cycling. Members organized group rides, night tours, and training sessions. The club aligned with USA Cycling (USAC) and competed in the Southwest Collegiate Cycling Conference (SWCCC) in various disciplines, including road, mountain, cyclocross, and BMX racing. Though currently inactive, the UNM cycling club left a legacy of supporting health, camaraderie, and competitive opportunities for students. Its mission emphasized teamwork and growth, reflecting a deep connection to the sport and fostering a vibrant campus cycling community.

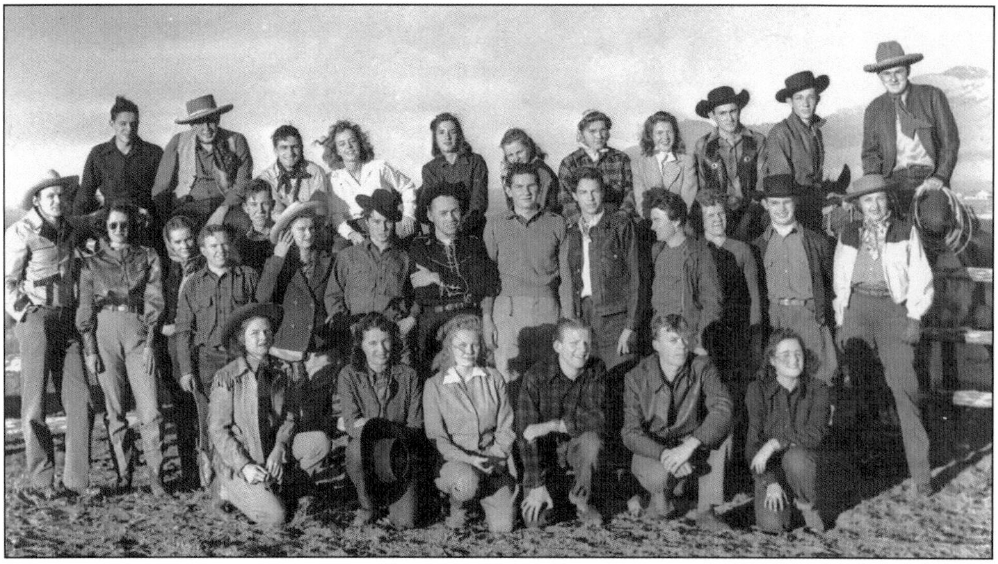

The Boots and Saddle Club was an energetic group that celebrated Western culture through rodeos, participation in the state fair parade, and themed social events, such as Western saloon parties. The group, which encouraged members to wear Western attire, sponsored its first rodeo and horse show with the Rodeo Club in 1941, showcasing their commitment to preserving and promoting rodeo culture.

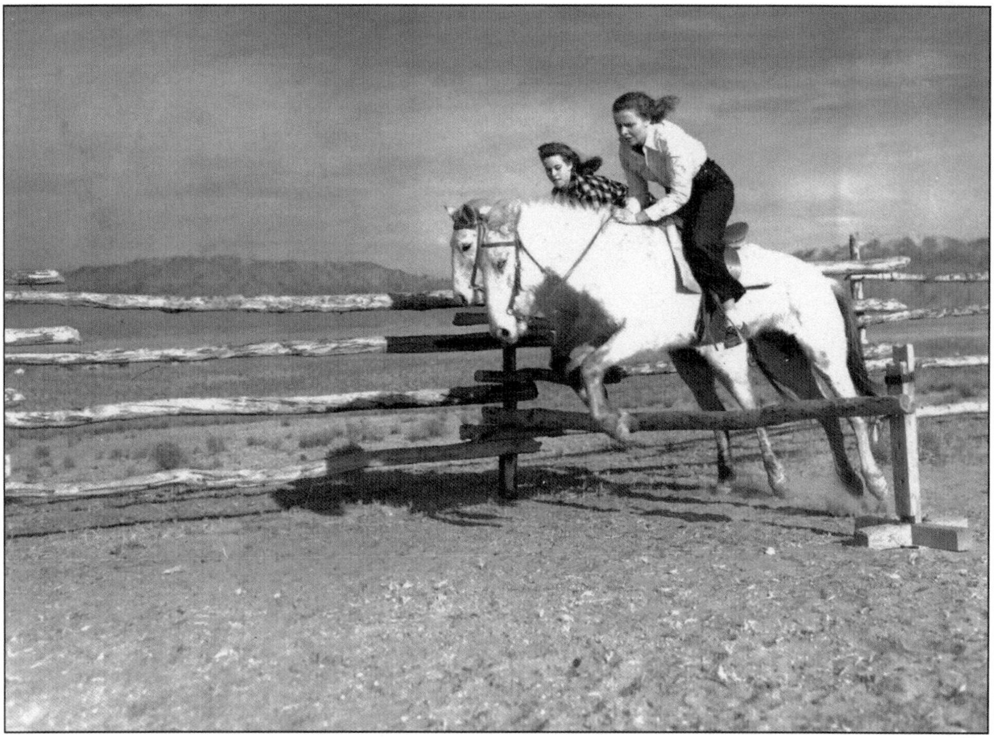

In 1940, the university joined its first intercollegiate rodeo at the University of Arizona, and by 1941, UNM hosted its own first on-campus rodeo. Organized by the Riding Club and the Boots and Saddle Club, the event was limited to university students, with an admission fee of 25¢. Activities included calf roping, relay races, and other traditional rodeo competitions. The Rodeo Club often joined the parades during Fiesta Days.

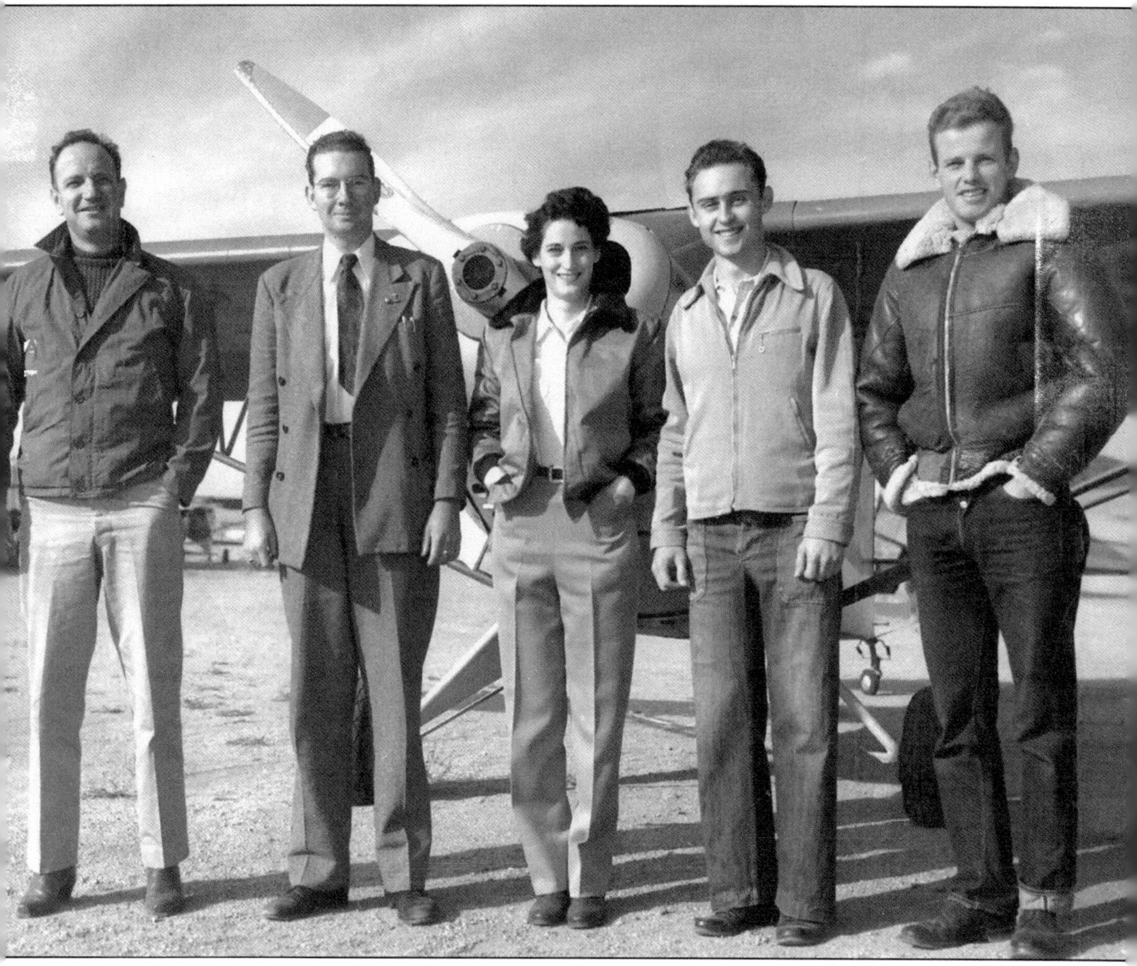

Starting in the fall of 1939 in Hadley Hall, students enrolled in the civil aeronautics flying course were the charter members of the UNM Flying Club. The club was affiliated with the National Aeronautics Association. The group typically met twice a month; the first meeting was social, and the second was for lectures on aviation. The one-year course was sponsored by the US government, and in this first year, three women were accepted into the program. The program had a contract between the university and the federal government, and flight instruction would be held at the municipal airport. Students who completed the training would be able to pass any tests for a private pilot's license.

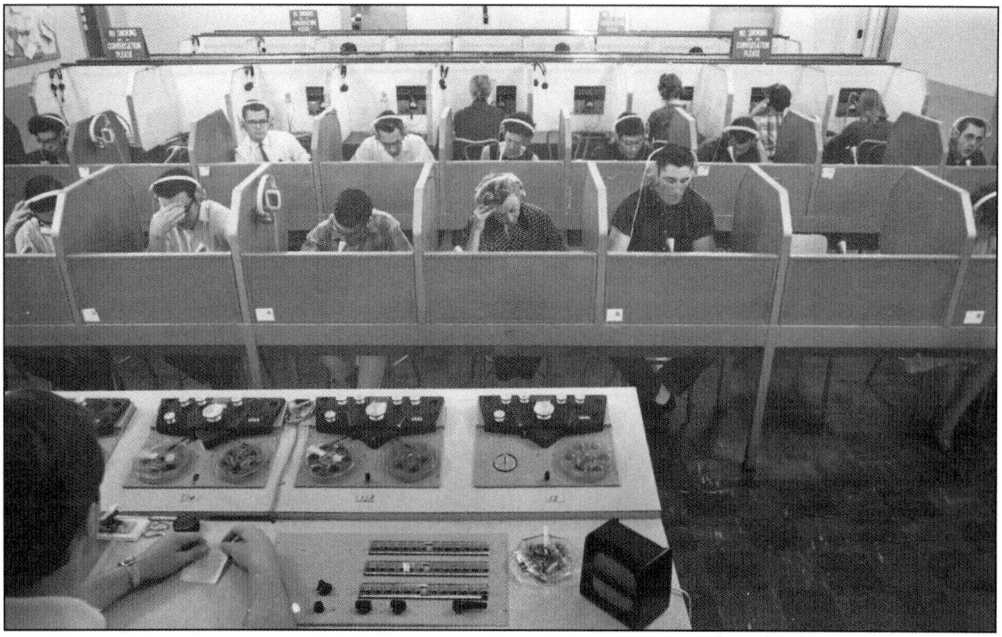

Language has been at the heart of UNM's history since 1889. Due to the long-standing significance of Spanish and English in New Mexico, three out of six early faculty members were language professors. Toward the 1960s, the UNM language lab was a cutting-edge facility designed to enhance language acquisition through immersive learning. At the time, Spanish was the most widely studied language, and Portuguese programs were among the largest nationwide.

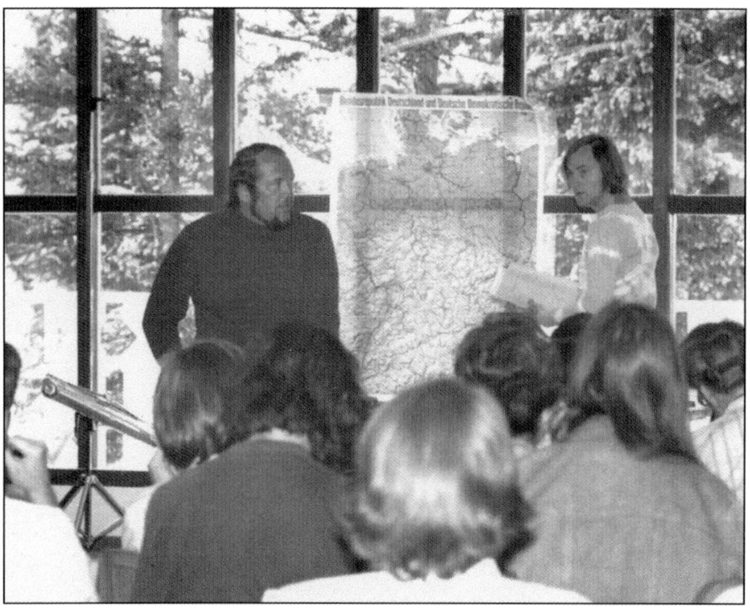

The German Summer School of New Mexico was founded in 1975 by UNM professors Peter Pabisch (left) and George Peters. The summer school is an immersive German-only one-month program where students can practice and improve their skills in the alpine-esque Taos Ski Valley. The summer school moved to Kingston, New Mexico, in 2022. (Courtesy of Peter Pabisch.)

Don Perkins (second from right), a three-year letterman from 1957 to 1959, was a standout running back for the University of New Mexico. After his senior season, he earned All-American honors and became a key player for the Dallas Cowboys, turning many New Mexicans into Cowboys fans. Perkins was part of the 1960 Homecoming Reunion Committee alongside Turner Branch, Sandra Strong Fritz, Jerry Prohaska, and Janet Sutton Nixon.

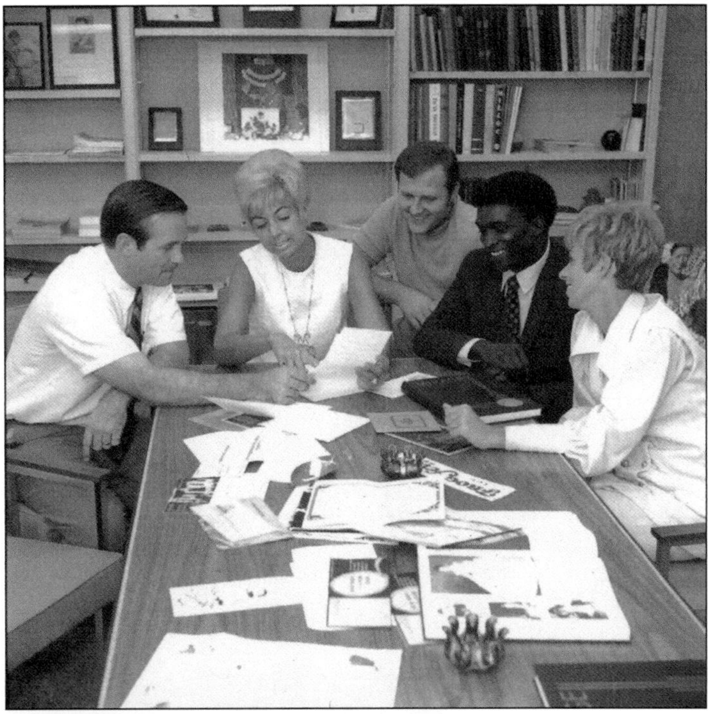

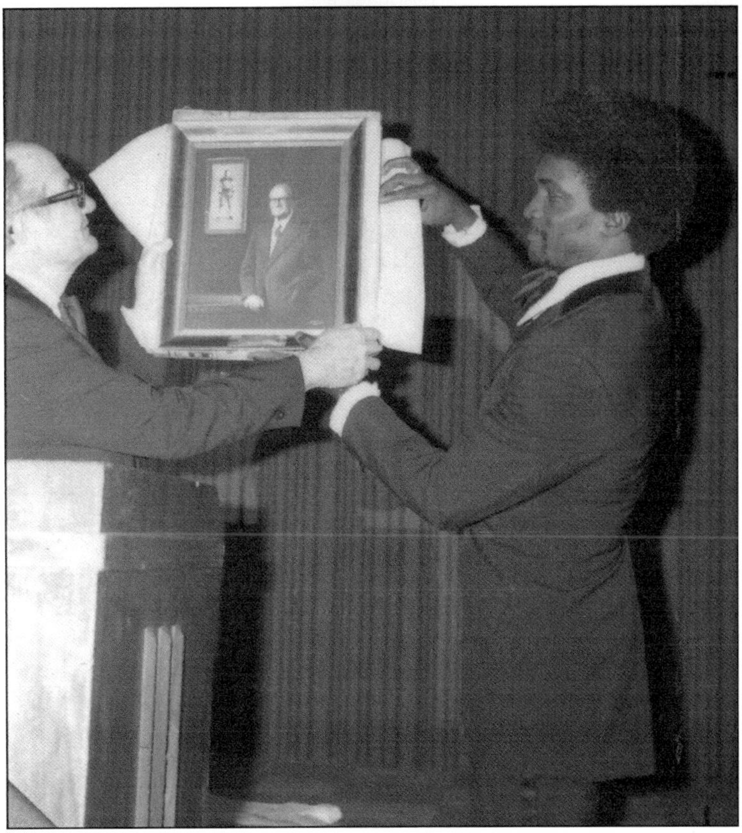

Don Perkins, a New Mexico football legend, was coached by future hall-of-famer Marv Levy, who called Perkins one of the greatest players he ever coached. Perkins's jersey number 43 was retired—the first such honor in UNM history. He was later inducted into both the New Mexico Sports Hall of Fame and the University of New Mexico Hall of Honor, solidifying his legacy in Lobos football history.

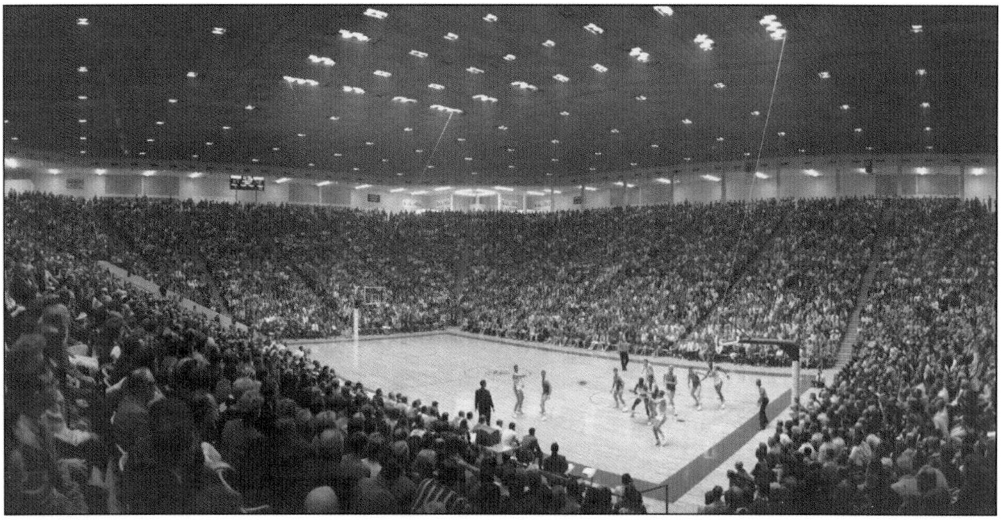

Built in 1966, the Pit is a subterranean basketball arena on UNM's south campus known for its acoustics and unobstructed views from any seat. It has hosted numerous NCAA regional championships for both women's and men's basketball. The sports complex also includes a football stadium, track and field stadium, and soccer complex. The Lobos' opening game was against Abilene Christian College on December 1, 1966.

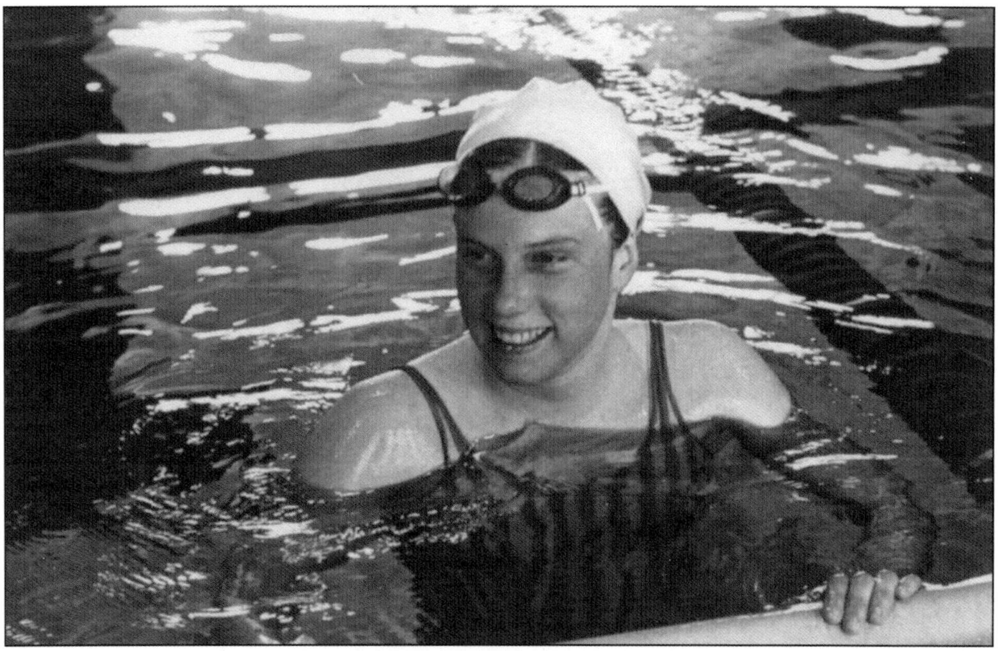

Cathy Carr, born in Albuquerque, New Mexico, and a graduate of Highland High School, represented the United States at the 1972 Summer Olympics in Munich. There, she triumphed in the women's 100-meter breaststroke, securing a gold medal and marking a significant achievement in her swimming career. Carr was the first female student-athlete at UNM to receive an athletic scholarship under Title IX, and she was inducted into the UNM Athletics Hall of Honor in 1989.

Adolph Plummer, a trailblazer for UNM track and field, broke the world record in the 440-yard dash in 1963 with a time of 44.9 seconds, shattering a psychological barrier. A two-time All-American, Plummer's achievement put New Mexico on the map and set the stage for Lobo track and field's future success. His record-breaking performance propelled the program into national prominence.

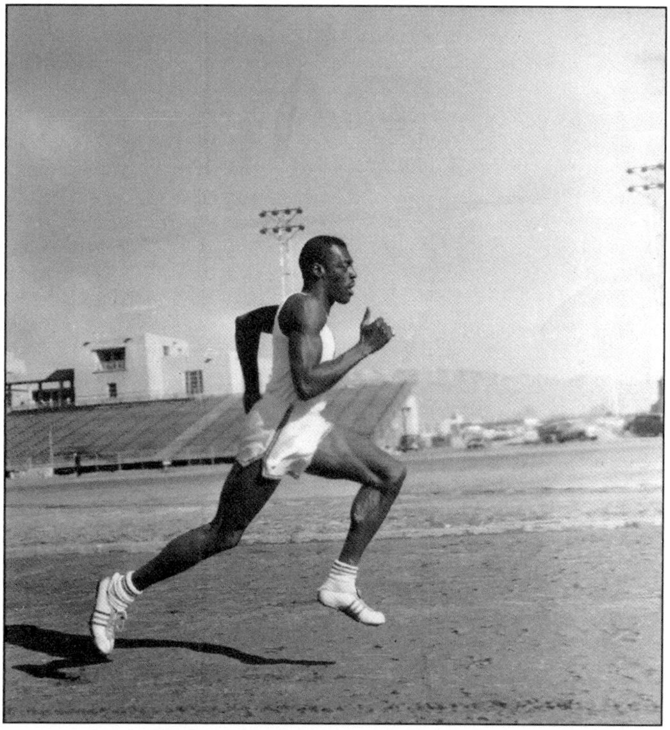

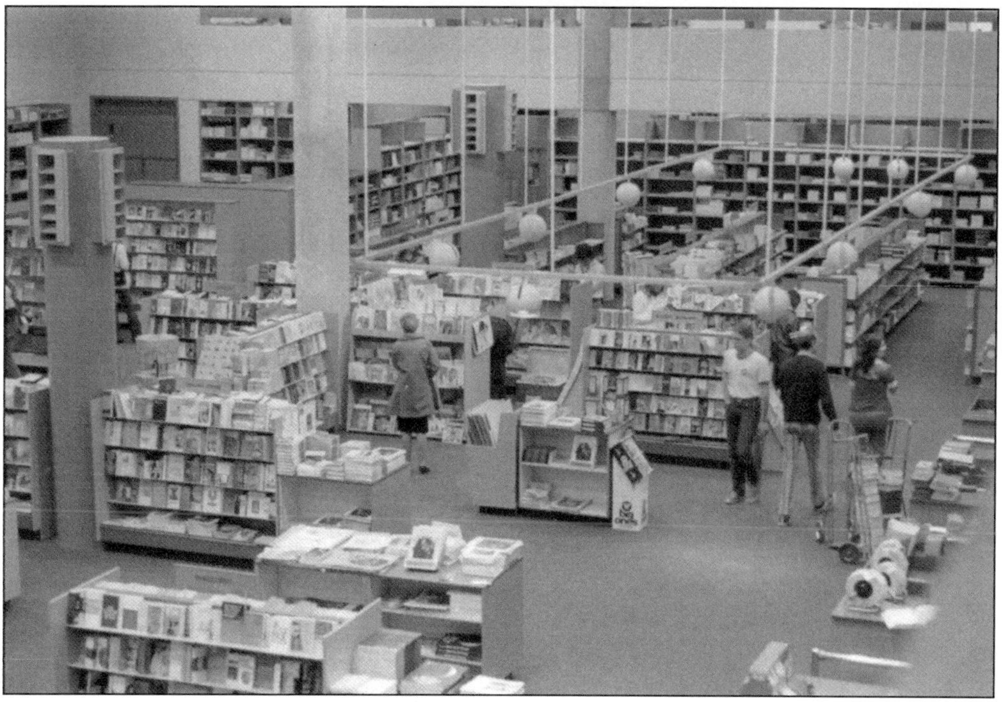

The UNM Bookstore began in an army barracks and moved frequently across campus. By the late 1950s, it was called the Associated Students' Bookstore and operated in the Student Union Building basement. In the early 1970s, it relocated to what is now the Biology Building. Since July 1996, the bookstore has operated from its current location next to George Pearl Hall, adapting to the evolving needs of the university community.

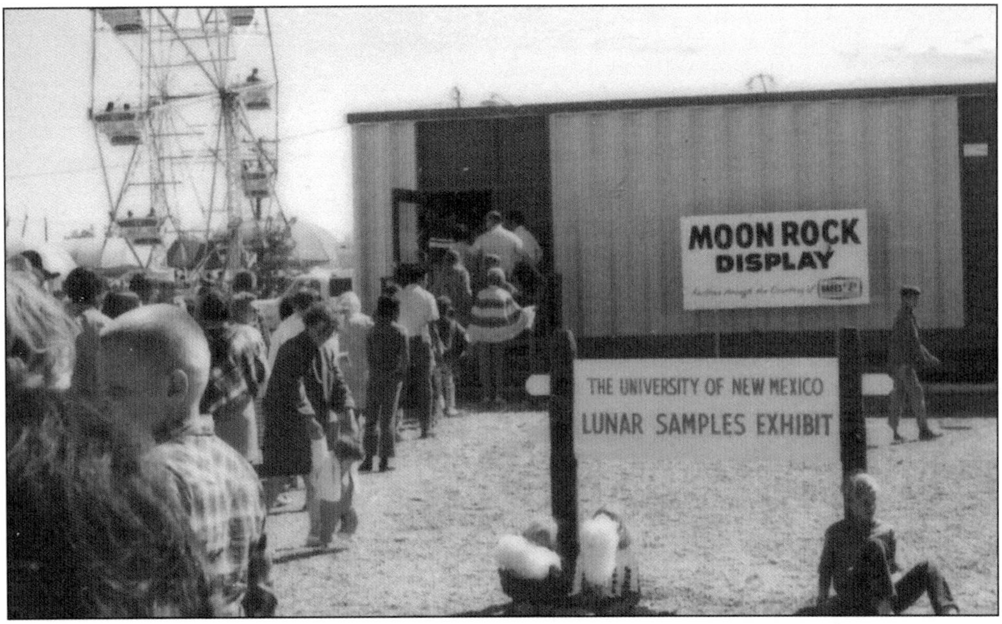

In 1970, the University of New Mexico showcased lunar samples at the New Mexico State Fair, marking a significant moment in the state's engagement with the Apollo program. This exhibit allowed the public to view firsthand materials collected during the Apollo 11 mission. The display aimed to foster interest in space science and inspire future generations of scientists and engineers while also celebrating the achievements of the US space program.

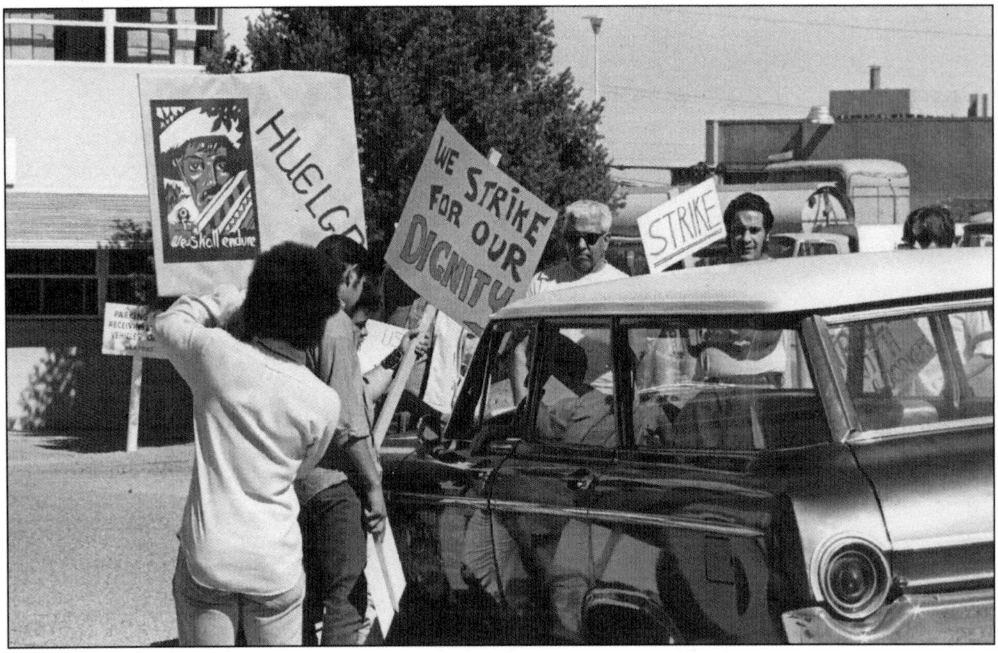

In September 1969, workers at UNM's Physical Plant Department (PPD) went on strike, led by Adolfo Padilla, to protest the unfair treatment and low wages of Chicano/a employees. The strike highlighted the systemic discrimination faced by Chicano/a workers and became a pivotal moment in the broader fight for equality and labor rights at the university.

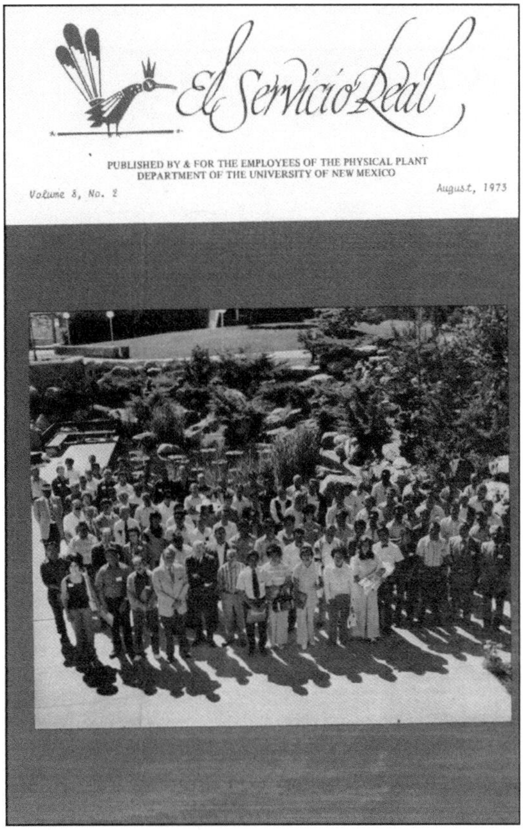

The university's Physical Plant Department, now Facilities Management, has maintained campus buildings since the late 1800s. Its history begins with Mathias Lambert Custers, a Civil War veteran and UNM's first custodian. Renowned for his skills in mathematics and surveying, Custers also served as UNM's first unofficial librarian and later joined the faculty. By the 1960s, the department had expanded significantly, employing hundreds of people. In July 1965, it launched *El Servicio Real*, a newsletter highlighting employee achievements and personal histories, such as that of Jesus Montoya, who retired in 1972. Today, Facilities Management continues this legacy, ensuring the sustainability and functionality of campus buildings while honoring its rich history of dedicated service. Its efforts remain essential to the university's operations and growth.

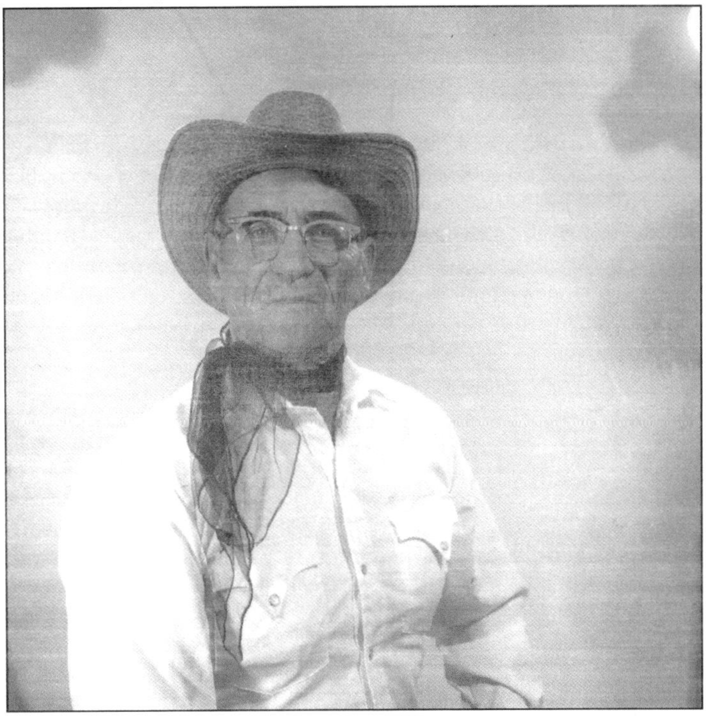

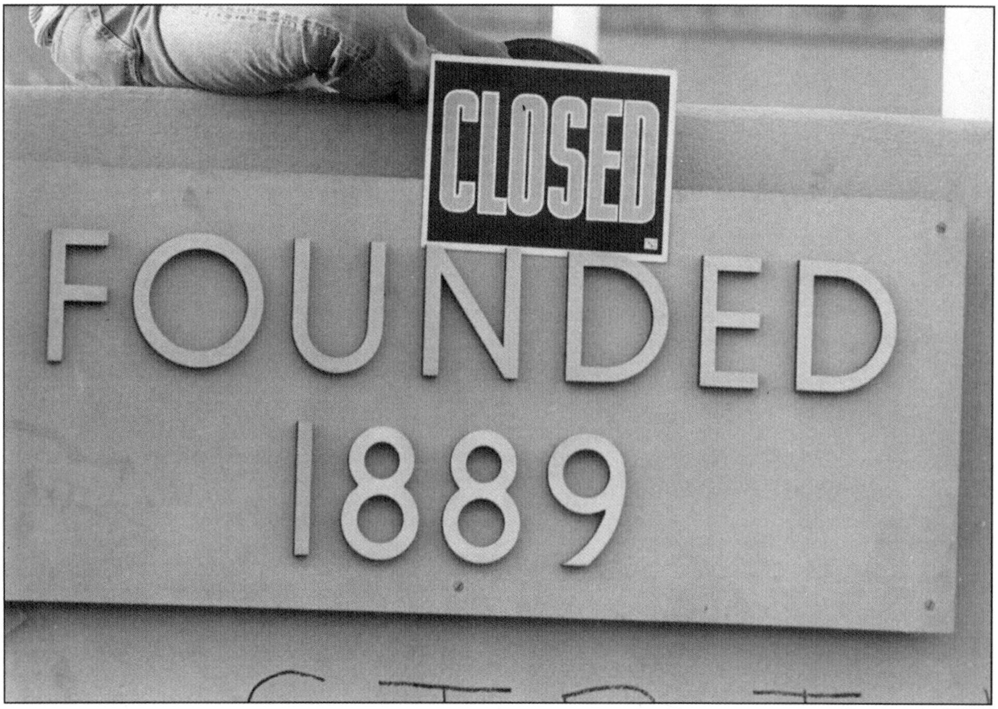

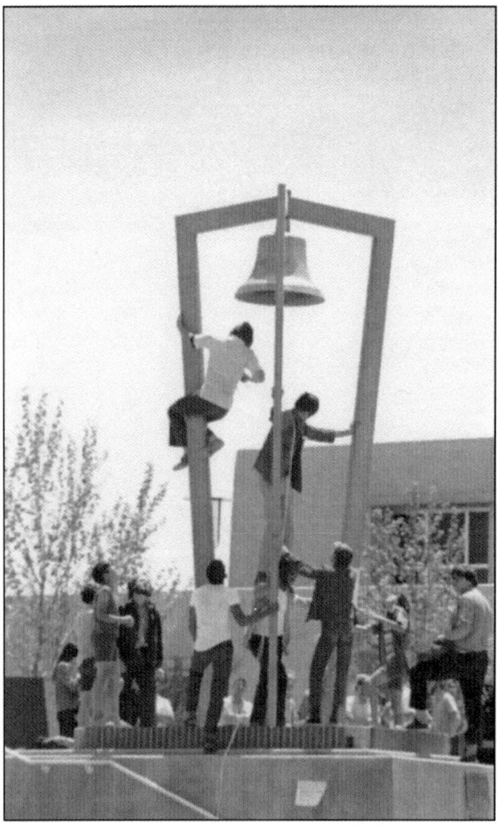

Protests at UNM began in October 1968, with only a handful of the institution's thousands of students actively involved. As the war in Vietnam increased in intensity and the draft became a threat to male students, the hostility began to shift towards the Navy and Air Force ROTC units on campus.

The USS *New Mexico*'s bell arrived at UNM in 1948 as a gift after the ship was decommissioned. In the 1960s, architect Max Flatow designed a bell tower to house it on Union Square. On May 9, 1970, the bell tolled to mourn the students murdered at Kent State a few days earlier. The bell is now located in a more prominent display in front of Zimmerman Library for greater public visibility.

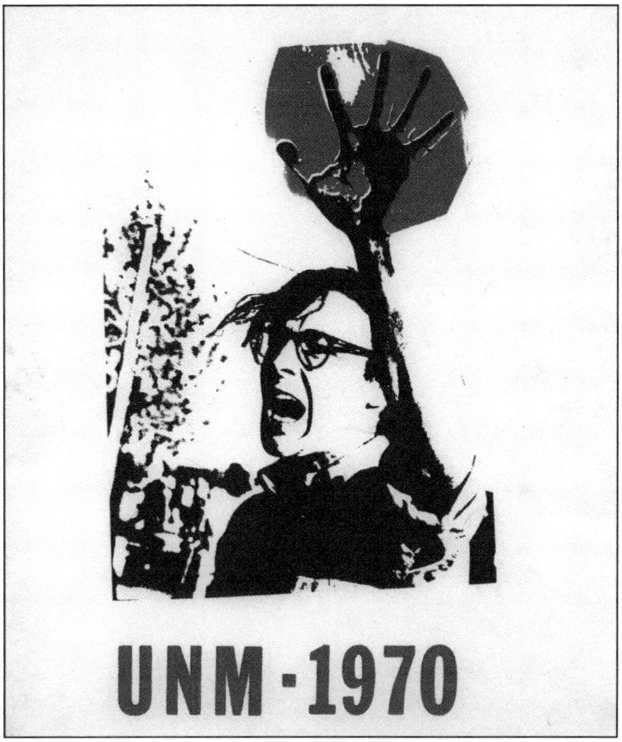

Under the guidance of Van Deren Coke, art students at UNM channeled their outrage over the Vietnam War and associated protests into powerful protest posters. One notable image depicts a student who had been stabbed in the hand with a bayonet, symbolizing the violence faced by protesters. This poster exemplifies the merging of artistic expression and political activism during a turbulent era in US history.

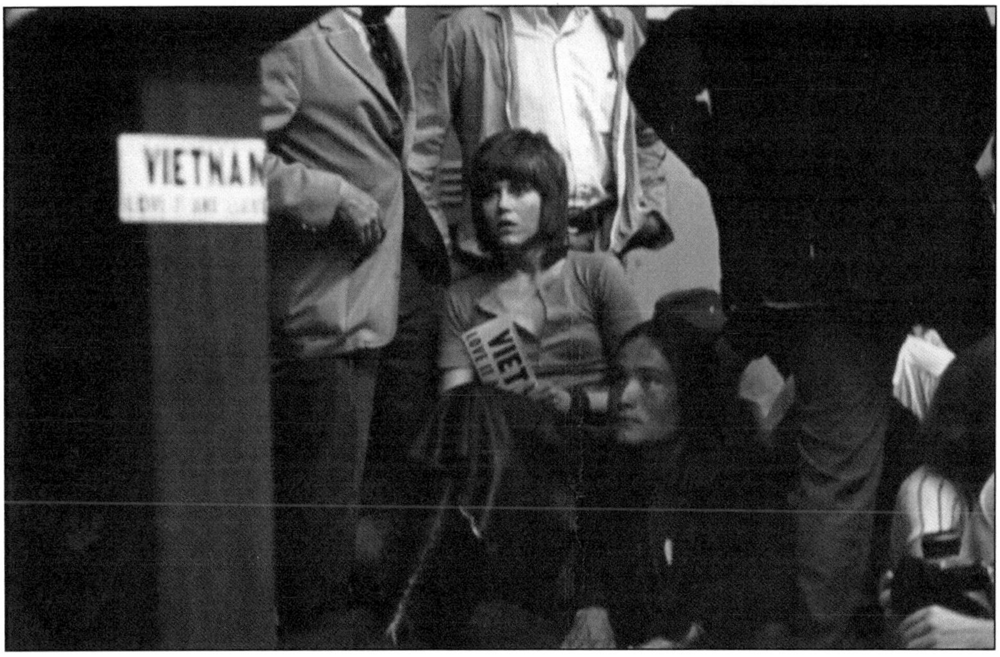

Events leading to the most violent event in UNM's history began on May 4, 1970, after the Kent State murders. That evening, actress Jane Fonda delivered an anti-war speech on UNM's campus, urging peaceful protest. Inspired by her words, an ad hoc group devised a plan to shut down UNM. Their demands included the withdrawal of US troops from Cambodia, the elimination of ROTC programs on campus, and increased scholarships for Native American students.

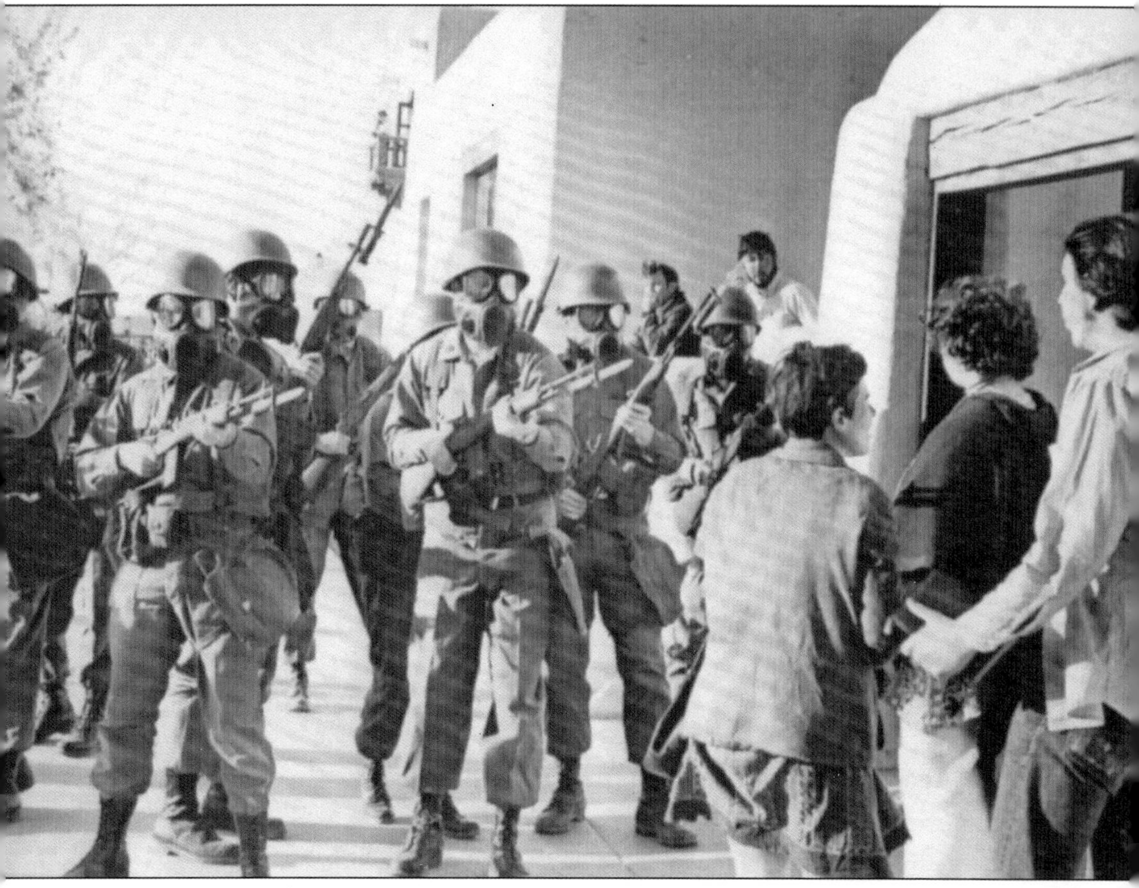

On May 6, 1970, following the flagpole incident, student strikers at UNM occupied the Student Union Building, claiming it as a space for students in protest against the US invasion of Cambodia. This was part of a broader wave of student activism across the country. Initially, university officials and state police adopted a nonconfrontational stance, as the protest remained peaceful and posed no immediate threat to the building. However, tensions increased over the following days. By May 7, the UNM Board of Regents declared the occupation illegal and secured a court injunction to have the protesters removed. The next day, Vice President Travelstead attempted to address the demonstrators, urging them to vacate the SUB. Some stayed, while others left on a peace march in downtown Albuquerque. The National Guard was deployed to enforce the court order, entering the building with bayonets drawn. This marked a significant escalation in the standoff, as tensions between students and authorities heightened.

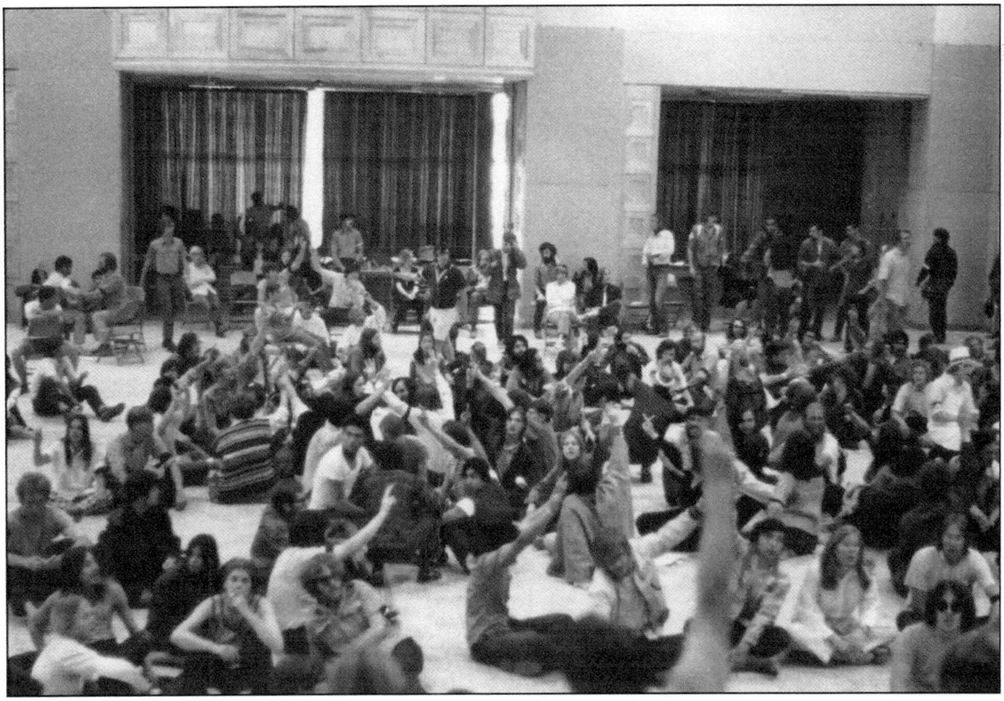

On the evening of May 8, 1970, a total of 131 students at UNM refused to vacate the Student Union Building, defying a court order. The National Guard, alongside state and local police, forcibly removed the protesters. During the confrontation, 11 people, including KOB-TV correspondent Bill Norlander, were injured by bayonets. Despite the force used, students did not resist arrest. Calvin Horn, later a university regent, described the students as an unarmed, nonviolent group, with no need for gas masks or bayonets. National Guardsmen cleared Cornell Mall of protestors and spectators and left around midnight. The incident highlighted the tension and escalating violence between students and law enforcement during the era of protest against the Vietnam War.

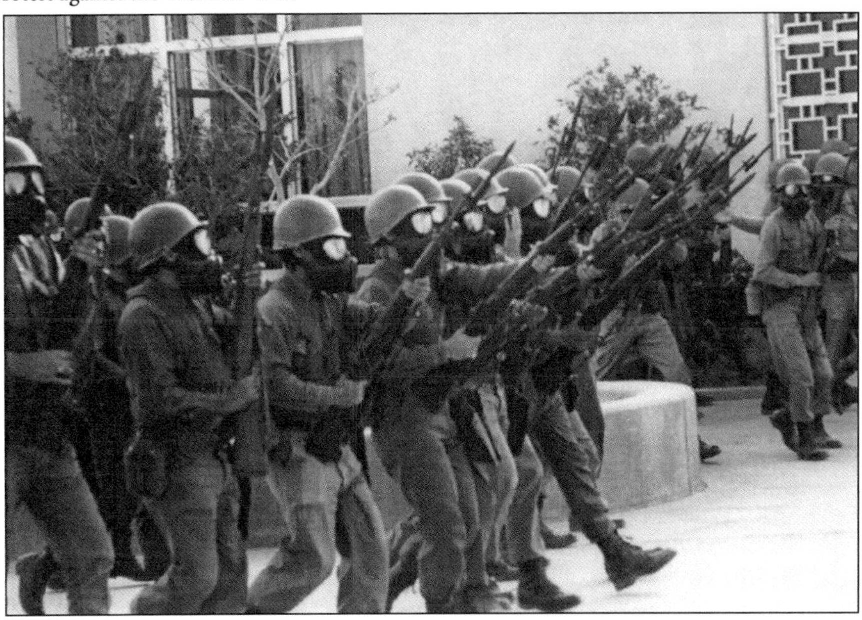

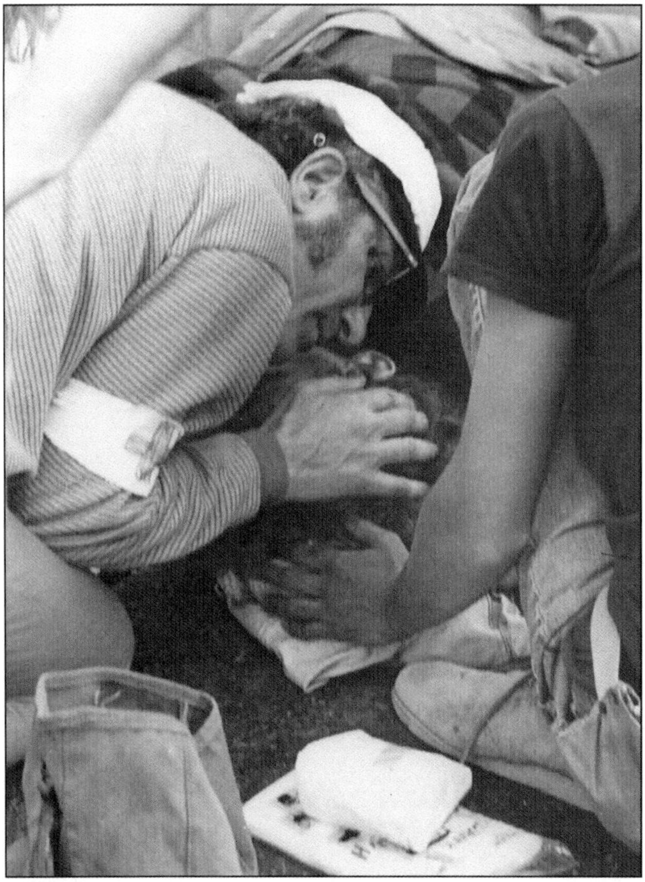

The wounded were taken to Zimmerman Library, where Dr. Leonardo Garcia-Buñuel and medical students organized a makeshift MASH trauma unit. The Student Health Center closed, sending staff home due to safety concerns, which Dr. Garcia-Buñuel condemned as "incredible negligence." Among the injured was graduate student John Dressman, who sustained a severe bayonet wound to the leg while running away; without immediate care, he might not have survived.

A state police major read a court order, resulting in 131 arrests for trespassing, and 20 additional were charged for injunction violations. The violent arrests, particularly the shocking use of bayonets, garnered national attention, cementing the incident as one of the most brutal episodes of student activism at UNM. The events left a profound mark on the campus community and highlighted the broader tensions of the antiwar movement.

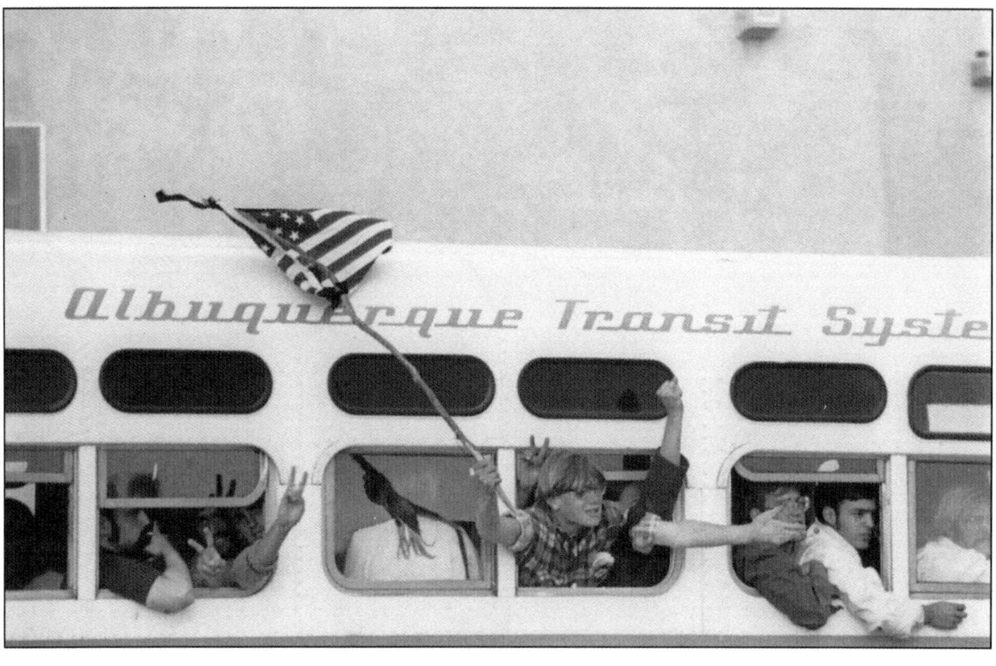

Author Tony Hillerman, a University of New Mexico alumnus and professor, is renowned for his novels set in the American Southwest. His works, often blending Navajo culture and traditional beliefs with gripping mysteries, have drawn attention to Native American communities and their rich heritage. Hillerman's novels continue to influence writers and readers, cementing his place as a key figure in both literary and cultural history, especially in the Southwest.

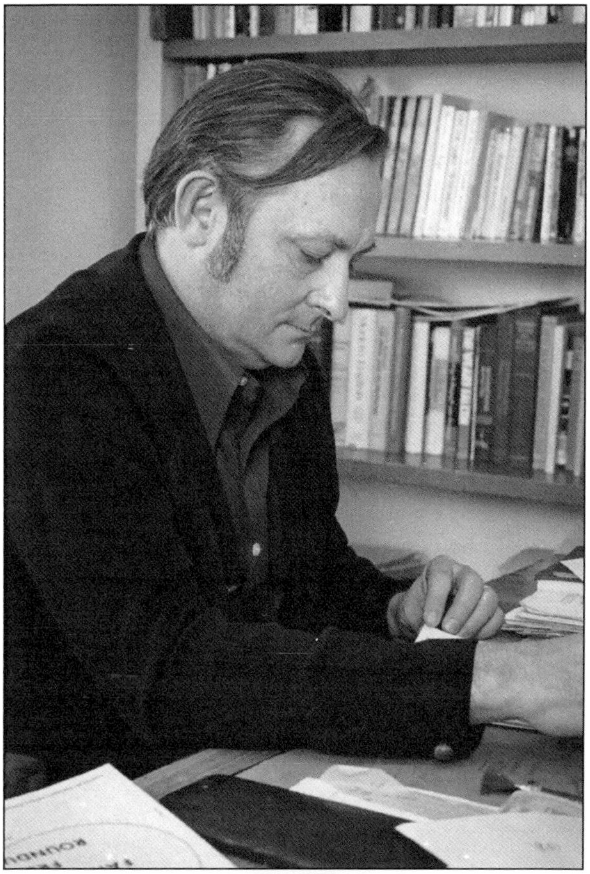

Rodolfo Anaya, a University of New Mexico alumnus from the class of 1963, is a cornerstone figure in Chicano/a literature. His impactful writing, including *Bless Me, Ultima*, has inspired generations and earned him two national medals. As a humble professor at UNM, Anaya influenced both students and the broader literary community, leaving a lasting legacy in the world of American literature.

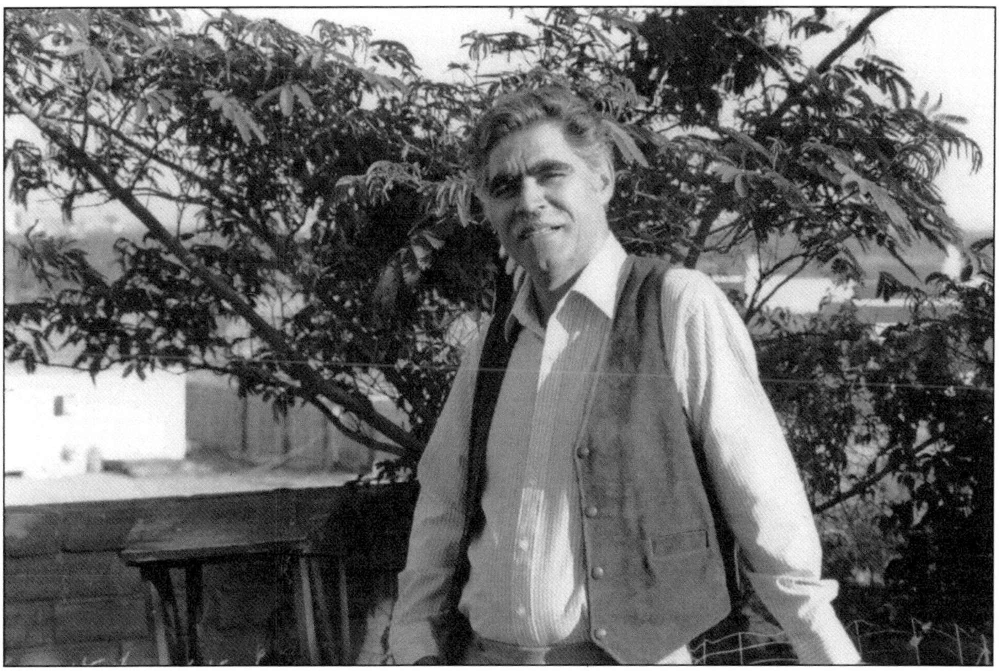

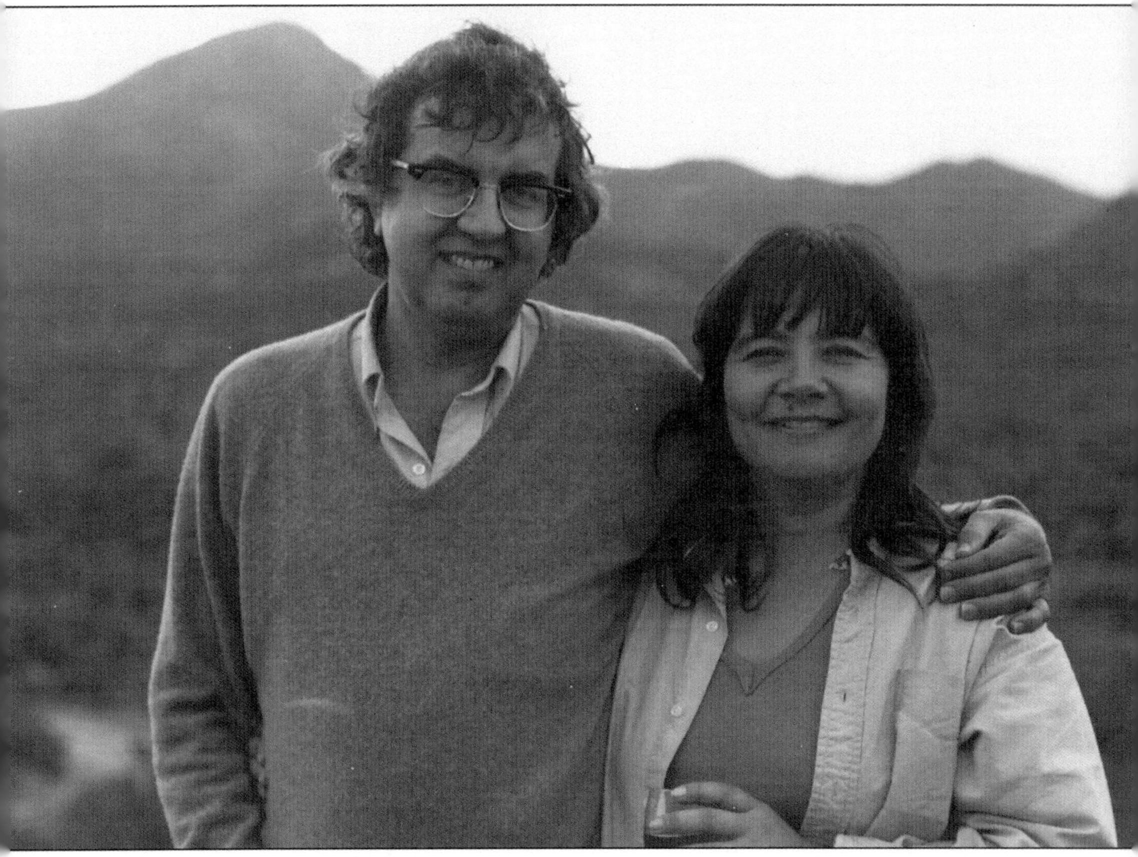

Leslie Marmon Silko, pictured with Larry McMurtry in Albuquerque, is a celebrated UNM alumna. Her first published work, "Tony's Story," appeared in *Thunderbird*, UNM's student literary magazine, in 1969. In 1969, she graduated from the University of New Mexico with her bachelor of arts in English. In 1991, her largest piece, *The Almanac of the Dead*, was published. Silko is renowned for illustrating the strength and passion of women in her storytelling. Recognized as one of the 135 most important women writers in history, she has earned numerous literary awards, cementing her legacy as a vital voice in American literature.

Four

Museums and the Arts on Campus

The University of New Mexico is home to an impressive array of museums and cultural institutions that enrich its academic and cultural fabric and community engagement. The University of New Mexico Art Museum (UNMAM), established in 1962, is New Mexico's largest art collection and a key teaching resource. Renowned for its photography and printmaking, the museum's legacy was shaped by figures like Van Deren Coke and Beaumont Newhall. Milestones include the 1970 integration of the Tamarind Institute, adding extensive lithography archives, and the acquisition of the Raymond Jonson collection in 1982, solidifying its reputation in art preservation and education. The Maxwell Museum of Anthropology, established in 1932, is Albuquerque's oldest public museum, dedicated to the archaeology and human history of the Southwest. Initially created to display artifacts from UNM's excavations, its collection has grown to over three million items. Renamed in 1972 following a generous donation by Dorothy and Gilbert Maxwell, the museum collaborates with the Hibben Center for Archaeological Research and houses the National Park Service (NPS) archives related to Chaco Culture, underscoring UNM's commitment to preserving the region's cultural heritage. UNM's influence in cultural preservation dates back to Edgar Lee Hewett, the university's first anthropology professor, who played a pivotal role in the passage of the Antiquities Act of 1906, which helped protect ancient sites like Chaco Culture. In addition to its anthropological focus, UNM is home to the Meteorite Museum, part of the Institute of Meteoritics, which opened in 1974. This museum showcases a diverse array of stony, stony-iron, and iron meteorites, including a one-ton fragment of the Norton County meteorite. With a collection of over 5,000 specimens, it draws thousands of visitors each year and serves as a valuable resource for academic research. The Silver Family Geology Museum, established in the 1930s, showcases minerals, fossils, and rocks from the Department of Earth and Planetary Sciences. Meanwhile, the Museum of Southwestern Biology (MSB), a university-based natural history museum, advances scientific study and student training across eight divisions, including Mammals and Arthropods. The UNM Arboretum, a sprawling collection of over 320 native and non-native plants, reflects the university's ecological commitment. The arts thrive at UNM through programs like the opera and music departments, which boast faculty members such as Marilyn Tyler. Tyler elevated the program to international acclaim with award-winning productions and a legacy of training global talent. Together, these cultural and academic endeavors underscore UNM's dedication to education, heritage, and creative expression.

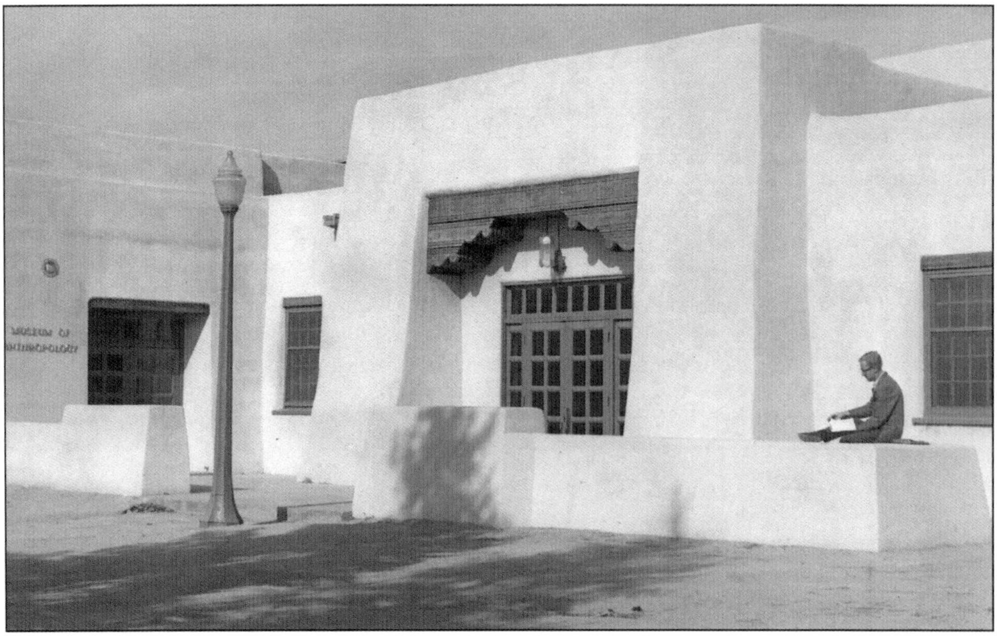

Since its establishment in 1932 as Albuquerque's first public museum, the Maxwell Museum of Anthropology has become a vital center for research and education on the diverse cultural heritage of the Southwest and beyond. Initially serving as a repository for archaeological collections from UNM's field schools, the museum has grown significantly over two decades. The building is the former SUB.

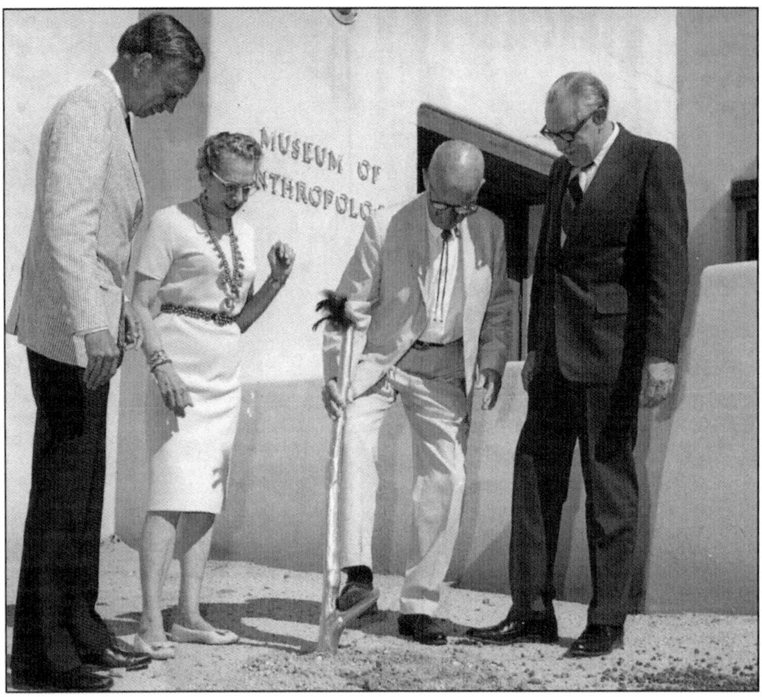

Renamed in 1972 in honor of Dorothy and Gilbert Maxwell, whose support led to its expansion, the museum continues to engage the UNM community and the public through exhibitions, educational programs, and ongoing scholarly discussions about our shared human history.

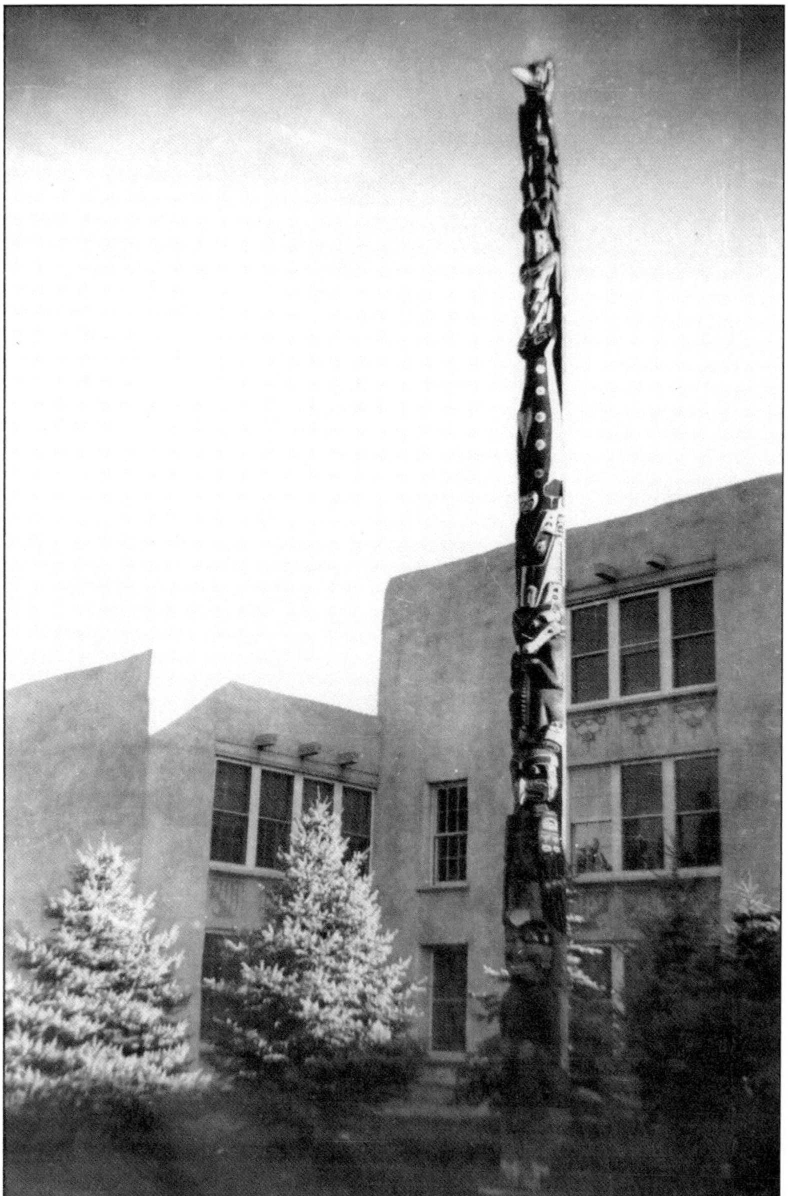

The Smith Family Totem Pole, brought to UNM in 1941, reflects anthropology's complex history with colonization in the Americas. In the late 19th and early 20th centuries, anthropologists often aggressively acquired cultural artifacts through dubious means. During fieldwork in May 1941, Frank Hibben negotiated for a totem pole and other items in the village of Kalagwees. However, the acquisition of the pole was later revealed to be illegal, prompting objections from the Tlowitsis Nation, who reported the theft to Canadian authorities. In the mid-2000s, the Tlowitsis Nation was consulted about the pole's future. They requested that it remain at UNM, be restored and renamed for the Smith family, and include proper contextualization. In 2017, Chief Danial Smith and the university reached an agreement for the pole's relocation, restoration, and reinterpretation. Restoration was led by Kwakwaka'wakw carver Tom Hunt Jr. and Bertram Smith, who restored and recreated missing sections following early traditional styles, with turquoise added to honor its new home. After extensive work, the pole was raised in the Hibben Center on May 20, 2017.

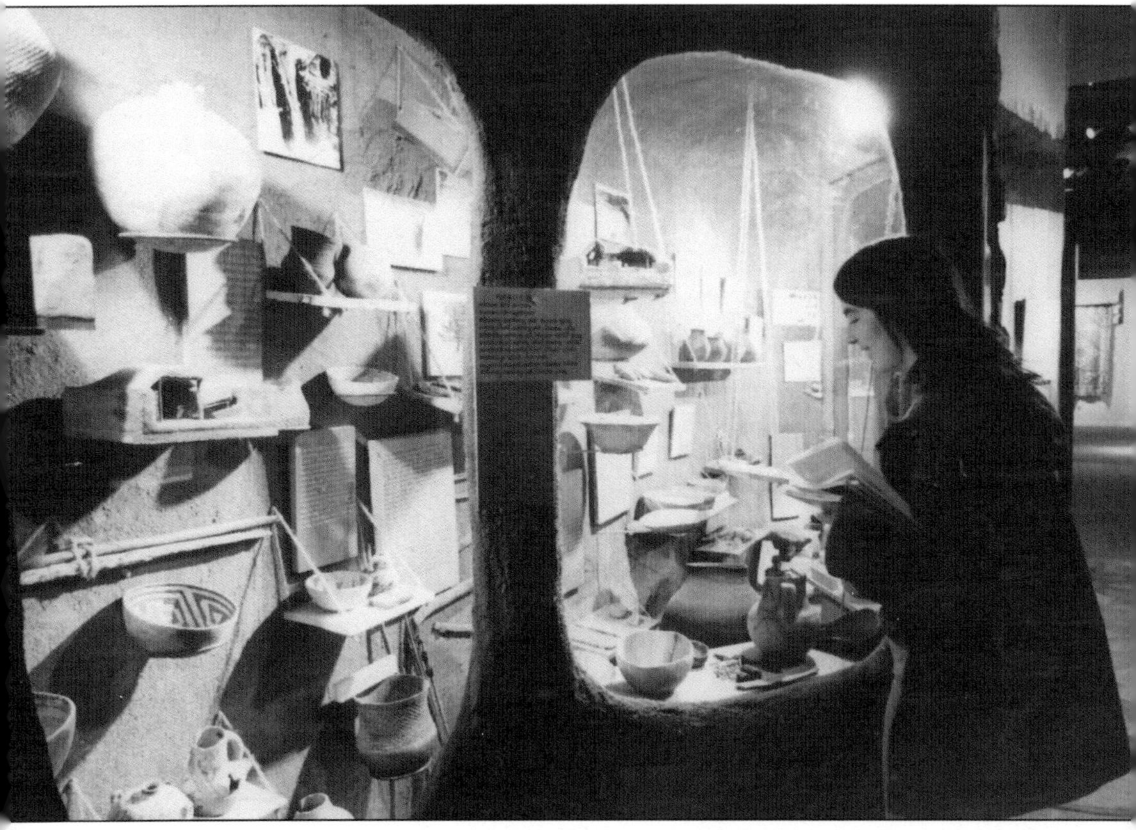

The Native American Graves Protection and Repatriation Act (NAGPRA) was signed into law on November 16, 1990, to safeguard Native American burial sites, human remains, and sacred cultural items. It mandates that federal agencies and institutions like museums protect and return certain items to their rightful tribes. This includes funerary objects, sacred items, and objects of cultural patrimony, all of which may include human remains, burial artifacts, and other sacred objects. NAGPRA applies to federally recognized Native American tribes, Native Hawaiians, and Alaskan groups. Museums collaborate with tribes to assess the cultural significance of their collections and repatriate these items accordingly. The Maxwell Museum is actively involved in the NAGPRA process, working with various tribes to repatriate and ensure the proper handling of cultural items in their collection, emphasizing the importance of respectful, ongoing relationships with the tribes they serve.

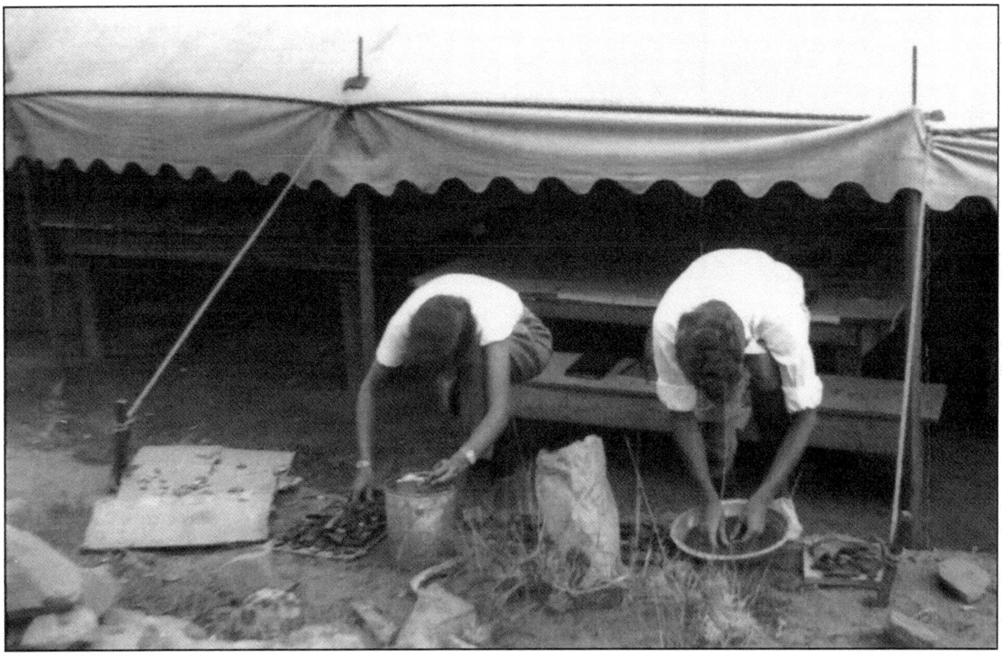

The university has been instrumental in preserving Chaco Culture, guided by Edgar Lee Hewett's contributions to the Antiquities Act of 1906. This advocacy led to the establishment of Chaco Culture National Historical Park in 1907. While the National Park Service manages the site, much of the early archaeological research was conducted by the university's Department of Anthropology, with findings archived at the Maxwell Museum and now the NPS Archives at the Hibben Center.

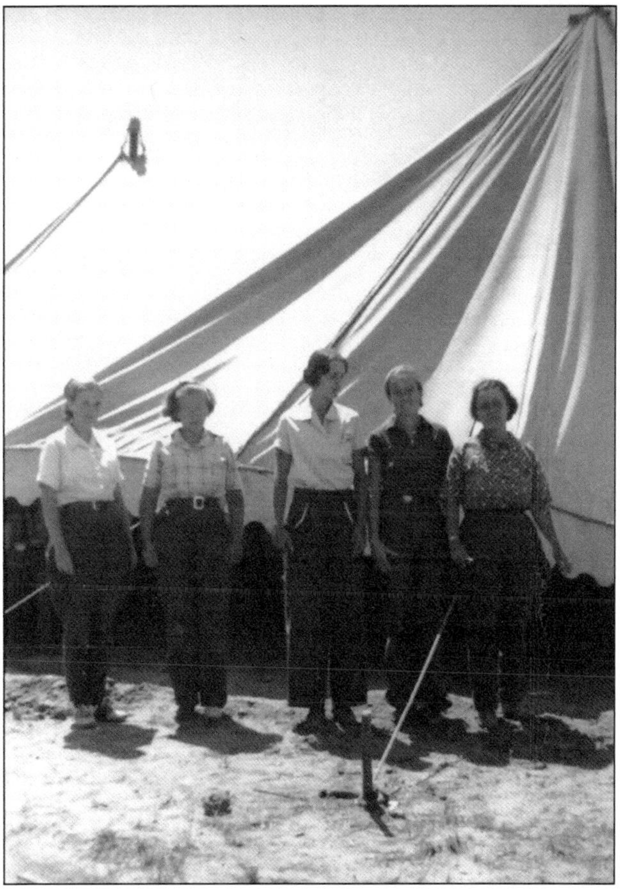

Beginning in 1929, the university's Department of Anthropology conducted field schools at Chaco Culture National Historical Monument, fostering a long-standing connection between Southwestern archaeology and the university. The first field school, led by Hewett, emphasized the need to protect the site from archaeological looting. Collaborations with other institutions led to key research projects, including WPA-approved student facilities and infrastructure improvements in 1938.

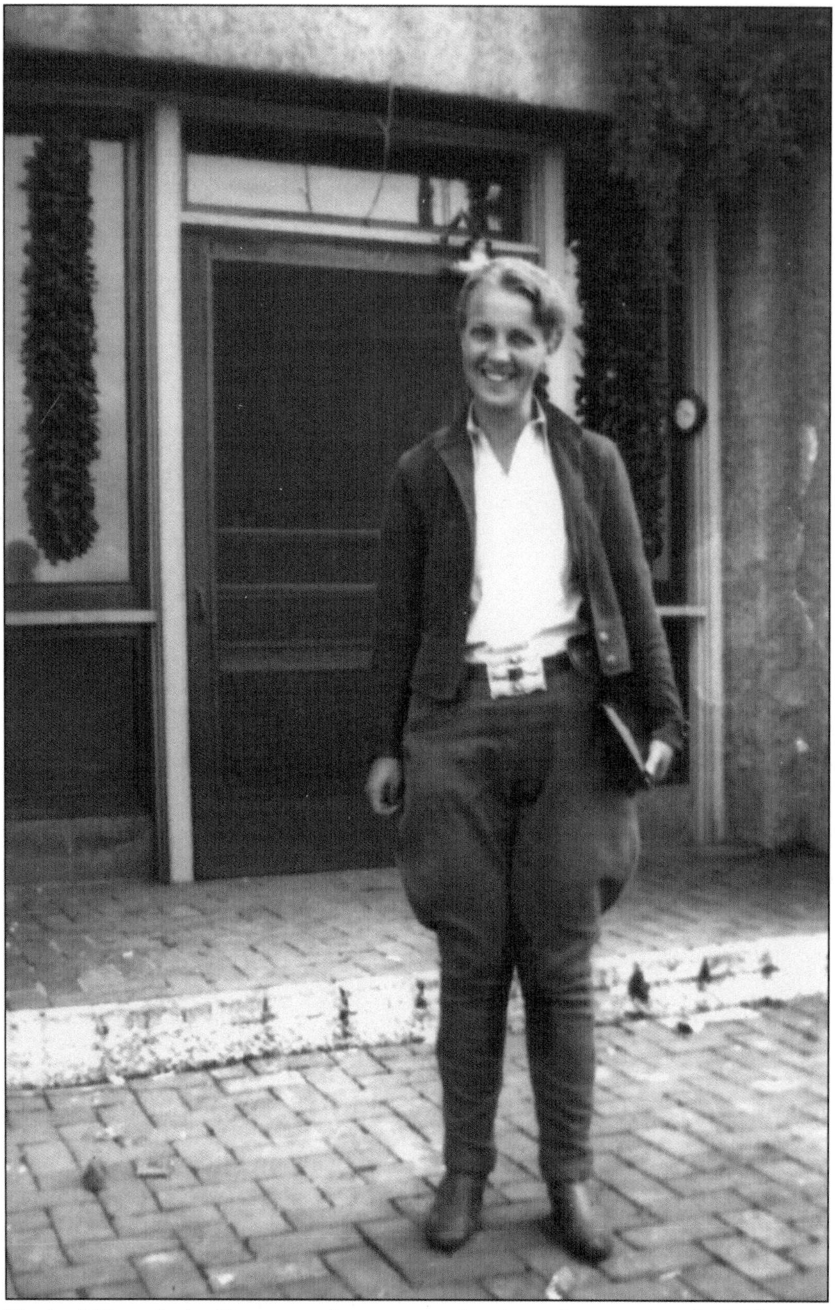

Florence Hawley Ellis made significant contributions to archaeology after attending the field school at Chaco Culture in 1929, led by the University of New Mexico's Edgar L. Hewett. Hewett was notably progressive for his time, actively encouraging female participation in a field traditionally dominated by men. Ellis pioneered innovative techniques in archaeology, utilizing dendrochronology, statistical analysis, chemical analysis, ethnohistory, and ethnoarchaeology in her research, often integrating these methods for more comprehensive insights. A strong advocate for women's rights and equality, Ellis's work not only advanced archaeological practices but also paved the way for greater inclusion of women in the field. She taught at the University of New Mexico in the Department of Anthropology beginning in 1934 until her retirement in 1971.

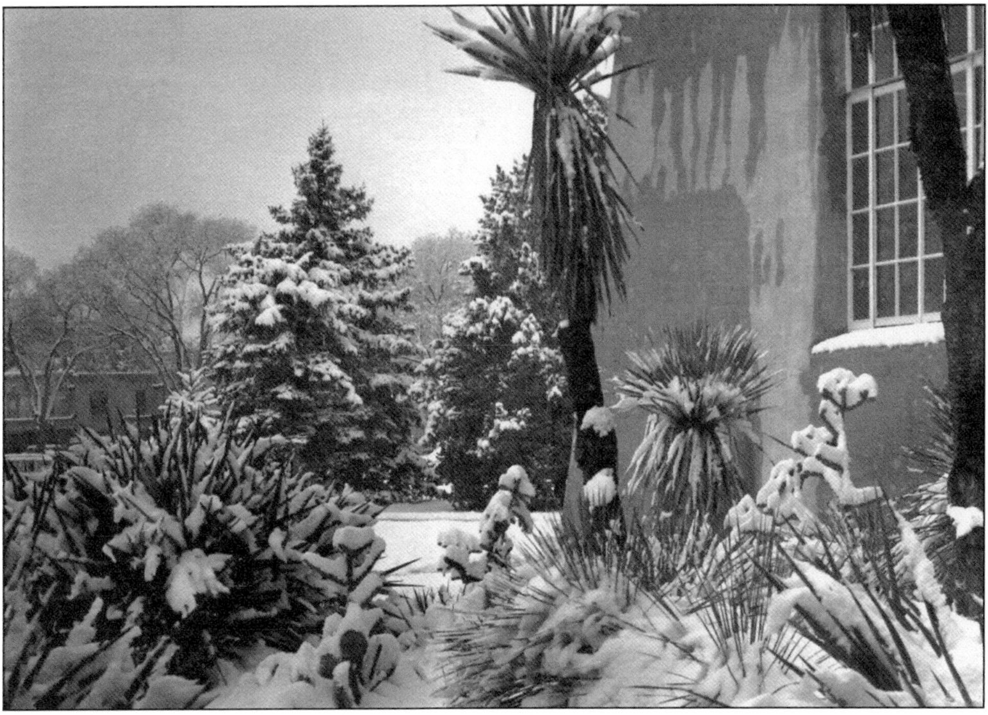

The Castetter Succulent Garden, located on the west side of Zimmerman Library, was designed by UNM biology professor Edward F. Castetter and his students in 1941. Highlighting native desert plants, the garden includes century plants, prickly pear, cholla, and yucca, among others. Castetter, a pioneer in ethnobiology, incorporated varying heights and colors into the design. The garden, featuring a central flagstone path and stone retaining wall, remains a campus focal point.

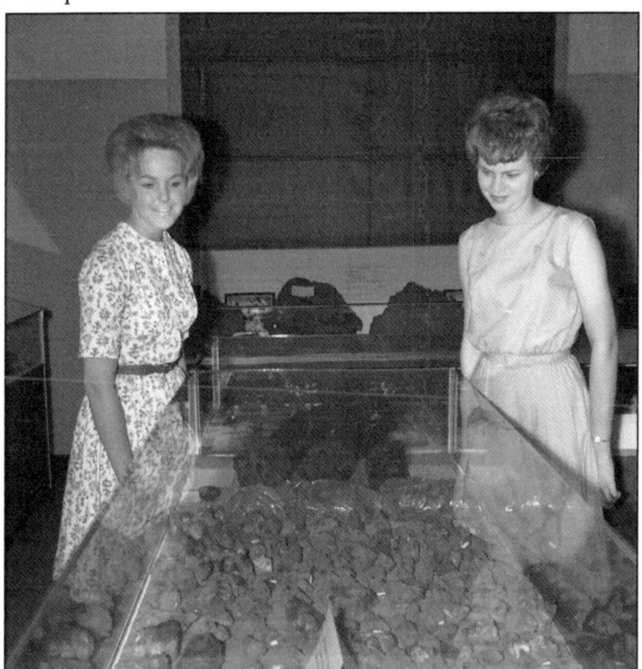

The Silver Family Geology Museum, established in 1937 by Stuart Northrop, showcases public exhibits of rocks, rare minerals, and fossils. The displays represent only a small portion of the vast geological collections from the Department of Earth and Planetary Sciences. The museum, along with the Meteorite Museum at the University of New Mexico, offers students and visitors unique insights into the origins of meteorites, minerals, and fossils.

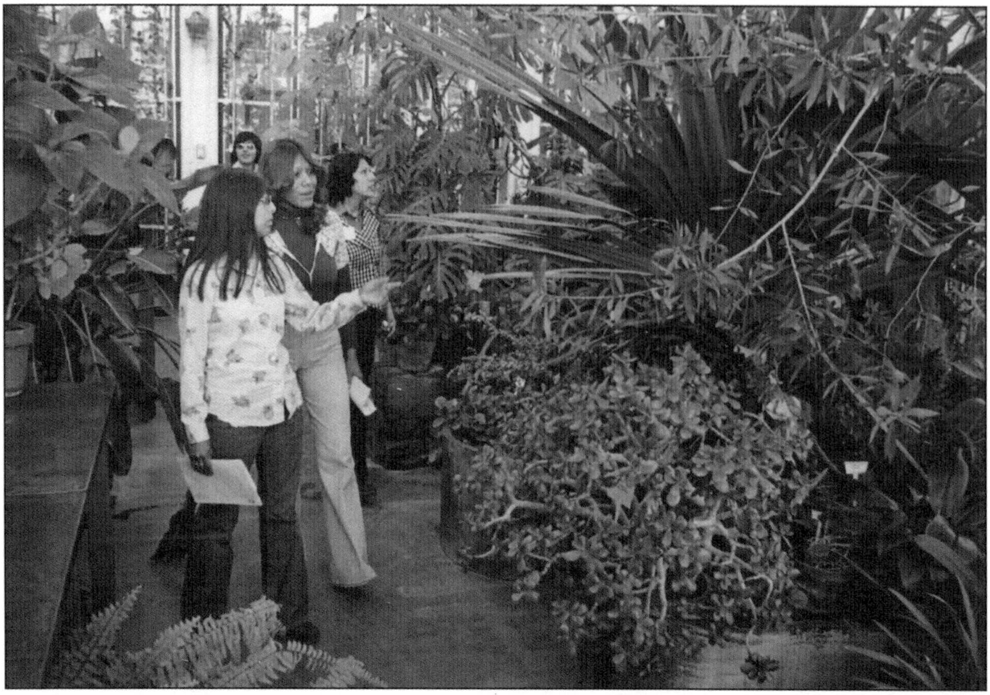

In 1968, the Biology Building at the University of New Mexico received a distinctive addition: a large, two-story greenhouse at its main entrance. Designed to serve both as a public space and a scientific resource, the greenhouse featured a tropical botanical display with water elements, birds, fish, and flowering plants. The adjacent patio showcased native New Mexico plants, while the round pond housed fish, frogs, and turtles, offering valuable hands-on opportunities for students and faculty. Though a 1969 incident occurred when the greenhouse's insecticide spraying temporarily affected some birds, they recovered. The greenhouse quickly became a popular spot for campus tours. In recognition of its innovative design, the Biology Building was later honored as the top architectural example in the state, symbolizing both aesthetic beauty and scientific utility.

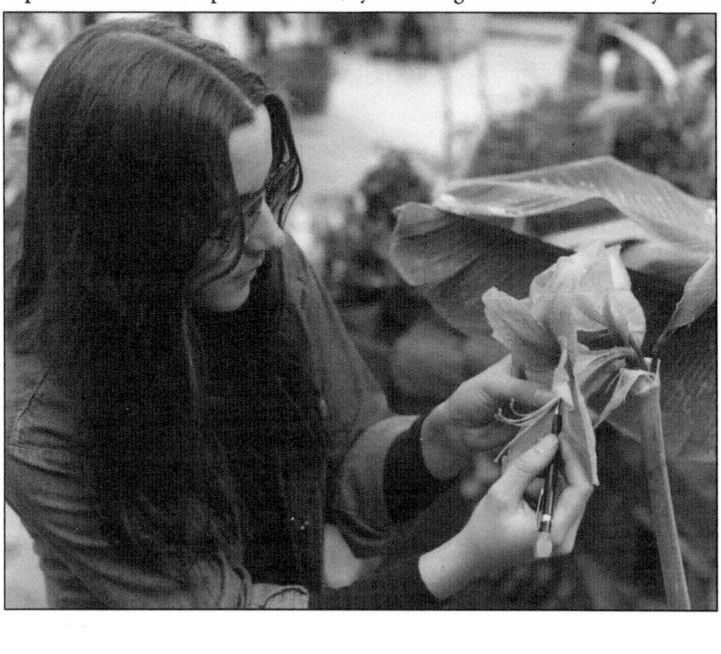

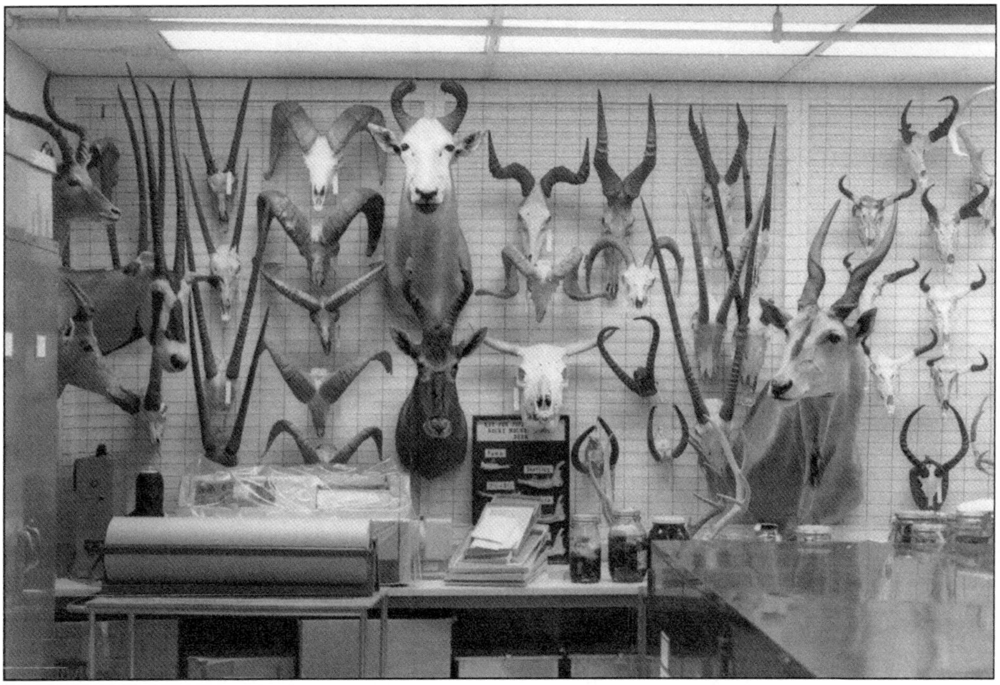

The Museum of Southwestern Biology is home to the state's largest herbarium, the oldest division within the museum, housing an extensive collection of approximately four million specimens, including plants, invertebrates, and vertebrates. The MSB collections trace their origins to the early work of Edward F. Castetter, beginning in 1928, with vertebrate specimens increasing in 1938. Today, the MSB's eight divisions—Amphibians and Reptiles, Arthropods, Birds, Fishes, Genomic Resources, Herbarium, Mammals, and Parasites—are recognized as the largest and most developed collections of their kind in the state and region. The MSB also manages the Natural Heritage New Mexico (NHNM) program, which is dedicated to the conservation and sustainable management of New Mexico's biodiversity. Through NHNM, a statewide database of rare species and ecosystems is used to inform conservation efforts by state and federal agencies.

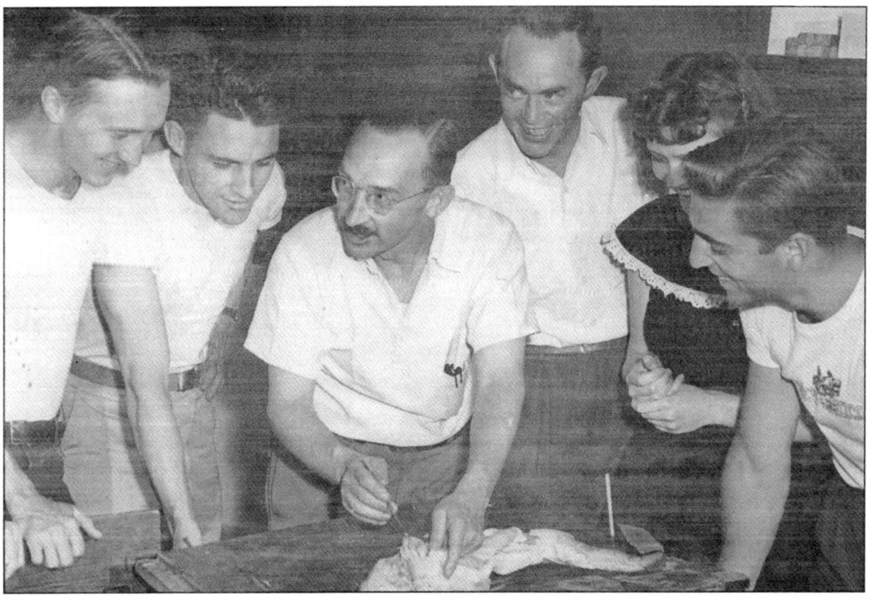

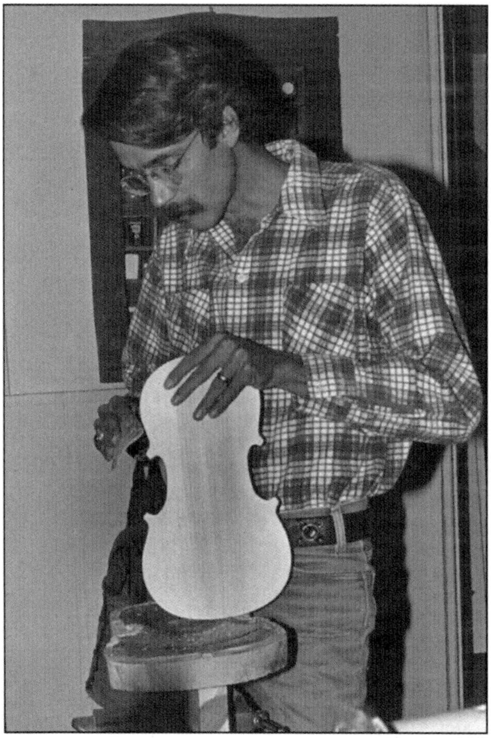

In 2008, UNM English and American studies professor Peter White, a trained violin maker, launched the only violin-making program in the United States. White, who studied in both the United States and Poland, believed that violins were made in the New World as early as the 16th century, introduced by Spanish missionaries. This tradition likely spread to the American Southwest before reaching the East Coast. Klarissa Petti, a student in the program, took over as instructor in 2015. The program is part of the New Mexico Musical Heritage Project (NMMHP), which combines violinmaking with learning Native American and Hispanic folk tunes. Making a violin typically takes 300 hours over several semesters, using traditional lutherie tools. Each violin consists of about 60 pieces of wood, including spruce, flamed maple, and ebony.

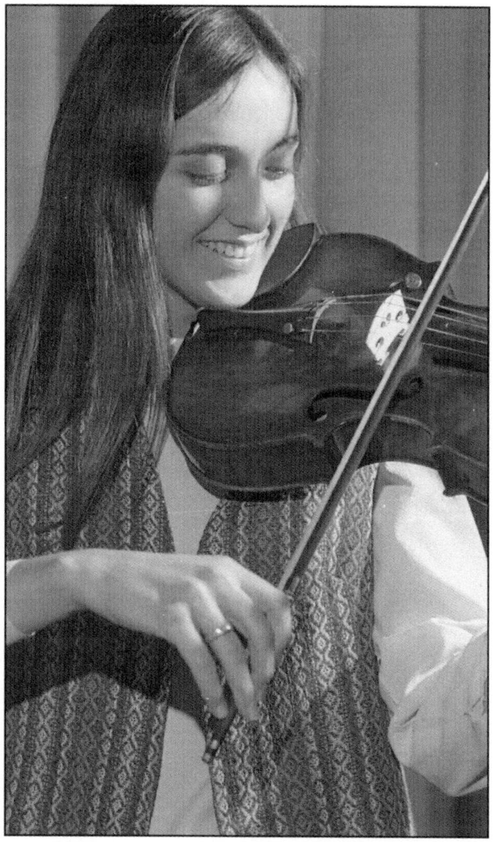

In 1942, Dr. Kurt Frederick, an Austrian-born violinist and conductor, joined the University of New Mexico's Department of Music, where he profoundly influenced Albuquerque's cultural landscape. He founded the UNM Symphony Orchestra, UNM Opera Workshop, UNM Madrigal Singers, Albuquerque Opera Theater (now Opera Southwest), and the Albuquerque Youth Symphony Program. As the first music director of the youth symphony, Frederick created an ensemble for students in grades seven through twelve, offering advanced symphonic training unavailable in school programs. The group met on Saturday mornings at UNM and inspired generations of young musicians. Under Frederick's leadership, Albuquerque's musical scene flourished, with KHFM emerging as one of the nation's few 24-hour classical radio stations. His Albuquerque Civic Symphony also presented the US premiere of Arnold Schoenberg's *A Survivor from Warsaw*, solidifying New Mexico's classical music legacy.

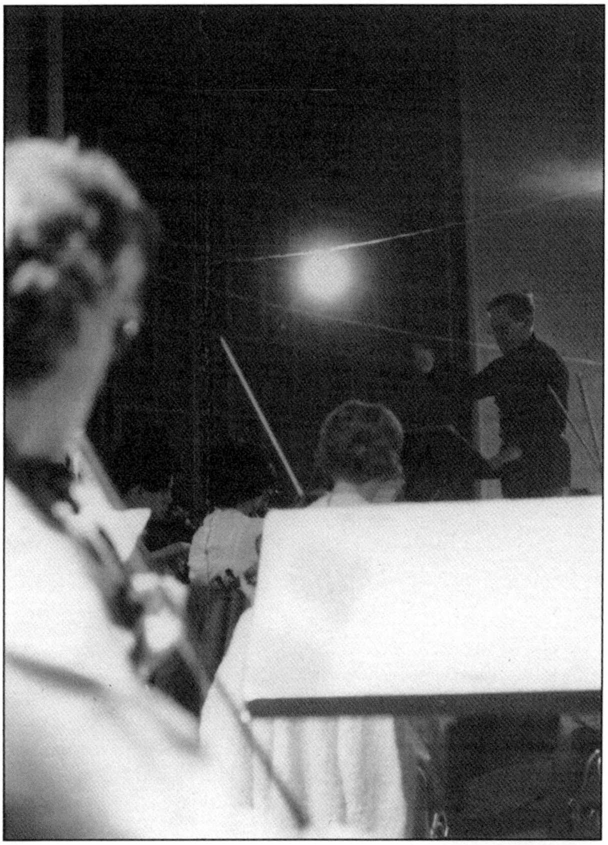

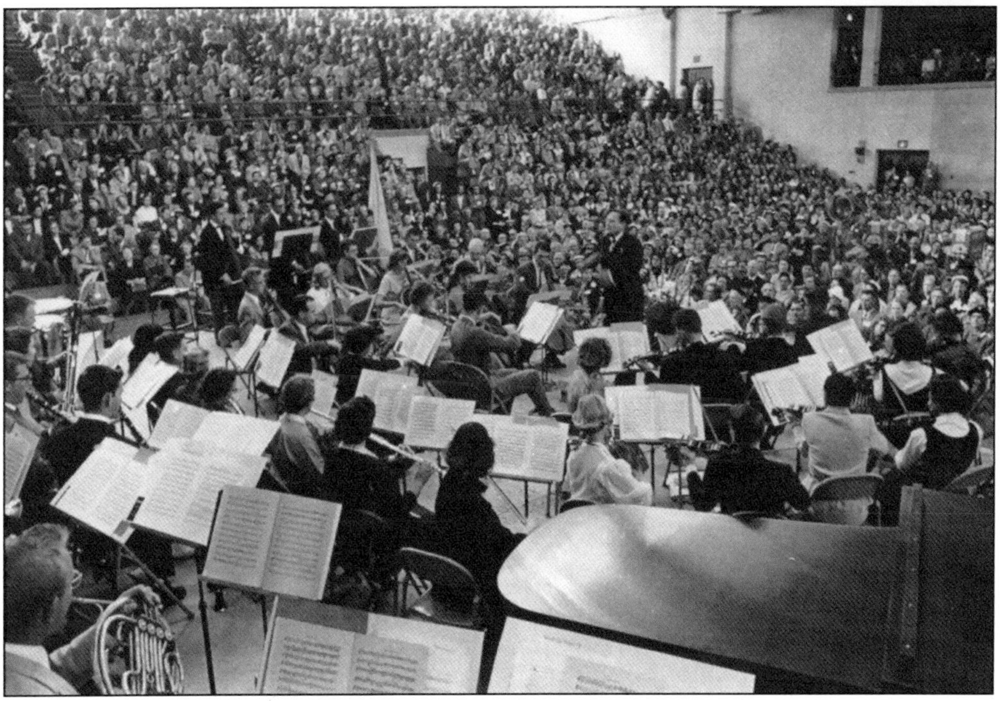

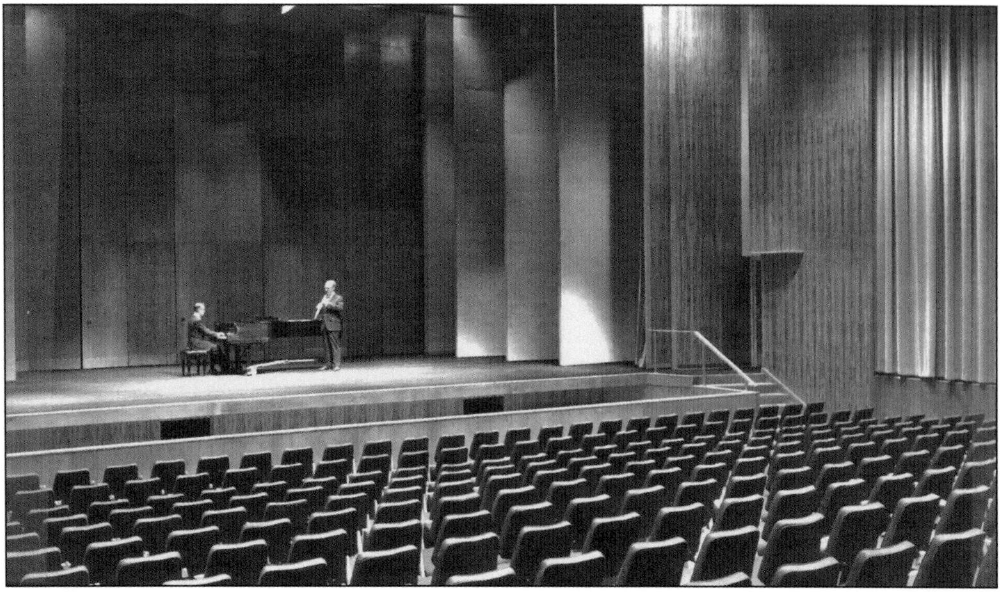

Keller Hall, located in the Center for the Arts, serves as the primary recital venue for the UNM Department of Music. Over 170 recitals take place annually, showcasing faculty, guest artists, ensembles, and students. Opened in 1966 and originally named the Fine Arts Recital Hall, it was renamed in 1971 in honor of Dr. Walter Keller, a former music faculty member, head of the piano area, and former president of the Albuquerque Symphony Orchestra. The hall seats roughly 2,000 people and is equipped with an orchestra pit, a green room, advanced recording technology, and the impressive Holtkamp organ, built in 1967. With 2,741 pipes, three keyboards, and 51 ranks, it is one of New Mexico's largest organs.

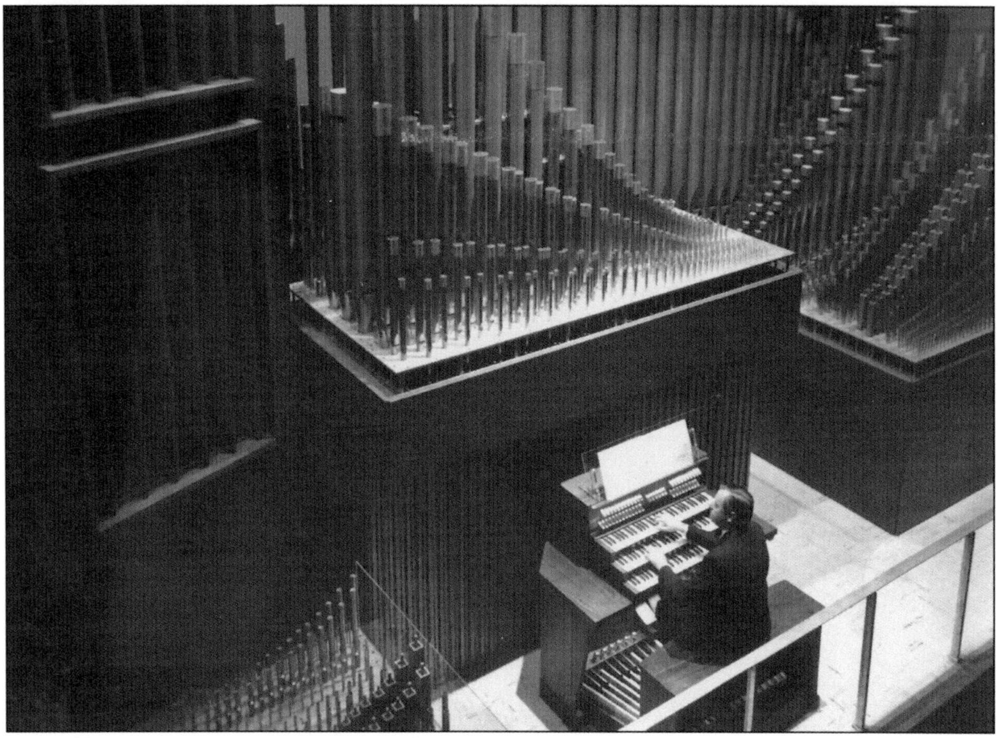

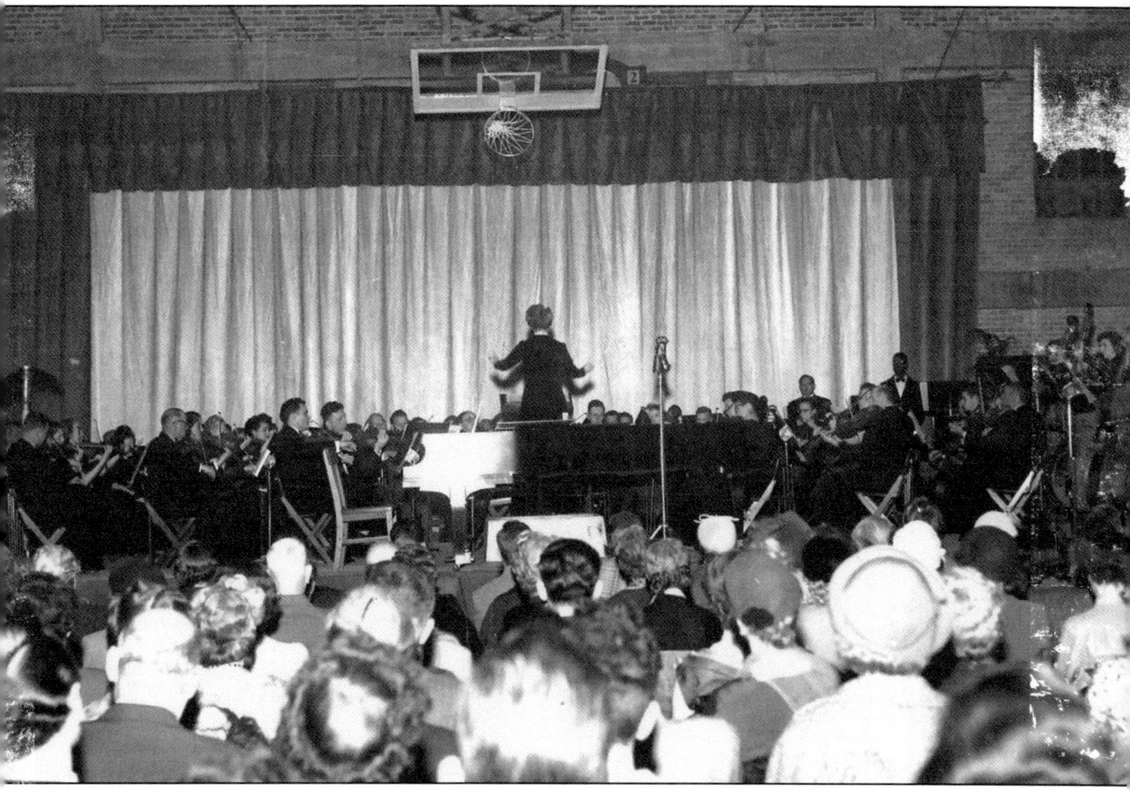

Under the leadership of Grace Thompson Edmister, the university orchestra became renowned for its performances, a result of countless hours of practice. Many members also played in the Albuquerque Civic Orchestra, conducted by Edmister. The orchestra's talents were showcased on local radio. Edmister, the first woman to conduct a city symphony, made history with the Albuquerque Civic Symphony's debut performance in 1932 at Carlisle Gymnasium. A prodigy, she earned a bachelor of arts in music at 17 from Defiance College and later studied at Juilliard and the Chicago Conservatory of Music. Beginning her career at UNM in 1923, she became head of the music department by 1925 and held the position until 1942. She recorded traditional Pueblo songs and continued her musical contributions, including conducting at the Albuquerque Symphony's 40th anniversary in 1972. In 1974, she received a Governor's Award for outstanding service to the arts in music.

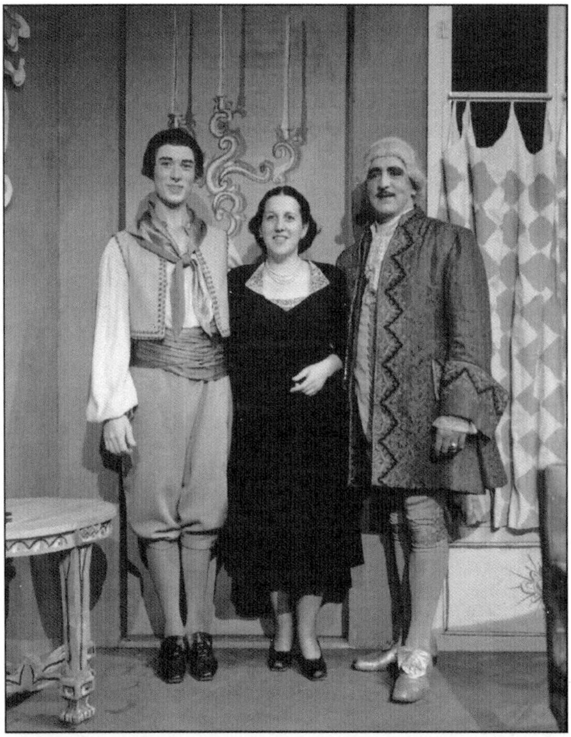

Jane Snow, a prominent voice and opera teacher at UNM, was instrumental in shaping the university's opera program. Collaborating with conductor Kurt Frederick, she directed over 22 fully staged operas through the Opera Workshop. Her reputation attracted professional opera singers, allowing students to perform alongside them. Snow's influence during the 1950s and 1960s greatly enhanced the quality and reach of the university's opera productions.

The 1960 *Don Giovanni* Opera Workshop at UNM, one of Mozart's most popular operas, took place on April 26 and 27 in the SUB ballroom. The performances were highly praised, with particular acclaim for the actor playing Leporello, who was said to have stolen the show. However, the acoustics posed challenges, as the UNM Orchestra occasionally drowned out the singers. Despite this, the performances were considered magnificent.

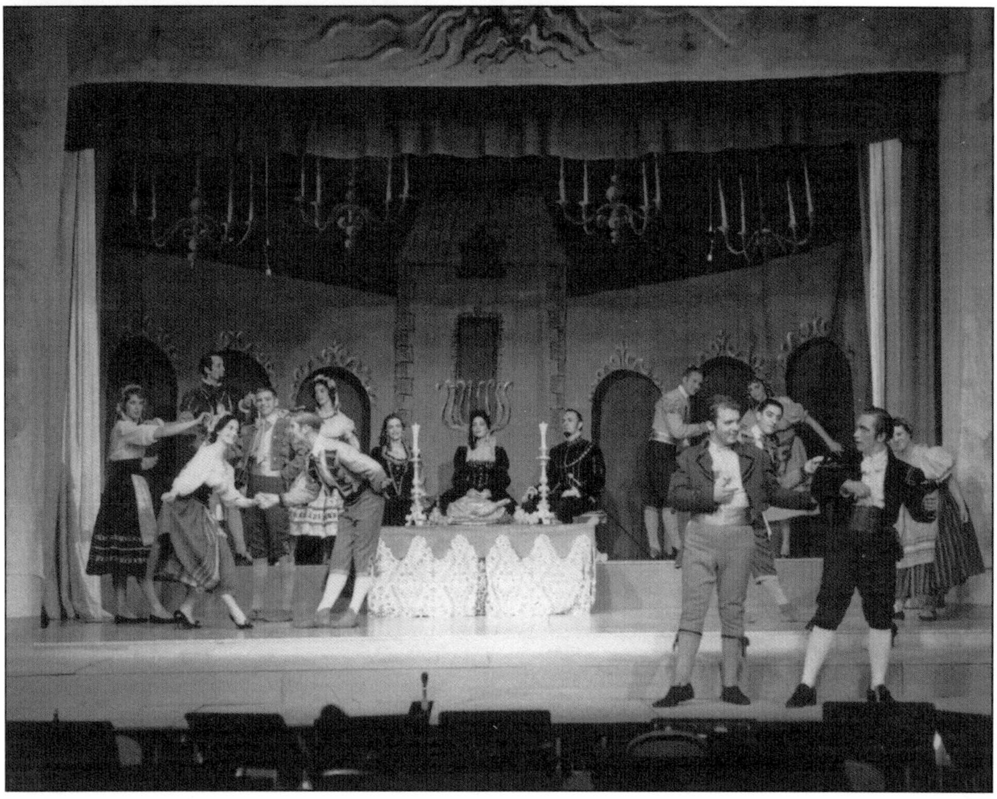

Elizabeth Hannah Waters, the "First Lady of Dance" in New Mexico, pioneered modern dance at UNM, shaping the art form statewide. Joining UNM in 1946, she taught modern dance through the Division of Adult Education when the style was virtually unknown. By 1961, she secured a full-time position and transitioned modern dance into one of the first fine arts majors in the United States, choreographing over 50 works inspired by New Mexico's culture and landscapes.

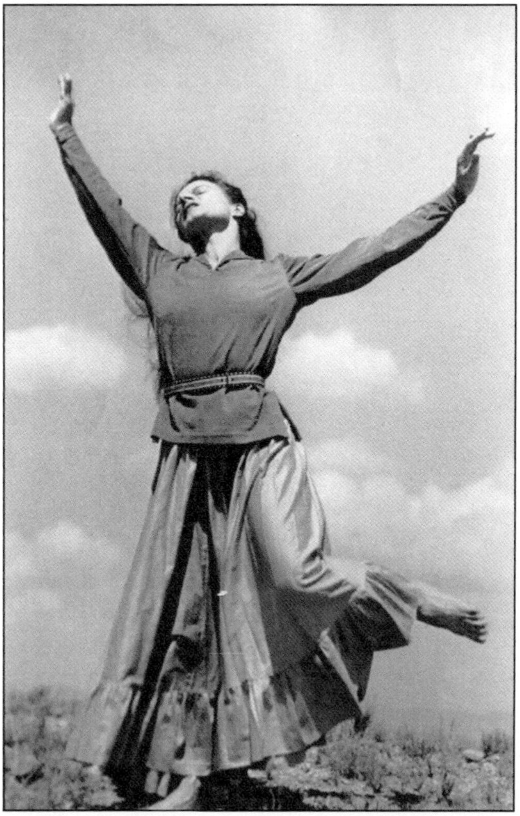

The Dance Program at the University of New Mexico has focused on enhancing physical health through dance, encouraging artistic exploration with interdisciplinary approaches, and fostering critical thinking to connect theory and practice. It has created a multicultural, dynamic environment that celebrates dance history as a legacy for contemporary scholars. Through cutting-edge choreography curriculum and international faculty connections, the program has enriched students' academic and professional journeys.

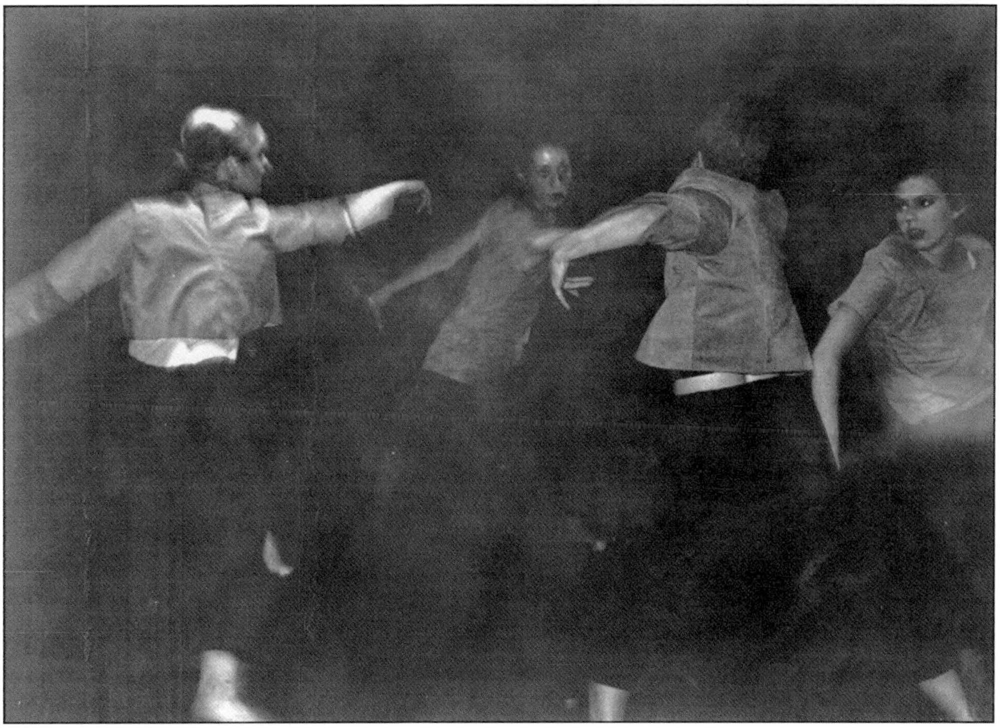

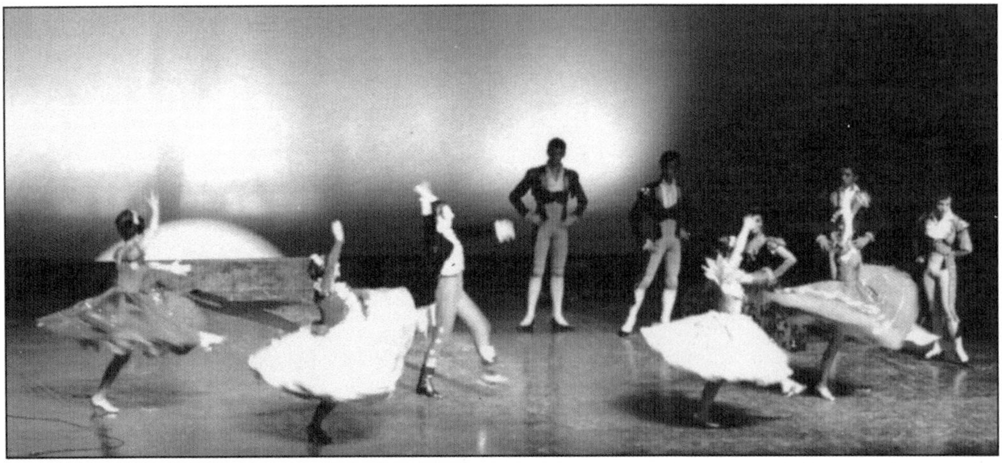

The Department of Theatre and Dance has partnered with the National Institute of Flamenco for decades, copresenting Festival Flamenco Alburquerque since its 1987 inception by Prof. Eva Encinias. Celebrating the College of Fine Arts' 50th anniversary, the festival has become one of the largest flamenco events outside Spain, featuring performances, workshops, and conferences with over 50 artists. This partnership continues to enrich cultural and educational experiences in New Mexico.

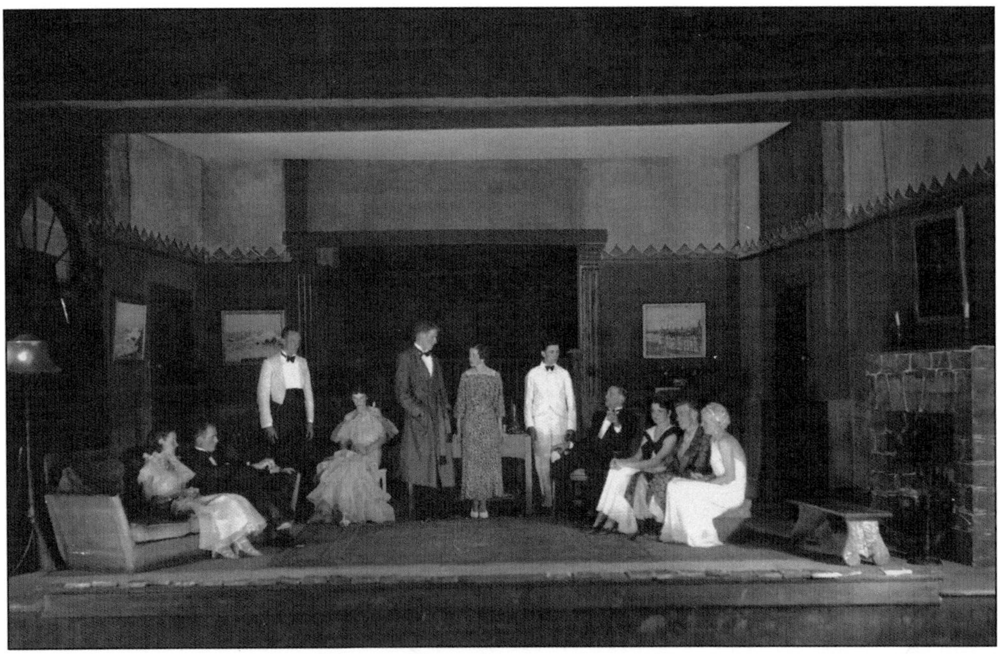

In the fall of 1919, a new initiative aiming to bridge the gap between the university's students and the local community began with a staging of *Mystery Murder*. Rodey Hall was outfitted with curtains, scenery, and lighting to create a "little theater." This effort stemmed from the Dramatic Club's growing popularity, which had been successful since 1907 with performances like *Snobson's Stag Party*. Under Dr. George St. Clair's direction, the club achieved financial and artistic success, operating independently through ticket sales and a small membership fee.

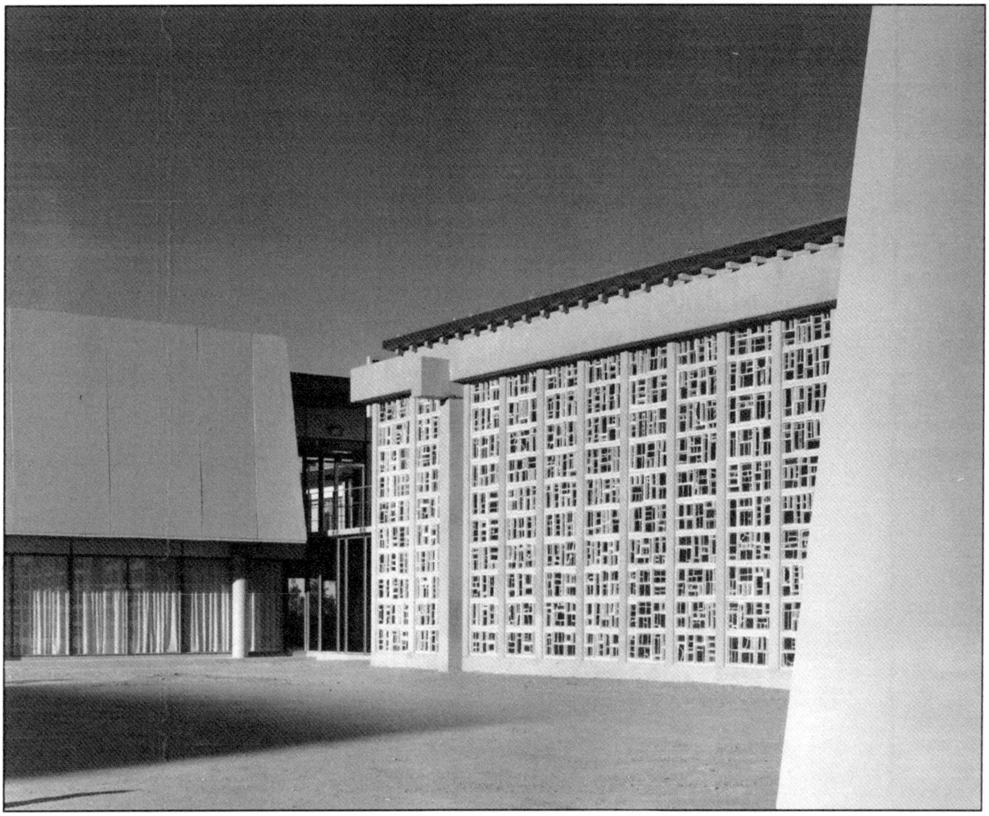

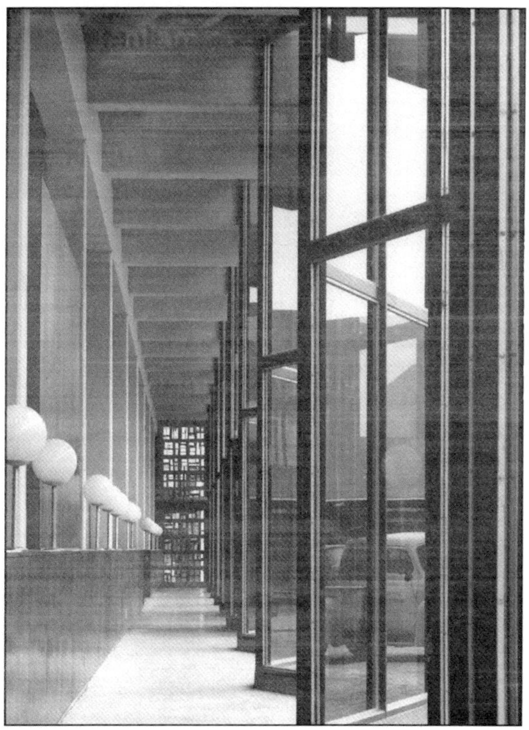

Upon its completion in 1963, Travelstead Hall stood as a bold departure and sharp contrast from the traditional Pueblo Revival style that dominated the campus. Max Flatow's design preserved the essence of New Mexico's architectural identity but pushed boundaries by abstracting regional Pueblo influences and incorporating modernism. Travelstead Hall, in particular, exhibited the least obvious use of Pueblo Revival elements within the Education Complex. Instead, it showcased a striking modernist approach, omitting the usual clichés, like vigas, with its western facade defined by a dramatic stained-glass wall designed by art professor John Tatschl. This was one of the first significant incorporations of artwork in a campus building in many years, cementing the building's status as an iconic piece of architecture. The complex won several awards, including being named Building of the Month by College and University Business in April 1967.

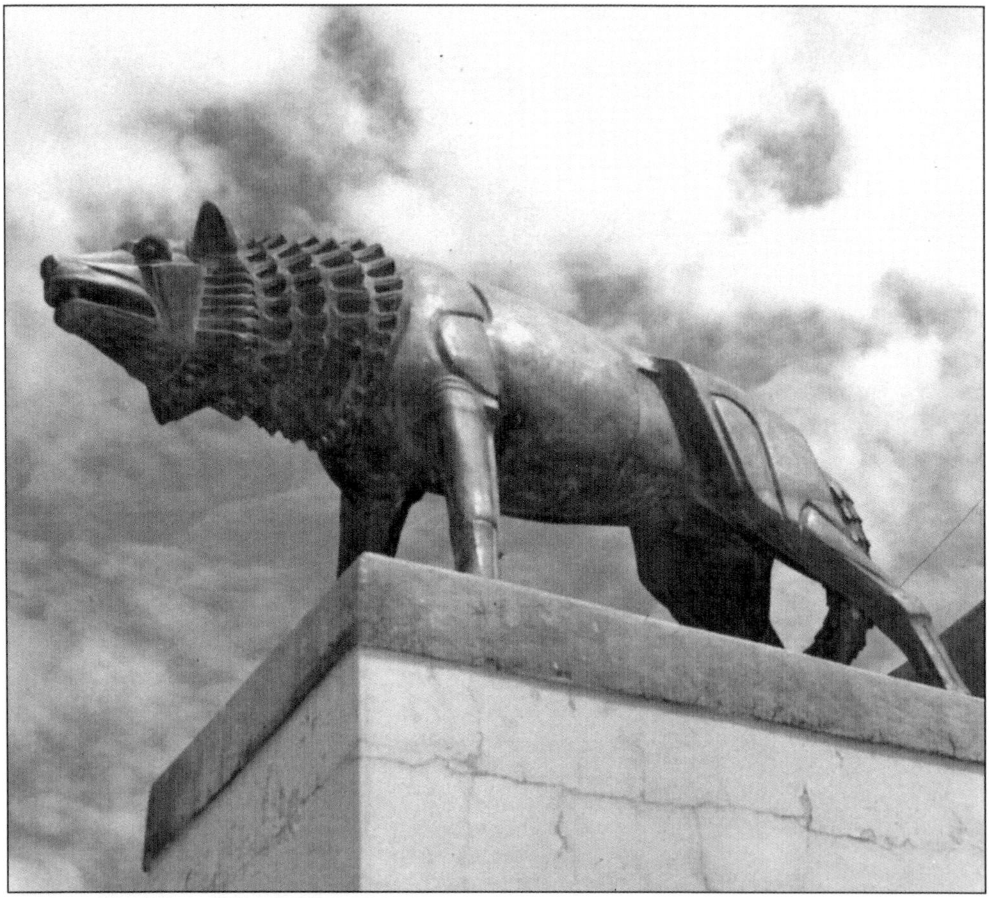

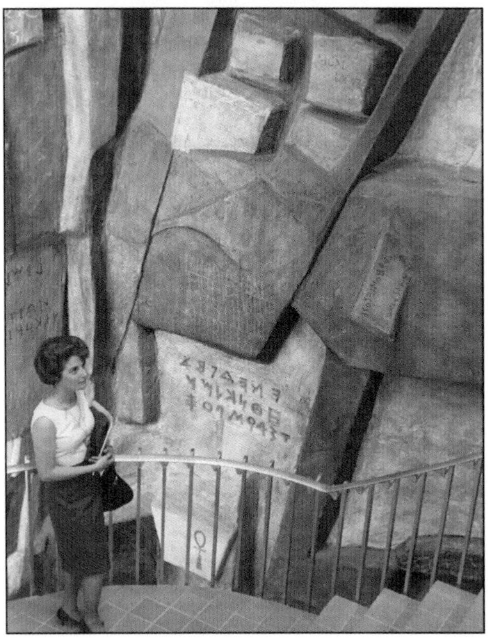

The bronze *Lobo* statue by art professor John Tatschl, created in 1947, serves as a memorial for the 158 UNM students and alumni who died during World War I and World War II. Its abstract representation of the wolf reflects the streamlined, mechanized aesthetics of postwar modernism. The design connects the human experience to the mechanized era, bridging the war's impact with artistic innovation.

The four-story mural *A History of Writing* in the center stairwell of Zimmerman Library, designed and executed by art professor John Tatschl in 1967, celebrates the history of writing. The mural spans 53 projecting geometric masses, starting in the basement with simple scratches and line drawings, then evolving through proto-writing, hieroglyphics, ancient alphabets, and finally culminating with the Latin alphabet at the top. It is an artistic representation of writing's historical progression.

Van Deren Coke, the founding director of the University of New Mexico Art Museum (UNMAM) in 1962, played a crucial role in shaping its early identity. A photographer and art historian, Coke focused on building the museum's collections in photography and printmaking, which quickly gained national acclaim. Under his leadership, UNMAM became a leader in contemporary photography, elevating the medium as a respected art form and strengthening the museum's cultural impact.

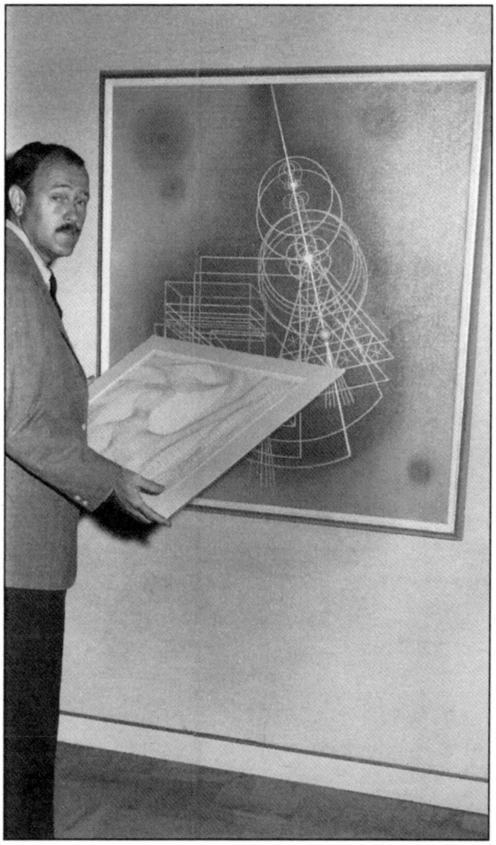

In 1970, the Tamarind Institute relocated to Albuquerque, where it established its archive at the University of New Mexico Art Museum. Founded in Los Angeles in 1960 to revive lithography, Tamarind became part of UNM's College of Fine Arts under the leadership of Clinton Adams. The Tamarind Archive has preserved all lithographs produced there, documenting the evolution of the art form from its early years to the present.

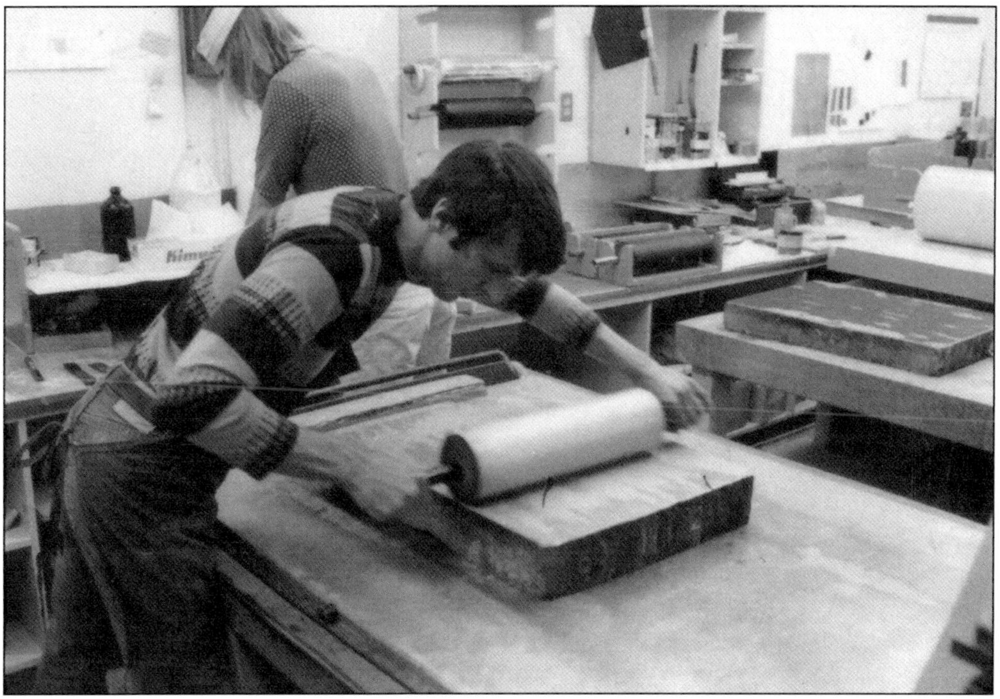

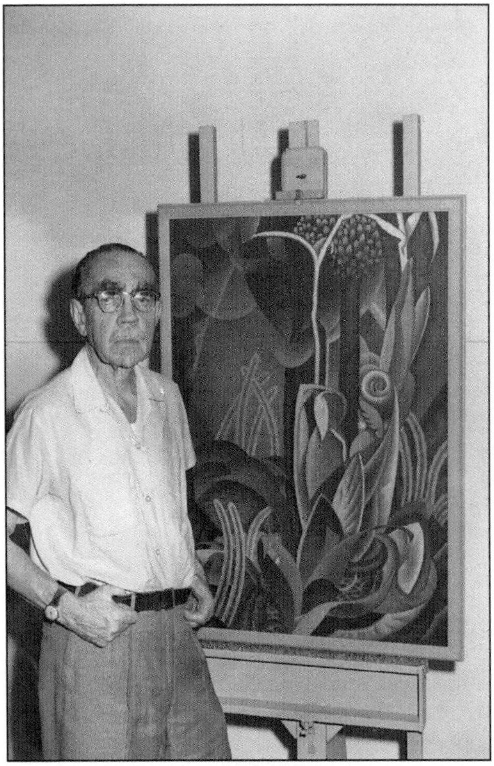

In 1982, Raymond Jonson, a modernist painter and cofounder of the Transcendental Painting Group, bequeathed a significant collection to the university. This gift included over 2,400 artworks by notable 20th-century artists such as Agnes Martin, Elaine DeKooning, and Richard Diebenkorn. The Jonson Gallery, designed by John Gaw Meem's associates in 1949, served as both a living space for Jonson and an exhibition space for his work.

The University of New Mexico Art Museum was founded in 1962 to serve as a teaching resource for the university. Initially focused on 19th- and 20th-century photography and printmaking, the museum's reputation is built on these mediums. In the 1980s, the museum expanded its collection to include more works, including 19th-century European and American paintings, sculptures as well as pieces connected to Spain, Latin America, and New Mexico modernism.

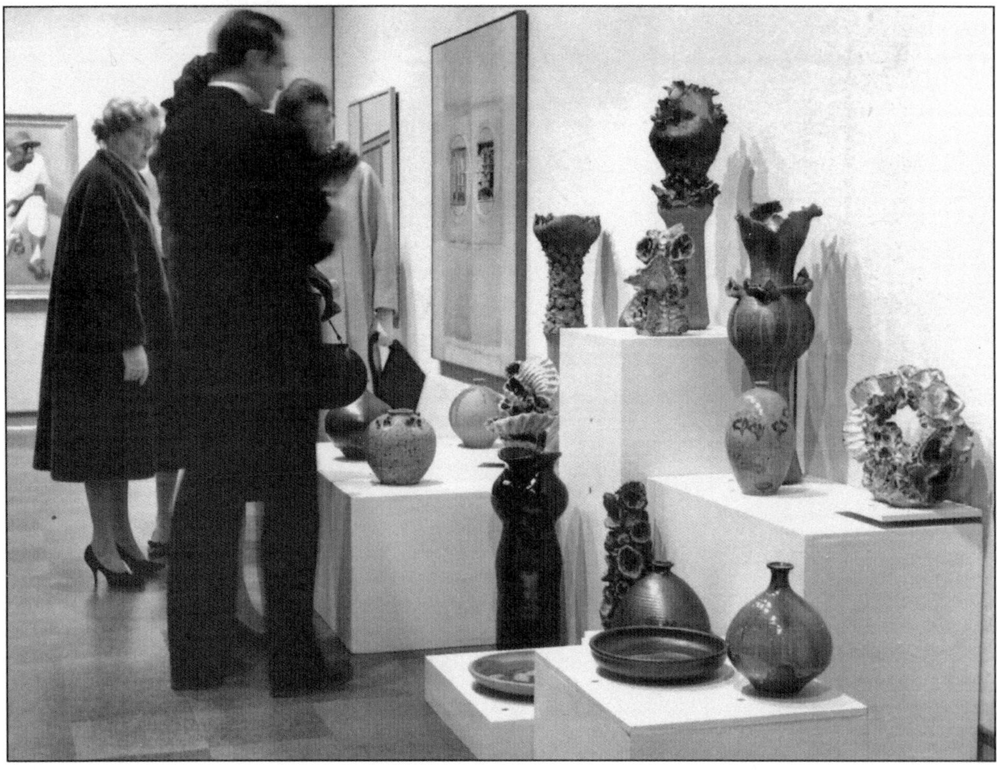

Georgia O'Keeffe received an honorary doctor of fine arts degree from the University of New Mexico in 1964. Her first New Mexico show followed shortly after, with a major exhibition held at the UNM Art Museum in 1966. This exhibition featured a collection of over 40 works, showcasing her profound connection to the region and university and her celebrated contributions to modern American art.

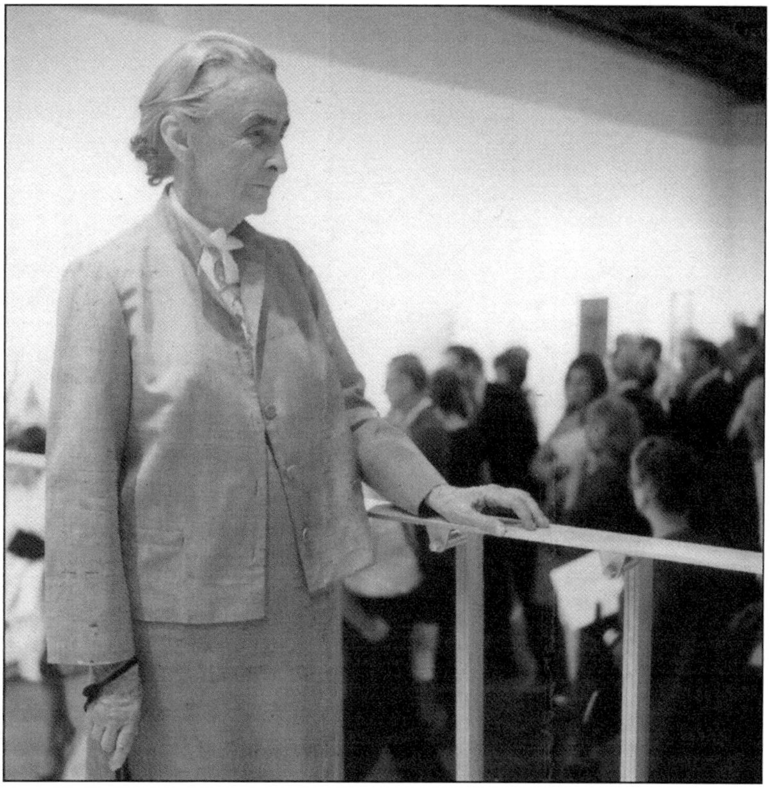

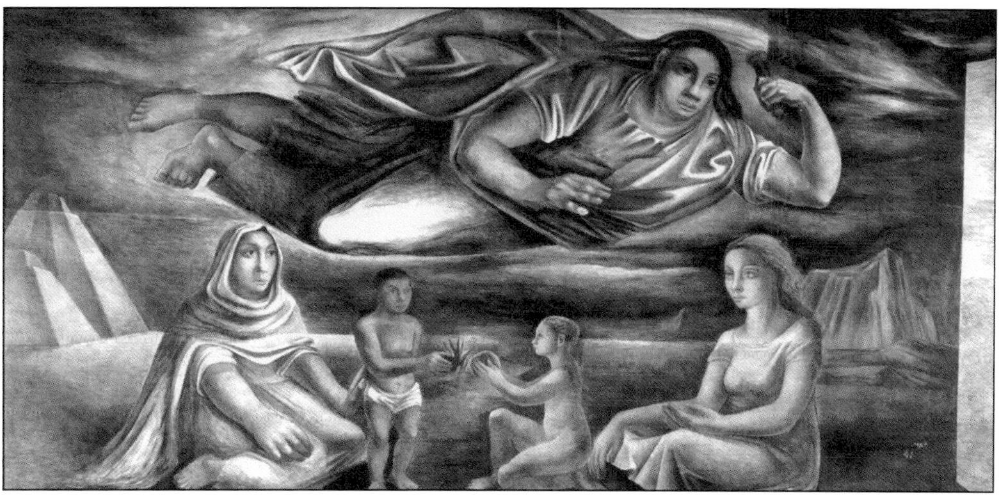

From 1942 to 1943, UNM president Zimmerman invited Mexican artist Jesús Guerrero Galván as an artist-in-residence. Funded by the Office of Inter-American Affairs, Guerrero Galván gifted *Union of the Americas* in Scholes Hall, reflecting Pan-American revisionary solidarity—a theme tied to Franklin D. Roosevelt's Good Neighbor Policy rhetoric. This initiative, part of UNM's engagement with cultural diplomacy, used art to foster hemispheric unity against the rise of fascism and Nazism.

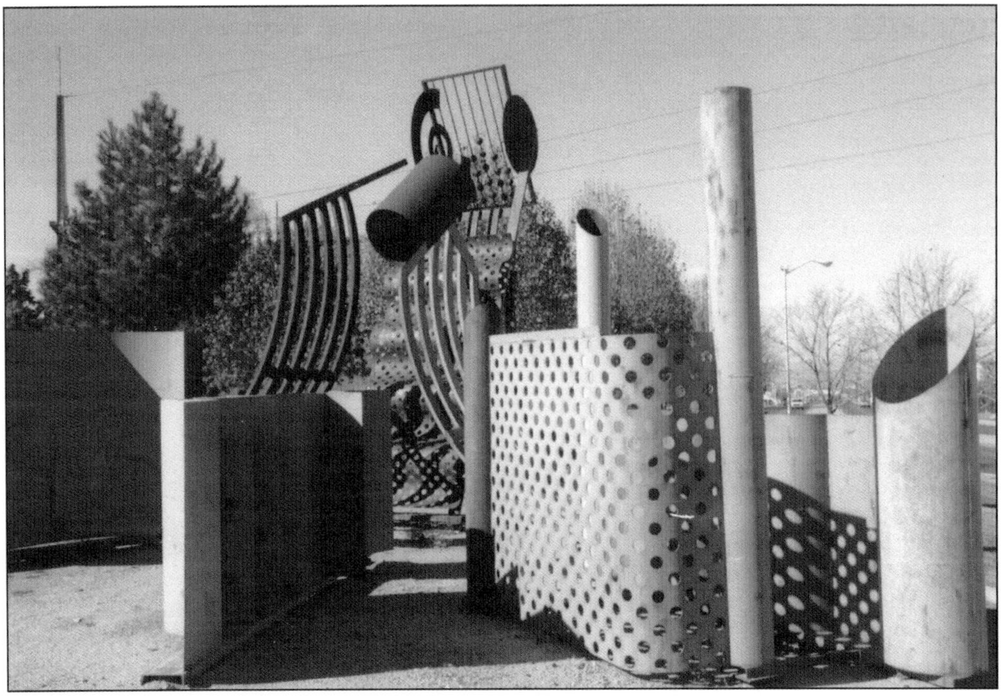

Dennis Oppenheim, a renowned conceptual, performance, and earth artist, was an artist-in-residence at the UNM Department of Art and Art History in the 1980s. In 1987, he created *Dreams & Nightmares: Journey of a Broken Weave*, a compelling piece of nonobjective art. With its geometric forms and thought-provoking title, the work encourages personal interpretation, merging abstraction and creativity. Constructed from steel and aluminum, the site-specific installation resembles a children's play structure, offering ever-changing perspectives. Its varied shapes, colors, and textures make it feel like multiple artworks in one.

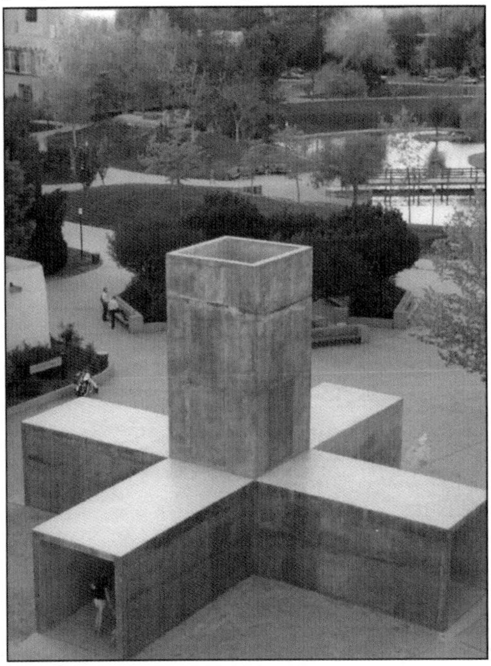

Bruce Nauman's *Center of the Universe* from 1988 embodies the x-y-z axes of a Cartesian coordinate system, placing the viewer at its conceptual core. This piece epitomizes conceptual art, prioritizing ideas over aesthetics. It prompts reflection on spatial relationships and one's place within a broader framework. The sculpture features plain concrete tunnels extending from a central plaque, one reaching skyward. Despite criticism for its stark appearance and disruption of space, Nauman welcomed strong reactions, emphasizing the importance of intellectual and emotional challenge in art.

Bob Haozous, a contemporary Native artist, addresses themes of race and culture through his provocative works. His 1996 sculpture, *Cultural Crossroads of the Americas*, commissioned by the University of New Mexico, contrasts pre-Columbian imagery with modern American symbols, connected by transportation motifs. Originally featuring barbed wire to evoke the US-Mexico border, its removal in 2000 sparked debates over artistic freedom and contractual obligations. The piece reflects cultural intersections and historical narratives, challenging viewers to consider complex social and political dynamics.

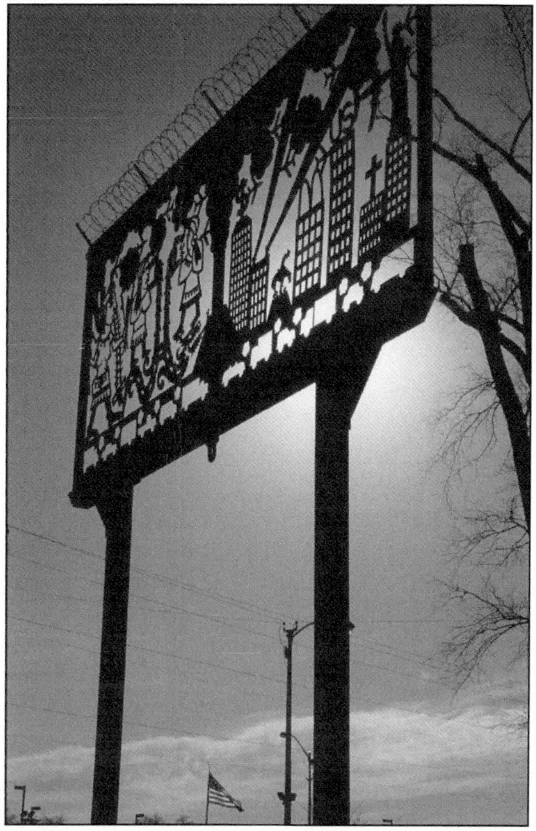

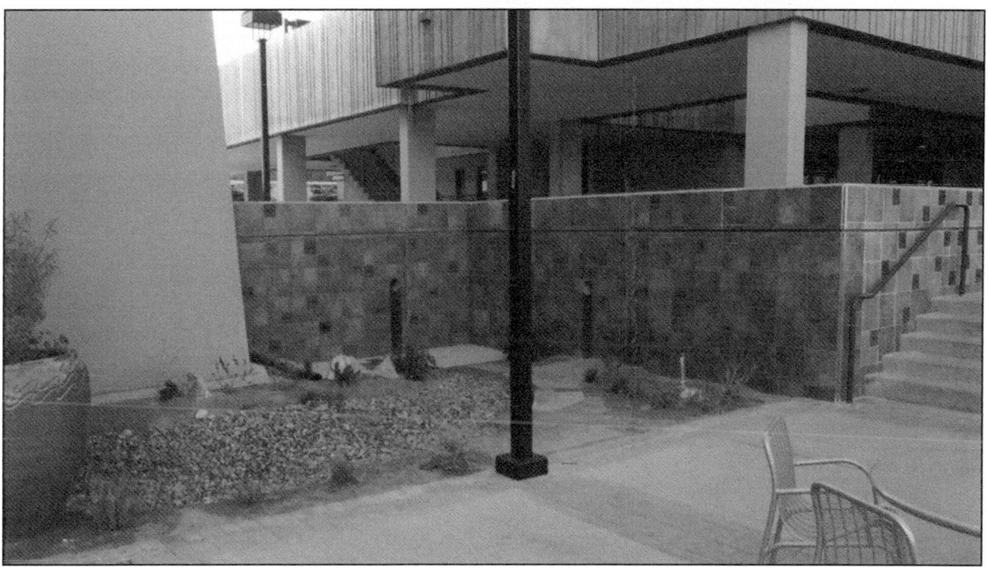

Basia Irland, professor emerita of the UNM Department of Art and Art History, is a renowned water and eco artist who founded the UNM Art and Ecology Program. Her *Xeric Fragrance Garden Rainwater Harvesting Project*, from 2004, captures rainwater from the Student Union Building roof, directing it to a low-water-use plant garden and eventually to the Rio Grande. Featuring a tiled wall with "water" in 64 languages, it underscores the importance of water conservation.

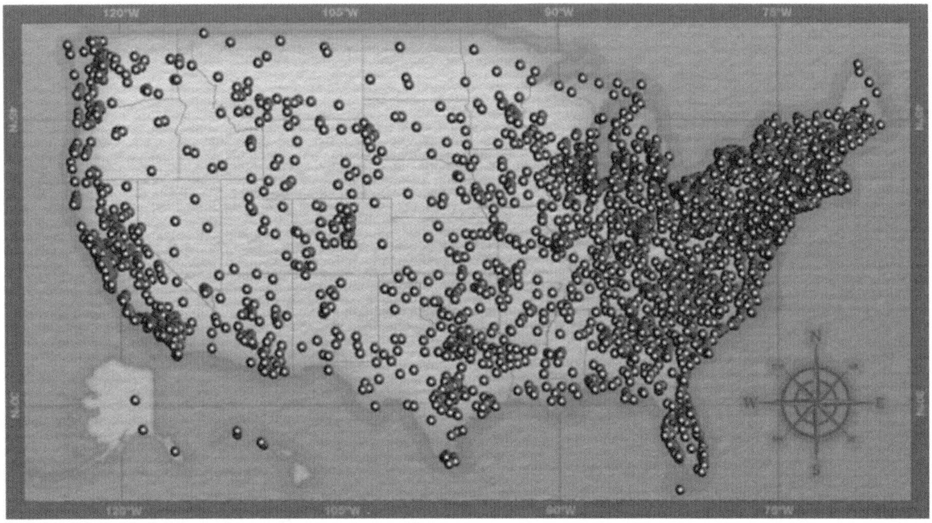